AF470875

ROCKY
MARCIANO

ROCKY
MARCIANO

THE
BROCKTON
BLOCKBUSTER

JOHN JARRETT

First published by Pitch Publishing, 2018

Pitch Publishing
A2 Yeoman Gate
Yeoman Way
Worthing
Sussex
BN13 3QZ
www.pitchpublishing.co.uk
info@pitchpublishing.co.uk

A CIP catalogue record is available for this book
from the British Library.

ISBN 978-1-78531-381-3

Typesetting and origination by Pitch Publishing

Printed in India by Replika Press

CONTENTS

For Mary, my sparring partner for
60 wonderful years

INTRODUCTION

YOU COULD knock Rocky Marciano out with a two-by-four but not with a boxing glove, and I still wouldn't bet on the two-by-four. The man was impervious to punishment – you could knock him down, only twice recorded in fights and twice in sparring bouts. But you couldn't knock him out.

He could knock you out. In an unbeaten run of 49 professional fights, Rocky only required judges to render a decision in six of those contests. In the other 43 fights his opponent was either saved by the referee, counted out by the referee, or scraped off the canvas by his handlers.

When Rocky died in a plane crash, *Washington Post* columnist Shirley Povich wrote, "He'd gotten there as heavyweight champion of the world in 1952 through absolute courage. It was the font of his success, a flaming valour that was the biggest thing he took into a prize ring. In style he was as unlikely a heavyweight champion as ever showed in boxing trunks and in physical stature he was too small for the task. Yet nobody ever walked out of the ring a winner over Marciano.

"Once it was written of him by an author who shall be nameless, 'Rocky Marciano can't box a lick, his footwork is what you would expect from two left feet, he throws his right hand in a clumsy circle and knows nothing of orderly retreat. All he can do is blast the breath from your lungs or knock your head off.' It was fairly descriptive."

Yet when he retired from boxing in 1956, Rocky Marciano could rightfully claim to be the only undefeated heavyweight champion of the world. He knocked out Jersey Joe Walcott in a 13-round thriller in 1952 to become world champion. Defending his title six times he brought the million dollar gate back to boxing in 1955 when he crushed Archie Moore in what would be his last fight.

As an ex-champ, he criss-crossed America making public appearances. He travelled any way he could without spending a cent, building a network of friends, businessmen and mob guys who willingly paid his way, fed him, dressed him and flew him from here to there and back again. Which is how he died, hitching a ride in a small plane that crashed in an Iowa cornfield in August 1969, on the eve of his 46th birthday.

He lived and died by his mantra, "If you want to live a full life then live dangerously."

1

A FLIGHT TOO FAR

ON THE evening of 31 August 1969, a green and white single-engine Cessna 172 took off from Chicago's Midway Airport and set a course for Des Moines, Iowa, a distance of some 310 miles. There were three men on board, including the pilot, who had been given a weather briefing that warned of stormy skies over Iowa with a low ceiling. At 8.50pm the pilot, who had decided to divert the plane to Newton, Iowa, contacted the Des Moines Radar Approach Control saying he was stuck in a cloud bank and was unable to find the Newton airport. Moments later, he radioed that he had broken through the clouds and was setting up to land. A flight service official at Des Moines stated that the pilot told him at about 9.00pm that he intended to land at Newton but gave no indication of trouble.

Mrs Colleen Swarts, aged 39, who lived across the road from the Henry Eilander farm, said she saw the lights of the plane as it passed overhead. She said the plane appeared to have reversed its westward course and 'seemed to be swinging toward the airport' when she lost sight of it behind a grove. But the sound continued. She said the plane's engine stopped, then 'kind of sputtered again. Then I heard this awful thud and I knew it had crashed.' Mrs Swarts's husband ran into the field where the plane had come down but couldn't find it in the dark. Mrs Swarts notified the police, and the sheriff's deputies arrived shortly afterward and found the plane.

It had hit a lone oak tree in the middle of a cornfield and skidded into a small creek bed. One wing had sheared off and wreckage of the plane, flight maps and weather charts were strewn all around. Federal Aviation Administration officials, who quickly sealed off the site, refused to speculate about the cause.

Deputy Sheriff Jim VeWere, with the aid of other deputies, found the bodies of two men who had been thrown forward more than 30 feet. Pilot Glenn Belz, aged 37, was found with the plane's motor on his chest. The other man was 23-year-old Frank Farrell. Under the smashed fuselage, still strapped in his seat, was the third man, later identified as the retired former undefeated heavyweight boxing champion of the world Rocky Marciano, aged 45. Debris had pierced his skull. Jasper County Medical Examiner Dr John Maughan stated all three men had been killed instantly.

The National Transportation Safety Board accident investigation concluded that the probable cause of the mishap was 'the pilot attempted operation exceeding his experience and ability level, continued visual flight rules under adverse weather conditions, and experienced spatial disorientation in the last moments of the flight.' Sheriff Darrell Hurley said simply, 'The engine conked out and they went down.'

The bodies of the three were taken first to the Toland-Wallace funeral home in Newton and later to the Dunn funeral home in Des Moines. Friends of Farrell said he and Belz, both of Des Moines, had flown to Chicago to pick up Marciano for a surprise birthday dinner party in his honour on Sunday night at the Charcoal Room in Des Moines. Rocky was to have flown home to Fort Lauderdale, Florida, the following day, Monday, 1 September, to celebrate his 46th birthday at a party organised by his 16-year-old daughter Mary Anne. An added surprise would have seen Rocky's adopted 17-month-old son, Rocco Kevin, showing his father how he had learned to walk since Rocky had left home.[1]

'It was late evening in Fort Lauderdale when the doorbell rang on North Atlantic Boulevard, Mary Anne heard her mother answer the door. She bolted to the staircase after she heard the scream. Jack Sherlock, the Fort Lauderdale police chief and an old friend of the family, was standing inside the door. "Are you sure it's him? Are you sure it's not Rocky Graziano?" [Marciano's wife] Barbara was saying, referring to the former middleweight champion of the world with whom her husband was often confused. "It can't be, are you sure?"

1   *Des Moines Register* 2 September 1969

Mary Anne started down the stairs. "Is my dad dead?" she asked. "I'm sorry," Sherlock said.[2]

A *United Press* man reporting from Brockton, Massachusetts, wrote, 'Rocky Marciano, the man who put this town on the map with his nickname, "The Brockton Blockbuster" comes home tonight. In the past it was a time for happy reunions with the old friends and his parents who still live down on Dover Street. Now it will be a time for sadness and last farewells. The people got up on Labour Day morning and read about it in the papers. At first there was only shock when they read about the plane crash and then the memories came pouring back. The Hickey Funeral Home, where Marciano's body will lie, can be seen through the windows of the Brockton Café, and the people cast uneasy glances towards it as they washed down their doughnuts with cups of hot, black coffee this morning.

"Sure, everybody in town knows Rocky," said Frank DiBarri. "He lived up the street. I used to play baseball down at Edgars Playground, and he would be there, too. You couldn't find a better guy."

'Naomi DeMaine was a schoolgirl when she'd watch him run down the street training to be a fighter. It's the same memory that others have. He was a fighter even in his youth. "There isn't any boxing here any more," one man said. "They used to have them down at the A.O.B. Hall, but not any more. Nobody's interested in fighting any more."

'Whenever Rocky would have a fight, the crowds would gather on Main Street and listen over speakers. "The place would go absolutely wild when he'd win," one old-timer said. "There were quite a few wild nights I can remember when he was fighting. We never went away sad because he never lost."

'Toni Costa didn't grow up in Brockton and she's too young to remember Rocky's bloody, hard-pitched battles. But she answers the telephone for the *Brockton Enterprise* and was learning a lot about him from the calls flooding the office. "I haven't had time to do anything but answer the phone all day," she said. "A lot of people heard it on the radio and don't believe it. They call and say 'I heard a rumour that Rocky Marciano was killed.' They really know, it's not just a rumour, but they don't want to believe it. And some of them break down when I tell them it's true."'[3]

---

2   William Nack *My Turf: Horses, Boxers, Blood Money and the Sporting Life* 2003
3   *Las Vegas Sun* 2 September 1969

A light rain was falling on 4 September as 11 priests participated in the solemn requiem high mass for Rocco Francis Marchegiano at St Colman's Church – site of his marriage – in Brockton. The service attracted a capacity crowd of 2,000 – including such pugilistic personalities as Joe Louis, Willie Pep, Paul Pender and Tony Zale – while another 1,000 mourners waited outside to pay their last respects. The sun also stayed away two days later for the funeral procession as Rocky was laid to rest in the Lauderdale Memorial GardensMausoleum at the Queen of Heaven Cemetery in his adopted hometown of Fort Lauderdale, Florida. About 500 mourners were on hand for this service, which concluded as Rocky's wife Barbara kissed the casket and then wept openly as workmen lowered it into the ground.[4]

The world in general, and the boxing world in particular, were shocked at Marciano's death. 'Joe Louis, the 55-year-old former champion, who was in Charlotte, North Carolina to referee some wrestling matches, said, "This is the saddest news I have ever heard. Everything I remember about him is good. When he defeated me, I think it hurt him more than it did me. He just had a good heart. Something's gone out of my life, but I'm not alone. Something's gone out of everyone's life." "No one can really appreciate at this point what Rocky Marciano has done. He was a man all youth looked up to, and a personal friend of mine," said Jersey Joe Walcott, mourning the death of the man who took away his world heavyweight title in 1952.'[5]

Columnist Shirley Povich wrote in the *Washington Post,* 'He'd gotten there as heavyweight champion of the world in 1952 through absolute courage. It was the fount of his success, a flaming valour that was the biggest thing he took into a prize ring. In style he was as unlikely a heavyweight champion as ever showed in boxing trunks and in physical stature he was too small for the tasks. Yet nobody ever walked out of the ring a winner over Marciano. Once it was written of him by an author who shall be nameless, "Rocky Marciano can't box a lick, his footwork is what you'd expect from two left feet, he throws his right hand in a clumsy circle and knows nothing of orderly retreat. All he can do is

---

4   *Boxing Illustrated Special* November 1969
5   *Post Herald* Beckley W. Va. 2 September 1969

blast the breath from your lungs or knock your head off." It was fairly descriptive.'[6]

'Bob Girard, now a fireman in Lynn, Mass., was one of Rocky Marciano's biggest fans and one of the only four men who ever defeated the Brockton Blockbuster. It is only 15 miles from Lynn to Boston's Prudential Center, where glass and steel have replaced old Mechanics Hall. Girard beat Marciano in the finals of the 1947 State Amateur heavyweight championship at the old arena. Girard reminisced, "I knew he'd be a champ that night. He was fantastic in the ring. If the fight lasted long enough, he was bound to get you. He could at any time – with one punch. I wonder to this day how I ever took his punch."

'In Weehawken, New Jersey, Emile Griffith, former welterweight and middleweight champion of the world, fought back tears when he heard the news. "I came back from the movies; my friend asked me, 'Emile, why are you crying?' And how could I explain. Rocky and myself were always good friends – that's what hurts me, and why I'm crying, because this man was a gentleman with me, a great champion and a perfect gentleman."'[7]

'Rocky's daughter Mary Anne knew well the perilous edge on which he lived. In 1965, on a trip from Los Angeles to Honolulu, Rocky had hitched a ride on a cargo plane and loaded Mary Anne and a friend of hers in the hold. "They put little jump seats in for my friend and me, and my father and his friend were sitting on top of the luggage," Mary Anne recalls. "A window blew in and we went into a nosedive and a red light came on and I thought, I'm 12 and I'm going to die. My father kept saying, 'Don't worry. You're gonna be OK.'[8]

Mary Anne would later disclose that the fatal crash wasn't the first time Rocky had been involved in an airplane accident. 'He walked away from two others,' she stated. 'He would fly in a tin can. My father was a fatalist and would say, "If it's your time to go, you go; everybody's number comes up."'[9] On that murky Sunday night in August 1969, Rocco Francis Marchegiano's number finally came up.

---

6   Shirley Povich *Washington Post* 2 September 1969

7   *Wisconsin State Journal* 2 September 1969

8   William Nack *My Turf: Horses, Boxers, Blood Money and the Sporting Life* 2003

9   *Boxing Illustrated Special* November 1969

2

GROWING A CHAMPION

WHEN PHILOMENA Mangifesti heard that the Marchegiano baby was ill with pneumonia, she made her way to the cottage at 80 Brook Street in the Italian section of Brockton, a town of some 60,000 people 20 miles south of Boston. Mrs Mangifesti was 90 years old, a distant relative of Pierino Marchegiano, and she knew that Pasqualena had already lost one son in childbirth. Dr Josephat Phaneuf had advised Pasqualena to wait a couple of years before having another child, but she wanted a big family and three months later told Pierino he was going to be a father. A boy was born on 1 September 1923 and christened Rocco Francis. He weighed a healthy 12½ pounds and one of the cards he received had little boxing gloves hanging from it. The message in the card read, 'Welcome to another champion.' Now 19 months old, Rocco was flat on his back fighting for his life.

When Mrs Mangifesti entered the room where the neighbourhood women were gathered around the crib, weeping, their lips moving in silent prayer, she remonstrated with them. 'Why do you keep looking at him?' she said in Italian. 'Why don't you do something?' One of the women answered her, 'There's nothing to do. He's too sick. Only God can save him.'

'No,' Mrs Mangifesti said. 'In Italy, I have seen the children with pneumonia. And if they are strong, they can live.' Then she ordered one of the women to bring her a dish of warm water and a small spoon. She forced the baby's lips apart with the spoon and let the water trickle into his mouth. And to the amazement of the women, the child blinked his eyes and began to move his lips. 'You keep making him drink,' the old lady said. 'This poor baby is all dried up. Give him some chicken broth, and if he doesn't want it, push it down his throat.'

That week, the crisis passed. The fever subsided and the boy Rocco started taking nourishment eagerly. 'You're going to have a healthy, strong boy on your hands, Mrs Marchegiano,' Dr Phaneuf said. Although it is quite possible that the pneumonia had taken its natural course, Pasqualena Marchegiano always credited the old lady with saving her son's life. Mrs Mangifesti died shortly after Rocco's recovery, never having really known the boy.[10] Dr Phaneuf was right – young Rocco grew to be a strong, healthy boy. 'I get my inner strength from my father and my physical strength from my mother,' he always said. His father was from Chieti, a little fishing village on the Adriatic. Pasqualena came from San Bartolomeo, near Naples. Pierino arrived in America in 1917 and a year later was in France with the Second Marines at Château-Thierry. He was injured by shrapnel and gassed and he was never really well after that. Brockton was the shoe manufacturing centre of America and Pierino spent the rest of his life working a Number 7 bed-laster machine. Young Rocco would take his lunch to him every day and his Pop would say to him, 'I want you to stay out of the shoe shops.'

Pasqualena had her hands full at home, with three boys and three girls. 'There was no central heating or hot water at home,' Rocky remembered some years later. 'Mom always had water boiling on the stove. She had a big washtub in the kitchen and we took turns taking a bath on a Saturday night – boys one week and girls the next.'

'Rocco,' his warmly, matriarchal mother sighed, 'was the best-natured child you ever see. He always want to be friendly. Always want to eat. He was 99 per cent boy!'[11]

Young Rocco wanted to be the strongest kid around and he was encouraged by Uncle Johnny Piccento. He had the boy chinning himself on a tree branch in the backyard, 15 times every morning and 15 every night. Rocco was playing baseball every day and his dream was to play in the big leagues. He played football for the school team and he fought

---

10 Everett M Skehan *Rocky Marciano: Biography of a First Son* 1977
11 *Time* magazine September 1952

in the woods with the local kids. He was about 11 when his uncle found a pair of boxing gloves somewhere and rigged up a punching bag for the boy in the cellar, a heavy sandbag. 'On account the ceiling was so low,' recalled Rocky, 'I had to crouch and hit the bag with a chopping motion. I knocked out Archie Moore and Ezzard Charles with a chop and it was the same punch I used when I hit that punching bag in my cellar … Pop was always tired after work and never took me any place. I went everywhere with Uncle Johnny – ball games, boxing, wrestling and swimming. Once he took me to see Primo Carnera, who had just won the heavyweight title. I touched Carnera on the elbow as he walked by me and I talked about it for weeks afterwards.

'I remember my first fight,' Rocky would recall. 'I was about 12 years old and I already had a reputation as the strongest kid around.' Allie Colombo lived next door and was Rocky's best friend. 'Allie's uncle set up a ring in his backyard and Allie promoted the fight between me and a kid named Jimmy DiStasi, who was older and bigger than me. We wouldn't hurt each other because we used great big gloves, but it was a good fight just the same. It was supposed to be a three-round fight but neither of us got tired so we kept going for ten. It was Jimmy's only fight and to this day he goes around saying he went ten rounds with Rocky Marciano.'[12]

Rocco was about 16 when Uncle Johnny figured it was time he got a job to help out at home. 'I know where you can make four dollars a day,' he said. 'Your folks can use the money, your father isn't too well.' However, Mom and Pop were not too happy about their eldest boy starting work. Mom put her foot down. 'No, no, you got to finish school,' she said. 'We want you to graduate.'

Rocco argued his case as Uncle Johnny stood by. 'I ain't a good student and I hate school. I can make 20 dollars a week and play so much baseball that I can be in the big leagues in a few years.' Mom wasn't convinced, saying, 'Everybody plays baseball around here but nobody makes any money at it.' Rocco and Uncle Johnny made their case and his parents relented when Rocco promised to go to night school. He started work on a coal truck at 50 cents an hour, hard work but he was using his muscles. He gave it three, four months before quitting. He worked in a candy factory mixing chocolate in a huge vat. It paid 60 cents an

---

12 *Saturday Evening Post* September 1956

hour but it was seasonal. He even tried the shoe factory, much against his father's wishes, but had to quit as he couldn't stand the smell. A job in a wire factory didn't last long, then he was a short-order cook in a diner. The pay was poor but he could eat as much as he wanted so he was happy, at least for a while. With the outbreak of the Second World War, there was work in defence plants with plenty of overtime. At last, Rocco was making decent money. One day he gave his mother his pay packet. It contained $150 for two weeks' work. 'I felt sorry for Pop that day,' he recalled. 'The most he ever made was $40 a week and he saw me, a 17-year-old kid, come home with all that money.'

Rocco had so many uncles that he forgot about the big one – Uncle Sam. He received his invitation in February 1943 and was off to Fort Lewis in Washington. 'They must have looked at my thick neck and said, "here's a guy we can work" because right away I was in a brand new Combat Engineers outfit, the 150th. You know, the guys who used to be there to shake hands with the first wave on an assault landing.'

Fort Devens to Camp Pickett to Camp Myles Standish and Rocco was soon aboard the *Mauretania* bound for Europe. Time for play … 'Some guy loaned me a quarter. In poker and blackjack I hiked it up to eight bucks. I moved over to a crap game. I went out of there with $1,200, but I loaned most of it out and never saw it again. That taught me a lesson. Ever since then, I've been very careful with my money. Twice I got into fights, once with a sergeant who quit in the first round, and then with a big Australian in a pub in Wales. One punch ended that one. After the war ended I was shipped home and started boxing at Fort Lewis in Washington, with eight months to do. I entered a competition and was nervous, but not worried. I was in shape. I beat the guy over three rounds and was thrilled to see my name in the post newspaper, first time in my life I saw my name in print as a boxer.'

Home on leave, Rocco went to see his friend, Allie, who was a sergeant. Showing his clippings, Rocco wondered if he could get a fight before going back to camp. Uncle Mike knew a guy named Gene Caggiano, who was promoting fights in Brockton at Hibernian Hall. He put Rocco on a card and paid him 50 bucks, bootleg boxing. Stuffed full of Mom's home cooking, Rocco went in the ring with Henry Lester, who had been a Golden Gloves champion three years in a row and fought in the New England championships. Rocco threw a million punches, missed most of them in the first round, then in round two, as Lester backed him into the ropes, which were slack, Rocco stumbled and accidentally kneed Lester in the groin and the referee ruled him out. First fight at home and he was beaten.

Back at Fort Lewis, Rocco had better luck. He qualified for the national junior AAU championships in Portland, Oregon. At the same time, the ball club he was playing for qualified for the AAU championships, but Rocco picked boxing over baseball for the first time. He won his first two fights in one round, and when his next two opponents refused to fight, 'the wild, powerful brawler' went into the final with Joe DeAngelis. Rocco had severely dislocated a knuckle in the forefinger of his left hand but boxed anyway. The fight took place in August 1946 and Rocco had his hands full. DeAngelis was more experienced and at 6ft 3ins towered over the boy from Brockton.

A couple of nights earlier, they had met in the cafeteria. Rocco walked up to DeAngelis and said, 'I've been reading about you. You're good. You'll make the finals here, and when you do, I'm going to stiffen you.' Joe was startled. 'When we got to the final and were receiving instructions in the middle of the ring,' he said, 'I got a chance to size Rocco up real close. He was the most solid, hard muscular man I had ever seen … I soon realised I was the better boxer and held him off with lefts. I saw a good opening for a right and belted him square on the jaw as hard as I've ever hit any man. He didn't even shake his head … The third round was the wildest. Knowing how hard Rocco could punch, I was very careful. I knew I had the fight won. Then my second yelled, "Fifteen seconds, Joe, you won", then bam!bam! Rocco caught me with a left and a right square on top of my head. I moved out and the bell rang. The referee raised my hand. Rocco hated to lose, but just the same he congratulated me. Later, in the dressing room, Rocco was sitting on a table, looking at his hand. He had broken a knuckle with the last two punches. He looked at me and said, "Joe, look what you did to my hand."

'So there I was with a busted knuckle,' recalled Rocky in 1956, 'and I had to go to the hospital [Madigan General Hospital, Tacoma, Washington]. An Army doctor, who was a Japanese-American, fixed up a special splint so my knuckle would heal right. He did a wonderful job. If he hadn't, I'd never have been able to fight again. I wish I could think of his name so I could thank him.' Marciano never could recall that doctor's name and often over the years he would attempt to contact this man he deemed his saviour, addressing him through interviews, pleading with him to make contact. Never. It remained one of his biggest regrets that he couldn't thank him personally for saving not just his hand but his future as well.

'Never, however, did that doctor come forward to claim his just credit for saving that private from the hum-drum existence that seemed to be destined to be his lot in life. To be fair, it is hardly surprising that he did, for the man in question was one of the most humble human beings to ever carve for himself a career in a profession beset by attention-seeking individuals, and his name, Shohiro Thomas 'Tom' Taketa.'[13]

* * * *

Two days after Christmas 1946, Uncle Sam dispensed with the services of Rocco Francis Marchegiano and sent him back to Brockton, a civilian. A civilian with a heavily bandaged left hand. He would make weekly visits to a local Veterans Association hospital and was encouraged at the rapid recovery of the hand, so much so that he began light training with his pal Allie Colombo. As March came up on the calendar, Allie said he could get Rocco a fight at the Valley Arena in Holyoke, Mass. A week later, 'he called to say he had booked me a fight against a guy named Lee Epperson for 50 bucks. I had started a job at the Brockton Gas Company but got the day off.'

It was 17 March, St Patrick's Day, and Allie had booked his pal as Rocky Mack to protect his amateur status. The promoter shook his head when Allie mentioned the 50 dollars. 'Four-rounders get 35 bucks round here,' he said. When Allie argued with the guy saying Rocky had taken a day off work and would lose money paying 15 bucks for the licence, the promoter finally agreed to pay for the licence and give Rocky the 35 dollars. There was a good crowd on hand and most of them thought the new guy was Irish. Weighing 192 pounds, Rocky struggled through the first two rounds, missing more than he hit, and Epperson gave him

---

13 John Cameron *Redemption: The Life & Death of Rocky Marciano* August 2012

a hard time. In the third, he knocked Epperson through the ropes with a right to the midsection and it was all over. The fans raised the roof as 'Irish' Rocky Mack was declared the winner. 'This is a tough racket,' he said to Allie in the dressing room. 'Too tough for me.'

'Marciano chose boxing only as the last means by which he could lift himself above the prosaic jobs open to him elsewhere,' wrote Tim Cohane, sports editor of *Look* magazine. 'He would have much preferred to be a football or baseball player. At Brockton High, he was a centre line-backer, a tremendous tackler impervious to injury whose strength and courage would have forced him on to any college football team. An athletic scholarship probably would have awaited him at Boston College, Holy Cross or Fordham, had he stayed at high school. But his marks were mediocre. This traced to two factors. Rocco thought of little else but sports, and realised he would have to leave school anyhow to get a job and help out at home. He left before the end of his sophomore year. So passed the dream of college football.

'In baseball he showed possibly even more promise. As a catcher, he would have had a strong chance to make it. His arm was powerful and accurate, he had good baseball sense and could handle a pitcher. He was a right-handed hitter and slammed a tremendously long ball. But in a service game at Swansea, Wales, he hurt his arm pitching. When he tried out with the Chicago Cubs farm team at Fayetteville, North Carolina, after the war, he discovered that his arm was gone. And so passed the dream of big-league baseball. It was only then that the Rock turned to the ring.'[14]

In January 1948, Rocco Marchegiano entered the Golden Gloves tournament at Lowell, Mass. He flattened his first two opponents in the first round and did the same to finalist Charlie Mortimer, who was unbeaten in 12 bouts. That put him on the train to New York City for the Golden Gloves All-East Coast Championships as the New England heavyweight champion. The bouts were held at the Ridgewood Grove, in Brooklyn, which was packed to the doors. Most of the 3,000 fans were there to see the sensational Coley Wallace, the Harlem heavyweight with 17 straight knockouts. His resemblance to Joe Louis would earn Wallace a starring role in the United Artists 1953 release, *The Joe Louis*

---

14 Tim Cohane *Look* magazine October 1956

Story. Coley looked like the Brown Bomber, but sadly he couldn't fight like him.

The New Yorkers had to smile as their favourite shaped up for his bout with the unknown slugger from New England. Wallace stood 6ft 2ins with a 78in reach. Marchegiano (The *Lowell Sun* spelt his name Markegiano, which was incorrect but was the correct pronunciation) stood only 5ft 10¼ins and had a 68in reach. The locals stopped smiling when the fight began.

'With all the stuff in the world,' wrote John F. Kenney, sports editor of the *Lowell Sun,* 'Rocco came out of his corner at the first bell and swished one of those uppercuts right at the giant's jowls. He missed. Wallace closed in to devour this presumptive New Englander, whereupon Markegiano slammed one into Wallace's stomach and threw a right to the dusky's face that you could hear as far as Beaver Brook in Dracut. Mister Wallace's expression changed. The fans began taking off their overcoats. If there had been any thoughts in the minds of the Lowell fans that Rocco acquired his Lowell victories too easily, well, they should have been here. Wallace beat Rocco back to the ropes by sheer power in that first round, but Markegiano wheeled quickly and put Wallace into the same spot, trying desperately to connect with that uppercut. Momentarily, the coloured behemoth put both gloves to his face for self-protection. The fans loved it. Apparently they had not seen this before from Wallace. They adopted Rocco, heart, gloves and trunks, from that moment.

'Markegiano couldn't knock Wallace. That was evident in the first round … The Brockton hope kept on whirring them in there but his Sunday punch was ineffective. It wasn't because he wasn't connecting, but because Wallace was too tall for the smaller Rocco's "whameroo." His big poke to the jaw connected often enough, but by the time it reached its objective, it had passed the radius of effectiveness … They were all in at close quarters when the last bell sounded. By that time the joint was going crazy. Gene Caggiano, who handles Rocco back in the Bay State, leaped into the ring with wild delirium. The fans were applauding the happy Markegiano to a point where the announcer could hardly be heard. The loudspeaker finally got its request for quiet. The announcer looked over the slips in the traditional manner, then spoke: "The winner," he said, "Wallace."

'Ridgewood Grove became pandemonium, also bedlam. A roar went up first and it was of one word: "No." It continued for a quarter-hour. Reporters demanded explanation. These were from Jacksonville and Buffalo and other spots unacquainted with Markegiano … A demand for the scoring sheets brought out the objective facts. Judge Rudy Keppler voted for Markegiano, while judge Delaney and referee Barney Smith voted for Wallace. The fight had not been finished more than 30 minutes when talk was general that Markegiano would be named alternate on the all-eastern team to meet Chicago's standouts in a later tournament. In the dressing room, Rocco smiled. "Why can't I go in as a number one heavyweight?" he asked. "I think I could lick Wallace again."

'The fans from Brooklyn, Manhattan, Bronx and Queens, who up to bell time didn't know Markegiano from a hole in the wall, milled their way from the back of the arena down to the very ropes after the final bout's decision was rendered. They raged for fully 15 minutes in fruitless protest, button-holing anybody who looked like an official, and at times even threatening violence … Fans picked up Markegiano, as a baby, and smothered him with pats on the back, handshakes, finally setting his feet on the Grove floor at Coach Tommy Rawson's insistence. All the way up to the far dressing room, the bewildered Rocco was pounded enthusiastically, his way impeded by fans who just wanted to shake hands with him. Hundreds of throats gave volume to the one yell, "You won that fight, son," or another, "The decision is only two blind men's – not ours, boy."'

The *Lowell Sun* had John Kenney's report on the front page the next day, in which he recorded, 'In one of the most putrid decisions ever handed down from a Golden Gloves tournament ring anywhere – and this writer has been watching boxing bouts from ringside since Jack Benny owned a Maxwell – Rocco Markegiano of Brockton was pencilled into the limbo of eliminated contenders after glorifying *The Sun* Charities New England team in the hearts of 3,000 fans by administering Coley Wallace, New York metropolitan champion, the pasting of that coloured goliath's career … In a word, it was a stinkeroo.'[15]

Back home in Brockton, Rocco would only say, 'Wallace is a good boy. He gave me the hardest fight of my experience.' That experience

---

15   John F, Kenney *Lowell Sun* 2 March 1948

was a mere three months. Two weeks later, Rocco declined the invitation of the *New York Daily News* to compete in the East-West Golden Gloves tourney at Madison Square Garden on 22 March. He said he would enter the New England amateur championships at Boston on the same date.

Rocco would lose four of his 12 amateur bouts. Bob Girard, a 6ft-plus heavyweight, was able to outbox Rocco, who was fighting one-handed after again injuring his left hand. His conqueror was modest about his victory, saying some 30 years later, 'How do you think I beat Rocco? I beat him because it was three rounds. There were a hundred guys who might have stayed three rounds with The Rock. But no man in the world was gonna beat Rocco in 15 rounds, not Dempsey, not Ali, not anybody. I knew he was going to be champ. I don't think anybody could hurt Rocco. Every time he hit you, you saw a flash of light. You either grabbed him or you moved back, because if he hits you twice you're gone.'[16]

---

16 Everett M. Skehan *Rocky Marciano: Biography of a First Son* 1977

3

THE BEGINNING

'IN THE Spring, a young man's fancy lightly turns to thoughts of love.'
That old sportswriter Alfred, Lord Tennyson, penned that line in a poem
called *Locksley Hall*, which hit the bookstalls in 1842. In the spring of
1947, the thoughts of a young Italian living in the town of Brockton in
Massachusetts lightly turned to thoughts of love for a 19-year-old Irish
girl named Barbara Cousins, the daughter of a local policeman. Still
nursing an injured left hand and dreaming of a boxing career, Rocco
Marchegiano was digging ditches for the Brockton Gas Company when
he met Barbara at a local dance hall. As in the ring, Rocco had two left
feet and usually sat out on the sidelines shooting the breeze with his
pals. But soon Barbara was taking the place of boxing and Rocco was
taking dancing lessons from the switchboard operator who seemed to
have his number.

Gene Caggiano was a Brockton bus mechanic who promoted amateur
boxing shows in the town and had been in New York with Rocco for the
Wallace fight. He hired a hall and promised Rocco and Allie $100 if they
sold tickets and helped set the arena up. They fixed the seats in place
and sold enough tickets to fill the venue twice over. Next day, Caggiano
offered the boys 40 bucks, and when Rocco refused to accept the money,
he put it in an envelope and delivered it to Rocco's mother.

'We were still arguing over that when it was time to enter the New
England Olympic tryouts in June 1948. In Boston, I knocked out Sal
Fischera in the second round and hurt my hand badly. I still beat a guy

named George McGinnis in the final the same night.' Fighting right-handed only, Rocco hammered McGinnis to the canvas twice in round three and took the AAU heavyweight title. But his hopes of going to the Olympics were shattered when the doctor examined his hand. The knuckle was out of place and the thumb was broken. He couldn't go to New York with the team and he had to take a leave of absence from the gas company.

They were still chasing Caggiano for the 60 bucks owed them and invited him to the house, now on Dover Street. Caggiano was outnumbered, with Pop, Allie, Uncle Mike Colombo, Uncle Dominic Prosper and Lester Cousins, Barbara's father, but he wouldn't give them a nickel more. 'Allie finally said, "Well, it won't make any difference, I think Rocco's going to turn professional anyhow. Aren't you, Rocco?" "Sure," I said. "I guess I'll turn pro." Caggiano said I wasn't ready, said I'd get murdered. It was like a challenge right there in that room. Pop said, "If my boy fights professional you can bet he'll make a good name for himself." Everybody nodded and Caggiano walked out. I was making 65 or 70 bucks a week at the gas company but I couldn't work until my hand healed. Uncle Mike said to Pop, "You want Rocco to be a pro? You know, if he does he won't make much money at first." "That's all right," said Pop. "If my boy wants to be a professional fighter, I want him to do it. We can get along all right for a while."'[17]

Allie had saved some money from his time in the army and agreed to give up his job and train Rocco. He could only use one hand on the bag and they walked a lot to keep in shape. It cost $125 for the doctor and hospital bills and the guys from the Ward Two Club threw a stag party to give Rocco some money. At Allie's suggestion, they went to see Joe Monte, an old fighter who lived in Brockton. It was a long haul from Brazil to Brockton and that was the journey two-year-old Joseph Montagano made with his family. The boy grew strong and became an amateur fighter, turning to the pro game in 1926. Managed by Johnny Buckley of Boston, who handled heavyweight champion Jack Sharkey among others, and fighting as Joe Monte, he put together a 39-fight career (26-11-2), meeting guys like Max Schmeling and Jimmy Braddock as a tough club fighter. In 1930, Joe suffered a torn retina in his left eye that ended his career. He

---

17 *Saturday Evening Post* September 1956

became a brewery representative, a job he held for 36 years. That's what Joe was doing when Rocco and Allie called on him for advice. Joe was happy to talk to the young men busting to get into the pro fight racket. 'You're a good fighter, Rocky,' he said. 'You got a great punch and you can go a long ways. Get yourself a good manager and give all your time to this thing. Give it everything you've got.' Joe looked at Allie, then back at Rocco, saying, 'Rocky, don't make the same mistake I did. I got a Boston manager and he didn't have the right connections. You got to get away from Boston. You want to hit the big time, go to New York and get one of them big-time managers. It's the only way.'

'Then a guy named Eddie Boland saw me fight amateur and told Allie he could help me get a good manager in New York. So one day, Allie went to Boston to see Boland. He came back that night and said, "Rock, this guy Boland thinks you got a good chance to make good. He knows Al Weill, Joe Vella, Charley Johnston, managers like that. Now he thinks that Al Weill would be the best of the lot. Weill's a tough guy, a hard guy to get along with, but the best. He can do the most for you. That's what Boland said. He's writing Weill a letter. I'll write him too."'[18]

Allie found Weill's address in the *Ring Record Book* and wrote, 'Dear Mr Weill, I'm writing in behalf of a young heavyweight fighter who I think has the potential to become the world's heavyweight champion. He is 5ft 11ins and weighs about 190 [pounds] and he just finished competing in the Golden Gloves, where he was robbed in a fight with Coley Wallace, who I'm sure you've heard of. Rocco Marchegiano is his name and I have known him all my life. He has been a football star and a good athlete. He's very strong and durable with plenty of determination. I'm sure with the proper handling he can win the title. If you are interested, please let me know.'

Armand 'Al' Weill was born in Gebweiler, Alsace Lorraine on 28 December 1893. He was only 13 when he and his dad, a horse dealer, arrived in America. 'We sailed steerage 'cause the old man didn't have any sugar,' he said. Young Armand worked at just about anything you could name in immigrant-teeming New York. He was a shipping clerk at 14, a salesman at 15, peddling chiffon and veiling for $5 a week. Then he won a $10 prize at a Yorkville dance hall one night and turned to

---

18 *Saturday Evening Post* October 1956

professional ballroom dancing. 'I wind up at the Canarsie amusment park in Brooklyn when I'm about 20 running the High Strike, where you hit the plunger with a hammer and try and ring the bell.'

Al found a two dollar furnished room with a guy called Andy Brown and got friendly with Charley Goldman, a little fellow who ran the Roll Down, a ball-throwing game with Kewpie dolls as the prizes. Andy Brown was a flyweight boxer, while Goldman had forsaken a ring career after 400-odd bouts because of bad hands. Weill became a fight manager with Brown as his first signing, and he and Goldman soon had a stable of more than 30 boxers.

Goldman was five years older than Weill and came from Russia to settle in the tough Red Hook section of Brooklyn. Only 5ft 1in and weighing 115 pounds, Charley was a tough little battler from 1904 through 1914. He fought guys like Kid Williams, Johnny Coulon, former bantamweight champion, and George 'KO' Chaney in 1912 in Baltimore in what Chaney called the toughest of his 170 fights. Charley boxed George Kitson an incredible 60 times, saying, 'We once fought 12 straight nights, including twice on the same night when we fought the opening bout at George (Elbows) McFadden's club on 135th Street, and then rushed over to 13th Street to fight the main event at the Summit Athletic Club.'

Charley got into boxing aged seven when he was the mascot of hero Terry McGovern, who was responsible for one of Charley's trademarks, the derby. He bought his first 'iron lid' to emulate his hero. His first pupil was Al McCoy, who took the middleweight title with a 45-second knockout of George Chip in 1914. He lost McCoy when 'Dumb' Dan Morgan discovered Al had no contract with Goldman and promptly signed him up. Charley invested in a string of concession stands at an amusement park in Canarsie, in Brooklyn, and it was there that he met a deep-voiced hustler named Al Weill. They became partners, running a stable of fighters. They split up during the Depression and Goldman ran the bar in O'Malley's roadhouse in Orange Lake, New York while handling a few fighters, among them heavyweight contender Johnny Risko. Weill's best fighter at this time was lightweight Lou Ambers, who lost a decision to Tony Canzoneri for the title vacated by Barney Ross. Al got Ambers a rematch and asked Charley to train him, and in 1936

Goldman had his second champion. He went on to train Weill's other champions, featherweight Joey Archibald and welterweight Marty Servo.

Al Weill was matchmaker for Mike Jacobs in 1931 and again in 1937/1938. Mike's ambitious promotion of the Carnival of Champions at the Polo Grounds in September 1937 proved a financial flop, mainly due to Weill getting an $82,500 guarantee for his lightweight champion Lou Ambers. Weill resigned as matchmaker rather than take a cut.

'Although he could be as unctuous as Uriah Heap, but without Heap's show of humility,' wrote Arthur Daley, noted sportswriter of the *New York Times,* 'Weill was more often rude, crude, and abrasive. But he was extraordinarily proficient as a manager, a genuine mitt Machiavelli. Some called him the Artful Alsatian, and Dan Parker, who flailed him regularly in print, referred to him as "The Vest". According to Dan, "The Vest got all the gravy".'

'The word dignity has a gleaming appeal to Al Weill,' wrote *Boxing & Wrestling* magazine in its July 1957 issue. 'That's how he got to be known as The Vest. Solid, responsible citizens wear vests [waistcoats].'

Jimmy Cannon, columnist for the *New York Post*, called Weill the most despised man in boxing, adding, 'There are few in the fight racket who know the angles as well as Weill. Deceit is his confederate. Stinginess is one of his characteristics.'

The brilliant boxing essayist A. J. Liebling of the *New Yorker* magazine wrote more kindly of Weill. 'Weill is a frugal man, and he likes frugal fighters. Every kind of serious trouble a fighter can get into, he says, has its origin in the disbursement of currency – rich food, liquor, women, horse-race betting, and fast automobiles. Once a fighter starts gambling, Weill doesn't want him. "A gambler thinks he can get money without working for it," he says. Weill had a big string of fighters before the war, and used to quarter them all in a lodging house near Central Park West, where the housemaster would issue to each boy a weekly meal ticket with a face value of five dollars and 50 cents, redeemable in trade at a coffeepot on Columbus Avenue. The tickets cost Weill five dollars each, cash … None of those fighters ever suffered a defeat that could be attributed to high living.'[19]

19 A.J. Liebling *The Sweet Science* 1987

Among the mail delivered to Al Weill's New York office at 1585 Broadway on a spring morning in 1948 was a letter from Allie Colombo extolling the virtues of his pal, Rocco Francis Marchegiano, heavyweight champion of Brockton, Massachusetts. Weill read the letter again, lit another cigar, and reached for the phone.

There was a baseball game in progress on the James Edgar Playground in Brockton, where you could always find Rocco and his pal Allie. On that spring morning, the game was interrupted by a young girl running from a nearby house, yelling, 'Hey, Allie, there's a long distance call for you – somebody named Al Weill! He's in New York or Washington or some place! Hurry up.' Allie ran all the way home, still wearing his gear, and they stopped the game. A short while later, he returned and the game started again. Allie didn't say anything to Rocco but when the innings was over, he said, 'Hey, Rock, that was Weill calling. He wants to see us the first chance we get to go to New York. When do you want to go, Rock?'

A few days later, Allie made the call to Weill and arranged a date. As usual, the boys were short of coin and they looked up a pal who drove a vegetable truck, leaving Brockton every other night about eight o'clock. There were two trucks going so Rocco rode in one and Allie in the other. Rocco's driver was a guy named Bill O'Malley and he said they were due in New York about three in the morning. 'I wanted to be a fighter some time ago, then this job came up and you got to eat, so now I'm a truck driver. I wish you luck,' said Bill as he dropped Rocco off in Yonkers. When Allie joined him, they found a subway station and rode the train into Manhattan, getting off at Times Square. They walked until they found Broadway, found number 1585, and waited for Mr Weill to arrive. It was around 10.30am when they saw a taxi pull into the kerb and a short, stocky guy in horn-rimmed glasses and with a big cigar get out and head into the office building. After ten minutes or so, the boys went up to Weill's office, where a guy said Al was on the phone. Allie asked him to tell Al that Marchegiano from Brockton was waiting for him.

'Finally the guy said to go in,' Rocco recalled. 'Weill was sitting by the window chewing his cigar with his hat on. "Who told you you could fight?" he said to me. "He won all his fights," said Allie. "How many amateur fights?" he asked. "About 12," said Allie. "Can you punch?"

"Oh, ho," says Allie. "Yah, with just the right hand?" Weill said. "No, both hands," said Allie. "How old are you, what do you weigh?" "Twenty-three," said Allie, "One-ninety." "I suppose you want to go right to work today." "Sure," says Allie.'

Weill picked up the phone and called a number. 'Charley, I'm bringing down a new kid, a heavyweight. Get somebody ready for him. I want to see him work a couple of rounds. Is Godoy around? OK, we'll be down.' They went down to the street and took a cab to the CYO Gym on 17th Street. The gym was up two flights and they met this 'tiny little guy, Charley Goldman, a teacher and trainer,' said Rocco. 'Godoy was still there but I didn't box with him. They had a guy named Wade Chancey, a kid with 11, 12 fights. I remember getting in the ring with no warm-up and Goldman saying, "Do what you know you can do." I go in there and nothing happens in the first round, then in the second I catch him with the looper and he goes into the ropes. Weill is shouting, "Kill him, kill him." Nobody else said a word until Allie says, "That's enough, he ain't in shape."'

Rocco went into the shower room and Godoy walked in. 'He says, "Boy, you got it. Weill's OK, you stick with him." Then he walked away still saying, "Boy, you got it."' Weill had signed Arturo Godoy, from Chile, and Charley trained him into two fights with Joe Louis for the heavyweight title. In the first fight, Godoy, awkward and fighting out of a crouch, returned to his corner after the first round. Goldman told him to crouch lower. 'Put your nose down like you was smellin' the floor and punch up at the fella.' Godoy did so well over the next 14 rounds that one of the judges gave him the fight by a 10-5 margin. Unfortunately for Godoy, the referee and the other judge gave it to Louis. Arturo wasn't so lucky in the rematch. Louis stopped him in eight rounds.

Back at the office, Weill told Marciano,'I want you to stick around here. You can live where Goldman lives, at Ma Brown's on 92nd Street.'

'I don't want to stay here,' Marciano said, 'I want to go home and get in condition for a couple of months.'[20]

Weill said OK, to let him know when they were ready and he would get some fights for Rocco. Providence, Rhode Island was about 35 miles from Brockton and Weill said he had a friend there who promoted fights,

---

20 *Saturday Evening Post* October 1956

Manny Almeida. They were headed down to the street when Al called Rocco back and gave him 20 dollars. They had a meal in a nice restaurant and got the bus back home to Brockton, where things were starting to look a little better. The boys were in the fight business. Every morning they were up at seven and pounding the roads, breakfast ten till eleven, then rest for two hours. They worked out in the afternoon then got home at five for dinner with the family. Rocco would see Barbara once a week and they would go to a show or spend time at her house before he went home to bed for 10.30pm.

Russ Murray owned a local dog track and there was a big gym there. He let Rocco train there, no sparring, just using the equipment. A fireman he knew, Art Bergman, gave Rocco a big punch bag that weighed about 180 pounds, the biggest he had ever seen, as the normal was around 40 to 50 pounds. He used to punch it with his bare hands and reckoned that was the way he hardened them. At the local YMCA, he used the pool, where he practised throwing punches under water.

Every once in a while, they went to New York to see Charley Goldman. The first time Charley saw Rocco in the gym, he told him, 'If you done anything right, I didn't see it.'

Weill and Goldman had never seen anybody so awkward. His idea of protecting his midriff was to lift his hands, expose the target and let the enemy punch himself out. When they put him in the ring with Chancey, Rocco missed and stumbled and floundered. But in the second round, he hit Chancey on the chin with a right hand. Chancey went down, colder than the corpse of the Egyptian high priest Imhotep the Magnificent. Goldman looked at Weill. 'This,' he said, 'could be the complete answer to boxing science.'[21]

In the early days, Rocco was so raw and awkward, Goldman frustrated him by not letting him spar for five days. Charley had him working the heavy bag, shadow boxing and skipping. When Rocco protested, Charley said, 'You got so much to learn, it ain't funny.' Charley believed that a trainer should not interfere with a fighter's natural style, but rather refine and improve it. Accordingly, he did not try to turn him into a slick, jabbing boxer. He also sought to turn Marciano's shortcomings into advantages. His adage was, 'If you got a tall fighter, make him

---

21 Tim Cohane *Look* magazine November 1951

taller. If you got a short fighter, make him shorter.' With Marciano, Goldman made him shorter by teaching him to fight out of a crouch. By having him stoop low, Goldman made the already low target offered by Marciano that much harder to hit. He also worked with Marciano to shorten his punches and narrow his stance, tying Marciano's ankles together with a piece of string. He taught him to throw combinations, rather than one big bomb at a time. Although the finished product was still crude and clumsy, Marciano became a formidable offensive and defensive fighter. As Charley pointed out, 'A lot of people say Rocky don't look too good to them, but the guy on the floor don't look too good either!'[22]

Rocco was happy to work at the CYO Gym rather than at Stillman's, the hub of boxing in New York that was always buzzing. 'I was very clumsy and always making mistakes and those guys would have laughed at me. But even Charley wanted me to go to Stillman's. That's where he hung out himself and it was a nuisance for him to have to go downtown to meet me at the CYO Gym. But Weill always said, "I want him down there. I want him to be kept away from all those other guys. When he makes a mistake, you can holler at him and tell him what he's doing wrong. You can't do that so well at Stillman's. There's too much confusion."'[23]

When Al figured his new tiger wasn't making too many mistakes, he figured it was time he started work. He put in a call to Manny Almeida in Providence …

---

22 *Wikipedia*
23 *Saturday Evening Post* October 1956

4

DIVINE PROVIDENCE IN NEW ENGLAND

MANNY ALMEIDA'S Ringside Lounge stood on Mathewson Street in the Rhode Island city of Providence, a welcome sight for thirsty fight fans attracted by the neon sign above, which flashed and blinked to make it appear as though the cut-out boxers were punching each other. In the 1940s through 1950s, Manny promoted fights at the Rhode Island Auditorium and the leading fighters of the day would often strut their stuff there on a Monday night, prices for the five-fight card ranging from $1.25 to $3.50 ringside. On a warm July evening in 1948, the first bout on the programme featured Rocco Marchegiano and Harry Bielazarian, four rounds, heavyweights. From Boylston, Mass., Bielazarian had lost six of his nine fights, five by knockout, and at 175 pounds he was giving Marchegiano ten pounds. With Allie crouched by the corner, the young man from Brockton stormed into his opponent with both fists, dropping him to the canvas twice and it was all over at 1.32 of round one. 'The first time he knocked me down he broke my tooth,' said Harry later. 'Then he knocked me down again. Then I don't remember anything.'

The fans loved Rocky that night and they were back a week later to see him go against John Edwards of New Haven, Connecticut. An overhand right sent Mr Edwards off for an early shower at 1.19 of the first round. Three weeks later, unbeaten Boston heavyweight Bobby Quinn, with five knockouts in his eight winning fights, was giving the new boy fits, taking the first two rounds easily. Coming up for round three, Marchegiano brought the right hand up from knee level to end the show after 22 seconds of the round, with Allie jumping up and down at ringside. Montreal's Eddie Ross brought an unbeaten record of 15 fights with 14 knockouts to Rhode Island but going home he had a headache and a KO loss on his record card, a murderous right to the jaw knocking Eddie's mouthpiece out of the ring and him out cold before he hit the floor. That one lasted 63 seconds and the auditorium fans knew they had to be there early if they wanted to see the new Providence pin-up puncher.

Boston promoter Sam Silverman was working with Almeida at the time and when he saw Ross go down like the *Titanic*, he said, 'When Rocky flattened this boy, I knew.'

After that fight, Manny Almeida called Weill and said, 'You got another Dempsey. You better send somebody up here or you might lose this guy.' After that, Weill sent Chick Wergeles, one of his team, up to Providence. When he fought Jimmy Weeks, a black New Yorker, on 30 August, Charley Goldman made the journey to Providence to work the corner. 'This is it, Allie,' Rocco said to his pal. 'We're finally on our way. If Weill sent Goldman, we must be ready for New York.' Rocco was ready for Jimmy Weeks. A blasting right hand dropped Weeks for a nine count and when he dropped again from the crusher, referee Sharkey Buonanno stopped it at 2.50 of the opening round.

When Jimmy Weeks got his head back together, he told a reporter, 'He has the heart. I tagged him with two solid rights and he took them gamely. He might have used his left more as he packs power with this mitt also. He looks like a big prospect.' Goldman said after it was over, 'He sure can punch. He's a little crude as yet to be sure, but what I like almost as much as his punching might is his poise. He has a fine temperament, reminds me of Lou Ambers. I believe he'll go far.' One guy who was impressed was Mike Thomas, sportswriter for the *Providence Journal*. 'If punching power will do it,' he wrote the next day, 'Rocco Marchegiano may one day become the world heavyweight champion.'

If Rocco was giving fellow heavyweights a headache, his name was causing reporters and Providence ring announcer Harold Warman some concern. Al Weill told Rocco he had to change his name and did he like Rocky March? No, Rocco was proud of his Italian heritage and he wanted an Italian name. About this time Manny Almeida called

Weill and when Al mentioned the name change, he yelled into the phone, 'Are you crazy? This guy's a sensation up here under the name of Marciano. What's the matter with that?' Almeida had chopped three letters h-e-g out of the middle of Marchegiano and a legend was born. Rocky Marciano.

Marciano's knockout parade continued into September 1948, with the Providence fans going crazy as he blasted out two more unfortunates. Jerry Jackson hauled his 254-pound bulk up to Rhode Island and it took Rocky only 68 seconds to stretch it on the canvas, courtesy of a left hook to the forehead. A local reporter noted that Jackson resembled Humphrey Pennyworth of the *Joe Palooka* comic strip, standing up or lying down! A week later, Rocky was promoted to the semi-final bout, not that it made much difference to him. He didn't need the six rounds to flatten Boston heavyweight Bill Hardeman, who was knocked out in the first. That made him 8-0, six by KO.

If the Providence fans wanted to see their favourite in his next fight, they had to travel to Washington, D.C. and stay over as his fight with Gil Cardone was postponed a couple of nights due to rain. The fight was scheduled for the open-air Uline Arena and with the delay Rocky got to know his opponent. Cardone told Rocky a hard-luck story about his family and how his father was sick, and when Rocky told Allie he felt sorry for Gil, Allie gave him some advice. 'Rock, you can't feel sorry for anybody like that,' he said. 'He's an opponent, a guy in your way. He's out there to hurt you!' Rocky got the message and Cardone got an early shower. His 36-second blowout was the fastest knockout in local ring history.

Four days later, Marciano was back in Providence and after 2.30 of round two, opponent Bob Jefferson was on his way back to Brooklyn. Boston heavyweight Patrick (Red) Connolly made the trip to Rhode Island and wished he'd stayed in Beantown. A right-hand smash to the head made everything go black for Red at the 57-second mark of round one and when he woke up he asked his second if he'd 'got the number of that truck!'

Six months after knocking out Jersey Joe Walcott in June 1948, heavyweight champion Joe Louis was in Philadelphia to box a six-round exhibition with old foe Arturo Godoy at the city's Convention Hall.

Godoy was managed by Al Weill and Al thought it a good idea to take his new boy along to meet the champ, and it wasn't a bad idea to get his new boy a fight on the undercard to help with the expenses. Gilly Ferron was 6ft 2ins and had won three against five defeats. He was bigger than the Rock but he didn't look so big lying on the floor. The referee stopped the bout in the second round. It was a win for Rocky but a costly one as he broke a couple of knuckles in his right hand that shelved him for three months.

'That was the night Joe Louis boxed an exhibition with Godoy and everyone was down from New York, all the big shot managers. In the dressing room Weill told me that Jim Norris was out there, the International Boxing Club boss, and how important it was for me to look good, so I could get a fight in the Garden. He told me I should go to the body, where I would look good. I hadn't been much of a body puncher, but I tried. I got excited because Al, working my corner for the first time, was hollering from the corner, "Go to the body, to the body." I didn't know what to do. I was just trying to knock the guy out.'

Rocky did that all right and he did get to meet his boxing hero, Joe Louis. Weill said, 'Joe, I want you to meet my new kid, Rocky Marciano.' Louis shook hands with Rocky and said, 'Good luck, boy.' 'I felt great,' said Rocky, 'and couldn't wait to tell the gang in Brockton.'[24]

Back in New York, Rocky and Allie went up to Al's office and when he saw Rocky's hand he said, 'Get over to the University Hospital and see Dr Ritter. Don't do nothing else until he looks at the hand.' Dr Ritter examined Rocky's right hand and when he saw the X-rays he shook his head, saying, 'It's a bad break. You'll have to lay off fighting for at least two or three months.' With the hand in a plaster cast, the boys headed home.

'I'm not letting this stop me, Allie,' Rocky said. 'We'll keep right on training.' 'Yeah, Rock,' Allie said. 'We'd be crazy to quit training, even for a week. We're too close to the big time now.' No matter how cold it was, they walked from five to ten miles every morning that winter. In the afternoons, they held long boxing sessions in Rocky's backyard on Dover Street with Colombo and Rocky's younger brother Sonny standing in as sparring partners. 'We left the house at eight every morning' Colombo

---

24 *Saturday Evening Post* September 1956

recalled. 'Even when it was snowing so hard you couldn't see the road. And in the afternoons, we shovelled out the yard and Rocky boxed. The Rock was keeping in top condition.'[25]

Marciano's hand was in the cast for three months and when the doctor saw it afterwards he said the hand would be stronger than ever. But when Rocky asked Weill for a fight, the manager made him wait another couple of weeks before sending him back to Goldman. Charley soon had him back at work, hitting the heavy bag with increasing intensity until he was happy the hand was healed. One of Rocky's sparring partners at the CYO Gym was the Austrian heavyweight Jo Weiden. Jack Dempsey had brought him over and he took him to Goldman's gym one day for a workout. Jack wanted to see if Weiden could take a punch and he said to Rocky, 'Kid, I want you to hit this guy right on the chin if you can, and watch out for yourself because he's a pretty good puncher himself.'

'We boxed a few minutes,' said Rocky, 'and then I landed a big left hook and opened a cut and Dempsey had to take him to the hospital. Weiden came back to the gym a month later but we never saw Dempsey with him again.'

Rocky was back to Providence in March 1949 to face Johnny Pretzie of Boston. Johnny had lost nine of his 14 fights and he would lose this one, although reporter Michael J. Thomas of the *Providence Journal* wrote that, 'Pretzie's performance impressed the 3,595 fans who paid in a gross of $6,821. He made Marciano miss by the proverbial mile with his smart boxing tactics, mixed it willingly with him in the early stages, particularly in the second round, and landed some hefty punches himself. Marciano hardly looked like another Jack Dempsey on this occasion. He showed no boxing skill whatsoever, left himself open to attack and his punching, dynamic as it was, was crude and aimless. He still must be regarded as a good prospect, but has much to learn.'

Fighting in his first ten-round bout, Rocky stopped Pretzie at 1.46 of the fifth round, putting Johnny on the canvas three times for nine counts before referee Dolly Searle stopped the fight. 'Weill was in my corner when I fought Pretzie,' recalled Rocky, 'and it was terrible. He got all excited, yelling and screaming. Once, when I had Pretzie in my corner trying to knock the guy out, I could hear him screaming, "Look at

---

25 Everett M. Skehan *Rocky Marciano: Biography of a First Son* 1977

him! He's a sucker!" Allie told me later Weill was giggling and laughing and sort of hysterical. He made everybody nervous.'

Manny Almeida had Rocky headlining his show a week later, against Artie Donato of Red Bank, New Jersey, a guy with a 7-5 pro record. He gave Rocky a boxing lesson for 22 seconds of round one, but in the 33rd second Rocky gave him a right to the jaw, dropping him in a heap. When referee Sharkey Buonanno got to ten, Artie was still there. Another New Jersey entry, James Walls, bothered Rocky for a couple of rounds a fortnight later, but in the third round the Walls came tumbling down when Rocky sent a series of right hands to his head and finished with a devastating left hook to the midriff.

Brooklyn heavyweight Jimmy Evans bobbed and weaved through round one to frustrate the boy from Brockton and outboxed Rocky in the second round before Marciano got his act together in round three. Heavy lefts and rights broke Jimmy's resistance and the referee put an end to the bout at 2.44 of the round. There was praise for the winner from Mike Thomas, who wrote, 'Marciano, sporting a new left hook, showed a much more polished attack. He didn't waste as many punches as in past bouts and handled himself well.' Loser Evans had kind words for his conqueror, calling Marciano a better prospect than the highly regarded undefeated New York heavyweight Roland La Starza, who had beaten Jimmy over six rounds in a Madison Square Garden bout in October 1947.

Rocky had a new experience in May 1949 when Don Mogard of Paterson, New Jersey, finished their ten rounds still standing, the first man to do so in Rocky's 17-bout career. A boxer rather than a puncher, Mogard covered well and bloodied Rocky's nose in the third round, putting a mouse under his left eye in the seventh. It was a unanimous decision for Marciano but he wasn't happy, despite Colombo's efforts at cheering him up. 'Don't be so downhearted,' he said. 'You won, Rock, that's what counts. You showed them you could go ten and win the decision.'

'I should have knocked him out,' was all Rocky would say. Promoter Sam Silverman consoled him, 'It done you good, Rocky. Every good fighter has to go ten rounds sometime.'

A few days before the Mogard fight, Rocky got a call at the gym. It was Al Weill. 'Come on right up to the office. Stop everything you're doing and get up here. It's very important.' Rocky remembered, 'When

I walked in the office, there were three other fighters there. Weill sent them out as soon as I got there. "I am the new International Boxing Club matchmaker," he said. "I just released those guys. I'm not managing them any more." He opened a drawer and pulled out a paper and passed it to me. "Sign it," he said. I didn't even read it. I signed it and Al put it away. Then he says, "That's a private agreement between you and me. But if anyone asks you who your manager is, tell them Marty."

'When I first came to Weill in 1948 looking for a manager,' Rocky would recall, 'he wanted me to get rid of Allie. Allie grew up next door to me, he encouraged me and worked with me. I couldn't get along without him, but Weill didn't want him around. "I want Allie with me," I says, "I want him to get ten per cent of me." "What?" Weill yells. "Ten per cent? Who do you think you're talking to? Nobody has ten per cent of my fighters. If you want Colombo, all right, but we'll throw him something after every fight."

* * * *

Al Weill let Rocky keep his first purses from the Providence fights, but when Rocky shaped up as championship timber, Weill gave him a 50-50 contract, with Al paying the expenses. Weill told Rocky when he and Barbara could get married. 'Every time Barbara would talk to me about it, I would talk to Al, and he would say, "Take it easy. You're just learning. Fighter's wives hurt fighters. When I think you're ready to get married, I'll tell you."'

Former featherweight champion Willie Pep was a close friend of Rocky's. He recalled a story indicative of Rocky's relationship with Weill. 'Trainer Charley Goldman once told Rocky that he wasn't getting the ten per cent of the purses he had been promised, so Rocky went to see Weill. When Marciano brought up the problem, Weill said, "Rocky, your business is fighting, so don't get involved in my affairs with Goldman." Then he slapped the heavyweight champion across the face. Marty Weill is Al's stepson. He's a nice guy and he had a few fighters. After Al and me signed that agreement, Marty was around for all my fights but he was never my manager. We weren't fooling anybody. Everybody knew my real manager was Al and he didn't try to hide it. He used to give me orders in front of everybody but he couldn't be a manager and the IBC matchmaker, so he never admitted anything publicly.'[26]

Allie Colombo was delighted with the news when Rocky told him that Weill was moving into the hot seat at the Garden. 'That is beautiful, Rock,' he said, 'With Weill calling the shots, how can we miss fighting at the Garden?'

It was about this time that Rocky was having trouble with his back and his family doctor was giving him shots and heat therapy, but nothing seemed to help and the stiffness was getting worse. Allie suggested he should have a rest but Rocky wanted another fight after the Mogard disappointment and he was happy when he got Harry Haft in the ring at Providence and blasted him out in round three.

Sam Silverman promoted a fight card in New Bedford, Mass., and put Rocky in his main event against Pete Louthis, a Rhode Island fighter with a decent record. Marciano got him out of there in the third round with a left to the jaw, but he was in more pain than his victim. His back was killing him.

'That night I could hardly get through the ropes into the ring,' Rocky would recall. 'Allie Colombo had to stretch the lower rope almost down to the canvas and hold the middle rope as high as he could get it. Allie and me thought it was just a muscle strain that would go away with heat treatment and massage, but it didn't. It kept getting worse.'

'Toward the end of the first round,' recalled Sam Silverman, 'Rocky bent down to get under a punch. The round ended and Marciano walked back to his corner like the Hunchback of Notre Dame.' Going out for round three, Allie's words were in his head, 'You can't fight like this, Rock. What're we gonna do?' Rocky did what he had to do. He sent a left hook to the jaw and Pete went down for the count, Marciano's 18th knockout in 19 fights.[27]

But he knew Allie was right, He couldn't carry on like this.

He went to see Dr Thomas B. Quigley at Boston and the prognosis was not good. Rocky had a slipped disc in his back and an operation was advised. No fighting for at least a year and then maybe never again. It was out of the question as far as Rocky was concerned. He could smell the

---

26 *Saturday Evening Post* October 1956
27 Everett M. Skehan *Rocky Marciano: Biography of a First Son 1977*

big time, he was a couple of fights from the Garden. He saw Al Norling at the YMCA, who massaged his back, and Allie had to keep pulling his legs to relieve the pressure. When he knocked out Tommy DiGiorgio in four rounds a few weeks later, the back didn't feel so bad. A family friend, Dr Michael Del Colliano, gave Rocky diathermy treatment, but told him the pain could return any time. Rocky could handle pain so he pressed on to his next fight, with Ted 'Tiger' Lowry, light-heavyweight champion of New England, a trial horse who had lost as many fights as he'd won.

'The only time Weill ever asked me if I wanted to fight someone was when I was offered a match with Ted Lowry, who fought out of New Bedford. I hadn't seen him but I heard he was a great defensive fighter. I told that to Al and he says, "Well, do you want to fight him?" "Sure," I says. "I don't want to duck anybody." Al made the match and I fought Lowry in Providence and the guy went the whole ten rounds with me. I won the decision and fought him a year later and he went ten rounds with me again. He had a funny style and I think if he fought me after I won the title he still would have gone ten rounds with me.'[28]

Michael J. Thomas watched most of Rocky's fights as reporter for the *Providence Journal* and he didn't like the Lowry fight. 'Marciano, in the first place, did not win the fight as this observer saw it. This reporter gave it to Lowry six rounds to four, but this wasn't the dilemma – hardly. There was some question as to whether Lowry, who came close to knocking out Marciano in the second, third and fourth rounds, deliberately bogged down in his attack after the fourth stanza. Many in the crowd felt he had. As it was, referee Ben Maculan warned Lowry three times to open up. In the fifth he bellowed, "Open up or I'll toss you out", and similarly threatened him twice in the seventh.' Thomas also wrote, 'Marciano was the much busier of the two, particularly after the fourth round. He landed three punches to Lowry's one from the fifth round on, concentrating wholly on the body. His aggressiveness and constant punching probably was what caught the eye of the three officials.'

In his next fight, Thomas was leading Rocky's cheering section again, calling Marciano an embryonic Dempsey in knocking out Joe Dominic of Springfield at 2.26 of the second round. Marciano dropped Dominic for an eight count with a right hook, sent him down again

---

28 *Saturday Evening Post* October 1956

with a left-right combination in the second round before finishing Joe off with a thunderous right.

'I figured I would knock him out,' said Dominic in the dressing room. 'I didn't dream he could hit like that. Marciano hits harder than Roland LaStarza, but I believe Bernie Reynolds hits as hard as Rocky.' In his 29 fights, Dominic had never been off his feet. He also had never been hit by Rocky Marciano.

As Rocky put it a few years later, 'When you have pride in your work, you appreciate it right away. When a fighter doesn't respect this, well, that's one of the reasons for me getting real mad a few times before fights. One of them was early in my career against Joe Dominic. He was out of Providence, where I was making my name, and he ridiculed me. He said I was nothing but an amateur – and maybe I was then – but when I got him in the ring I put him away in two rounds.'[29]

Six months after Al Weill landed in the matchmaker's seat at Madison Square Garden, he decided it was time for Rocky to hit the big town. He had Roland LaStarza fighting Cesar Brion in the main event and gave Rocky the eight-round semi-final bout, nothing too tough for son Marty's new signing, a chap called Irish Pat Richards of Columbus, Ohio, who had a 20-5-5 record. With a crowd of 12,035 in the Garden eager to see the new heavyweights, LaStarza beat Brion in a dull fight and Rocky demolished Richards at the 39-second mark of round two. He did the job but the opponent was glad to get out of there.

Back in the Providence ring, Marciano drew a record standing-room only crowd of 6,775 and they went home happy after seeing their favourite drop Phil Muscato of Buffalo to the canvas nine times before the referee got tired of counting and stopped the bout. Muscato was 56-20 coming to the ring and he had tangled with guys like Lee Savold, Joey Maxim, Lee Oma, Archie Moore and Arturo Godoy, but Rocky had him going up and down like a yo-yo until 1.15 of round five, when the referee allowed Phil to go back to his dressing room. Safely out of Rocky's reach, Phil told reporters, 'He's a good prospect and hits hard, but I still believe I can beat him.' On second thoughts, he retired after losing two more fights, aged just 26. 'He does hit hard, though,' Phil told his two boxing brothers when he got back to Buffalo.

---

29 *Saturday Evening Post* October 1956

Strange as it seemed, when Weill gave Rocky a ten-round bout at the Garden, it was not the main event. Al put three tens on the card, with Nick Barone facing Dick Wagner in the lighty-heavyweight feature bout; middleweight Lee Sala meeting Reuben Jones and Rocky Marciano in with Carmine Vingo.

5

TOUGH TIMES IN THE GARDEN

CARMINE VINGO'S dream of becoming heavyweight champion of the world began in a prison cell. A husky Italian kid from New York's Bronx, he was just 16 when he was caught behind the wheel of a stolen car and arrested. On his second day in jail while awaiting trial, Carmine was reading a newspaper when a familiar face looked up at him from the sports page. It was a picture of amateur fighter Jimmy Vingo, Carmine's brother. Boxing had never appealed to Carmine before but it seemed like a good idea now. When Jimmy came to see him the next day, Carmine said he wanted to be a fighter. Jimmy said he would send his manager, Billy Masselli, to see his kid brother, and as he was leaving he said, 'Look, you got lots of free time here. Why don't you exercise?'

Carmine Vingo began his boxing career doing push-ups and knee bends on the floor of his cell. The guards watched him and walked away, shaking their heads. Three days and already the kid was stir crazy. Carmine was in jail 12 days before they let him out with a year's probation. He swore he would never return and he never did. Billy Masselli bought the kid some equipment and he started training at Bobby Gleason's Gym in the Bronx, alongside such fighters as Jake LaMotta, Walter Cartier and Steve Belloise. One day, when sparring with Belloise, Carmine tried to knock out the middleweight contender. 'After that the ring got too small for me,' he said. 'Steve almost chased me out into the street.'

By March 1947, Billy Masselli was ready to unveil his new tiger. Fighting a prelim at Madison Square Garden, Carmine knocked out

Barney Melten in two rounds. He lost only one of his next 16 fights, with six knockouts, before he climbed into the Garden ring again to face Rocky Marciano, the new sensation who was undefeated in 24 bouts, 22 by knockout. By this time, Carmine was being managed by Jackie Levine, Masselli having decided to give all his time to his butcher shop, and he had won 11 bouts with Levine when he got the Marciano fight. The kid they were calling 'Bingo' Vingo turned 20 on 28 December 1949, two days before the fight that would be his first ten-rounder. Carmine wanted to marry his sweetheart, Cathy, and, with the $1,500 purse, they set a date in February for the nuptials.

A chilly night in Manhattan kept the Garden crowd down to 9,277. In the dressing room, as Whitey Bimstein taped his hands, Jackie Levine said to Carmine, 'Show him who's boss right away.' Then it was time to go and Carmine walked out with Jackie, Whitey and Freddie Brown, the other trainer, along the corridor and up the six big steps on to the floor of the Garden. Carmine's memory of the Marciano fight ended with those six steps. He didn't remember the walk to the ring or the fight itself. He didn't remember anything about the next 11 days when he lay near death in St Clare's Hospital. The kid's big dream had turned into a nightmare.

The fight that Carmine Vingo can't remember will never be forgotten by those who saw it. It was one of the most sensational heavyweight bouts ever seen in the Garden ring; a savage, no-holds barred brawl that had the fans on their feet throughout the almost six rounds it lasted. Looking back, Marty Weill realised the accuracy of the dark premonitions he had before the fight. 'I just didn't like the feel of the match. I guess I really believed someone would get hurt. Each fighter was too fearless and sometimes that can be bad.' Marty had voiced his feelings to his father when the match was proposed, but Al said, 'It's Vingo or you guys don't get on the show.' So the fight was on.

They came out slugging at the opening bell. A savage exchange of punches and Rocky nailed Carmine with a smashing right to the jaw, dropping him to the canvas with a thud. Vingo took nine before getting to his feet, and as Rocky came at him again with the fans already roaring for the kill, the kid stood his ground and traded lethal wallops with Rocky. Marciano was glad to hear the bell. In round two, they were at each other like a couple of stags locked in battle. Another vicious barrage of punches saw Carmine go down and again he took nine before getting back into the fight. The more he was hurt, the harder he fought back and his supporters yelled their heads off as he pounded Rocky back across the ring.

At the bell, Rocky dropped on to his stool, breathing hard. 'This Vingo is tough,' he said to Allie and Charley. 'I hit him with my toughest punch and he still got up.' Little Charley Goldman nodded as he worked over Rocky. 'Marty and I think maybe you should pace yourself, box him for a couple of rounds and don't take no chances. You've got to save your strength in case this thing goes ten rounds.' The third round was a repetition of the first two and the fans were already limp with excitement. The fighters were smashing each other with vicious blows, each one with 'KO' written on it. Vingo unleashed a terrific left hook that exploded on Rocky's jaw and sent him reeling into the ropes. Carmine tore in for the finish as Rocky hung on like a drowning man clutching driftwood. 'Hang on, Rocky,' they were screaming from his corner. 'Stay on top of him, stay on top of him!'

Marciano managed to hang on until the bell brought 60-seconds relief and Weill, Goldman and Colombo went quickly to work as he hit the stool. Across the ring, Jackie Levine was telling Carmine. 'You almost had him that round, kid, keep at him, he won't take many more of them.' Rocky had no intention of taking any more. 'That guy not only takes a real wallop,' he said in the corner, 'he can pack a real wallop, too. I've never been hit by anything that hard in my life.'

'We've told you to box him,' screamed Charley Goldman. 'So you'd better start.' Rocky did as he was told. Coming out for round four, he was more cautious, more defensive, and the kid was somewhat frustrated as he tried to nail Rocky with another good one. Standing 6ft 4ins, Vingo had height and reach advantages over Marciano; what he didn't have was Rocky's steely determination, experience and physical condition. That would make the difference. Levine and Bimstein lit a fire under their boy and he charged out for round six, hell-bent on destruction. Unfortunately, the guy coming from the other corner had the same idea. Rocky weathered Carmine's opening assault and fired a vicious left hook-right cross combination that dropped the big fellow to the canvas with a thud. As he sprawled there, referee Harry Ebbets broke off his count at three and signalled Dr Vincent Nardiello into the ring. The timekeeper finished the count, making Marciano a knockout winner at 1.46 of round six. But by that time, all eyes were focused on the group of men huddled around the stricken fighter. Dr Nardiello, the New York Commission physician, knelt before Carmine and jabbed a needle into his chest. There was no response. A stretcher was brought into the ring and Vingo was carried to the dressing room, where Dr Nardiello attempted to revive him, without success. When the ambulance failed to arrive within 20 minutes, the Bronx boy was carried, coats and blankets piled high on the stretcher, the two blocks to St Clare's Hospital.

Examination revealed a blood clot, concussion and a small tear on the brain. His chances were not good and a priest was called to administer the last rites.

'I went to my dressing room and showered,' said Rocky later, 'when the newspaper guys came in and one said, "That Vingo boy is in bad shape, Rocky, they think you better go to the hospital. They got him in St Clare's Hospital. Dr Nardiello's over there." Allie and Goldman and me went straight to the hospital. There was this woman sitting there. She was sobbing so hard she had a handkerchief in her mouth and I knew this was Carmine's mother. I just stood there and looked at her and said "I'm sorry." She didn't say nothing. A nun came along and I hoped she would say something. She touched my arm and said, "We're praying – all praying for this boy. I know you're praying, too, Rocky." Dr Nardiello came along and I said, "Doc, you got to do something for this kid. You got to pull him through for me." "Don't worry, Rocky," he said. "We're doing everything we can. We got this brain expert up here and we're going to stay with him until he's all right."

'About three in the morning, the doc told us to go back to the hotel. All the family was there, Uncle Mike, Uncle John, Uncle Dom and Pop. Barbara was there, too. She and I looked at each other and we both had tears in our eyes. She says, "I heard all about it", and she didn't say any more. Nobody went to bed, we all stayed up and talked all night. The others went back to Brockton in the morning. Allie and I walked over to the hospital and Dr Nardiello was still there. He gave a little smile and said, "We've got hope   good hope now, Rocky." Next day,

Dr Nardiello told us to go home and he would keep in touch. We went back to Brockton and I stopped at St Patrick's Church on Main Street. I prayed for Vingo every morning until one day the doc called and said Vingo was able to go home. Except for a slight paralysis on one side, he came out all right. We got to be real good friends. I gave him some of my purses from the next few fights and he was at my big fights after that.'[30] After the fight, referee Harry Ebbets, a former light-heavyweight boxer, told the commission, 'I was watching closely. He really got a very hard bang when he went down. I would not have let him continue if he had been able to get up. I took out his mouthpiece at the count of three.'

Carmine Vingo was in and out of a coma for the next ten days as his family kept a vigil by his bedside. He was in the hospital for six weeks before they let him go home. He was partially paralysed on his left side and he couldn't see out of his left eye. But he was alive and after a few weeks he threw his cane away. In March 1950, he and Cathy were married.

'Marciano,' recalled Vingo, 'by generously donating a percentage of each purse from his next few fights, gave $2,000 to the hospital and $500 to me. Rocky is one of my best friends today. Also I got $500 from the Garden, which was payment on an insurance policy they take out on fighters. So that makes $1,000 altogether that I received in cash. Oh, yes, just recently I ran into Jackie Levine, he pressed $200 on me. I didn't want to take it, but I needed the money too badly to turn it down.'

In his *New York Times* column some years later, Ira Berkow wrote of meeting Carmine Vingo at a large office building on Broadway, where the former heavyweight was working as a night-security porter. 'He speaks softly, hoarsely. His eyes are soft-brown and lingering. His nose is flat. He appears older than 41. Talking of the Marciano fight, he says, "Who'd ever believe it? I figured the worst that could happen was to get knocked out. Actually, I was figurin' on winnin".' Vingo was knocked out in the sixth round; he did not get up. He was paralysed for two years, his right leg is still stiff and he is partially blind in both eyes. "I can't drive a car no more, I can't walk so good no more. I can't even put my pants on without leaning against the wall. Imagine that! And all the neighbours thought we were rich because of the rumours that we

---

30 *Saturday Evening Post* October 1956

were collecting thousands from all over the place. What a laugh. The only money we got was from Cathy working. I couldn't hardly get out of bed for two years."

'Another belief was that Rocky Marciano was helping Vingo financially. In fact, after Marciano died in a plane crash on 31 August 1969, the *New York Times* obituary read, "Despite his reputation for conservative spending, Marciano had a list of beneficiaries to whom he sent money regularly. One of these was Carmine Vingo."

("The only thing we ever got from Rocky were promises," said Cathy Vingo recently. "He'd tell Carmine that he'd have something going for him soon, to put him in some business, that he had some property for him in Florida, that he'd have a benefit for him. Nothing. Each man is for himself in the fight game. That's the game.")

"I didn't care," said Carmine. "But my wife gets mad about it. I didn't push Rocky or Al Weill, his manager. Rocky, he was one of the nicest guys you'd ever want to talk to. I'd go up to his training camp in the mountains. And I was at his wedding and met his family, went to his funeral. Paid my own way … We ain't rich and we ain't poor but it's not easy, either. I think about what happened and I got to shake my head. 20 years old.'"[31]

About a week after Rocky knocked Carmine Vingo out of boxing and into a hospital bed, Al Weill phoned him to say he had booked a fight at Madison Square Garden for 21 January 1950. 'Rocky didn't even ask who his opponent was. "Forget it, Al," he said, "I'm not getting back into the ring until I'm sure Carmine is okay."

'Weill pleaded with him, but Rocky hung up. The next day Rocky packed his bags and went to New York to visit Vingo, who had asked to see him. Vingo was still in his hospital bed reading a newspaper and looked himself. He thought Rocky was stupid for thinking about quitting boxing.

"Anybody who has a punch like you, Rock, will be the next heavyweight champion," Vingo said. "I didn't see that left hook that sent me to the hospital. I just forgot to duck."

'Even after Vingo had apparently recovered and was released from the hospital, Rocky was not ready to fight again until a story hit the

---

31 Ira Berkow *New York Times* January 1971

papers that relieved him of all guilt. It seems a routine investigation by the New York State Commission revealed that Carmine Vingo had fallen from a window at his home when he was a baby and had suffered a head injury and partial loss of speech and hearing. He reportedly was told to quit boxing in 1947 because of this accident, but he refused to heed the warning. Dr Nardiello was quoted in the news item as saying had he known of Vingo's medical history, he would not have permitted him to fight because the slightest blow to the head could have caused injury or even death.

'The news brought great relief to Rocky, who paid $2,500 towards Vingo's medical bills and offered to help him in other ways. Carmine and Rocky eventually became close friends. Although Vingo was not permitted to fight again, he was at all of Rocky's remaining fights courtesy of the Rock and was a guest at the wedding of Rocky and Barbara later in 1950.'[32]

'I remember back around 1949,' Rocky recalled for the *Saturday Evening Post* in October 1956. 'I sat with Weill and watched one of Roland LaStarza's fights. When it was over, Al said, "What do you think of him?" I said, "That LaStarza is a good boxer, but I'd just as soon step in with him." "LaStarza's better than he looks," Al says. "Sometime you'll fight him, but you're not ready yet." By the spring of 1950, Al thought Rocky was ready for Roland LaStarza and made the announcement from his office at Madison Square Garden. The battle of the undefeated heavyweights would take place on 24 March at the Eighth Avenue arena: Rocky Marciano, undefeated in 25 fights, 23 knockouts, versus Roland LaStarza, undefeated in 37 bouts, with 17 by knockout.

'They have no objection to intelligence, but they do not care for educated fighters in the boxing business,' wrote W. C. Heinz in *Ring* magazine. 'They call them college fighters, and it is not a term intended to connote endearment. For years they have been citing Bob Pastor and Steve Hamas and Jack Torrance and Bob Nestell as proof that a knowledge of Chaucer, calculus and the chemical qualities of cadmium will do less than help a man in the ring. Now they have LaStarza, who put in two years at City College of New York.

---

32 Michael N. Varveris *Rocky Maricano: The 13th Candle* 2000

'LaStarza is the son of a Bronx butcher and as polite, personable and intelligent an athlete as you would care to find gracing any sport. He is a little short for a heavyweight – only 5ft 10½ins – but he has the clean, hard, well-trained look of someone you might find playing guard for Earl Blaik at West Point.

'When LaStarza first started to put together the wins that went to make up his string of victories, the savants of the sport raised their heads. Here was a well-built young man who, as they say, could hold his hands up better than most young heavyweights new to the sport. He could jab. He could hook behind it reasonably well. He had a good short right … Maybe this would be the one who, if he kept coming along, would give the division class and carry it and all boxing along on his ample shoulders.

'This enthusiasm or optimism was shortlived. It was found that while LaStarza improved, he didn't improve enough. He stood up too straight. He wouldn't step in with a right hand. He did the same things at the end of any 12 months as he did at the start. His basic trouble was that he couldn't or wouldn't improve on the book. That was when they dropped the college tag on LaStarza. Like all educated fighters, they reasoned, he was trying to get all his fighting, like he once got all of his English, his mathematics, his chemistry, out of a book. This was a book written for him, so to speak, by Jimmy Brown, who trains him, and Jimmy DeAngelo, who manages him, and by all the fighters he had ever seen and studied. None of his fighting came out of himself.

'There was one typical example. On 10 December 1948, LaStarza fought Gene Gosney in the Garden and Gosney knocked him down twice before he knocked Gosney out. Those who saw this fight liked LaStarza for it, because they saw him get off the deck, but this bothered LaStarza and he did not consider it flattering, and so he lost the lesson that should have come from it. "I can't understand that," LaStarza said several weeks after the Gosney fight. "Once I fought a perfect fight. Every move I made was perfect, and nobody said anything about it. Now I fight a bad fight and people seem to like me better for it. I did everything wrong in that fight and I chewed myself plenty for it. Here it had gone six rounds when I should have finished it in the third."[33]

____
33 W. C. Heinz *Ring* July 1950

For almost 40 years, Barney Nagler wrote a newspaper column devoted mainly to boxing and thoroughbred racing for the *Morning Telegraph,* and when it ceased publication in 1972 his column 'On Second Thought' moved to The *Daily Racing Form*. With all due respect to the esteemed Mr Heinz, Barney put the LaStarza puzzle more succinctly, writing, 'In boxing gloves, Rocky Marciano is dressed to kill. Garbed the same manual way, Roland LaStarza is dressed for a night's work.'

On a chilly night in March 1950, some 13,658 fight fans paid $53,733 to get into Madison Square Garden to see the boxer against the brawler in a ten-round bout that could decide the next challenger for the world heavyweight championship. The men who could decide were sitting ringside: judge Artie Aidala, judge Artie Schwartz and referee Jack Watson.

Both boys were fast out of the traps at the opening bell, with LaStarza catching the eye as he countered Rocky's awkward lunges with clever boxing. He gave the New Englander a boxing lesson through the first three rounds, with Rocky chasing, swinging and missing most of the time. But he was warming up and in the fourth round LaStarza's growing confidence was jolted by a thunderous right that connected with Roland's jaw. He dropped to the canvas as a roar went up from the Marciano supporters, who had hocked a few belongings to make the trip to New York.

'Rocky floored the 22-year-old New Yorker with a looping right to the chin in the fourth round,' recorded Jack Cuddy for *United Press*. 'The bell rang, ending the round at the count of seven. LaStarza then lurched to his feet and staggered to his corner. That was the only knockdown of the fight.'[34]

'When he decided to fight it out with Marciano, LaStarza had the better of the argument,' wrote Nat Fleischer in *Ring* magazine. 'Rocky, a wild swinger with either hand, in one round he missed eight attempts to land on his moving target, yet one looping overhand right, the kind one expects in an ordinary fist fight, felled LaStarza for a seven count in the fourth round.'[35]

---

34 Jack Cuddy *Dunkirk Evening Observer* 25 March 1950
35 Nat Fleischer *Ring* June 1950

'In that frame, the swarthy, short-armed New Englander cut LaStarza over both eyes, bloodied his nose and climaxed the round by decking his rival,' reported Murray Rose.

'In the fourth round he hurt Marciano near the Forty-Ninth Street ropes,' recalled Bill Heinz. 'Marciano stood for a moment, his hands down, an open target. Instead of stepping in, LaStarza stepped back, his hands high, the counter-fighter waiting for Marciano to throw the next punch. A fight that might have been ended early went ten rounds.'

Marciano tried his best to cash in on the knockdown, forcing the action in round five, but LaStarza had tasted his power and tied him up, taking advantage of Rocky's wildness. Marciano forced the fighting in every round, but his more skilled opponent beat him at in-fighting during their many clinches. LaStarza had such an edge in the in-fighting that most of the boxing writers scored in favour of the New Yorker. He also staggered Rocky with a straight right to the chin in the sixth.

Rocky was doing all the work through rounds six and seven, but LaStarza appeared to land the more effective punches as he was now making Rocky fight his fight. In an attempt to bring LaStarza's guard down, Marciano unleashed a vicious body attack in round eight, a bit too vicious, as a low right caused referee Jack Watson to take the round away from Rocky. The crowd was getting behind Rocky now and he slugged away in the ninth round with his dynamic right hand, desperately trying to bring his man down again, with Allie yelling from the corner. Little Charley Goldman had some words for his tiger before sending him out for the tenth and final round, and Rocky won it, surprising Roland with a left hook attack as the New Yorker looked for the right hand. At the bell, LaStarza walked to his corner, looking like a loser, blood coming from his nose, cuts over both eyes, his prestige damaged.

The excited crowd quieted down as ring announcer Johnny Addie took the microphone to read, 'Judge Artie Schwartz votes for Marciano, 5-4-1!' Rocky's hometown supporters were still shouting as Addie started to read the second scorecard, 'Judge Artie Aidala votes for LaStarza, 5-4-1!' There was hushed anticipation as Addie read out, 'Referee Jack Watson, five rounds for Marciano, five for LaStarza, six points for LaStarza, nine for Marciano. The winner on a split decision, Marciano!'

'Watson's card thus created the opportunity, unique under the New York State boxing rules, for him to vote further in points. In being scored on points in New York, a man gets up to four points for winning a round and none if he loses it. Thus Marciano's 9-6 victory. Things were never like this with Louis.'[36]

'In the ring, after Addie announced the decision, a bruised, battered and bewildered LaStarza rushed over to the ring announcer and asked, "Did Marciano win?" He had. Many years later, the New Yorker was still shaking his head over the verdict. "I won the fight," he maintained. "There's no doubt about it in my mind." LaStarza was also fairly confident about the reason he lost. "The fact that his manager was a matchmaker at the Garden I would say had a lot to do with the decision … That's what I think. That's what everybody thought at the time."'[37]

Indeed, many ringside observers in the Garden that night felt that LaStarza had not only won but had also won in convincing fashion. For example, Jesse Abramson, the boxing writer for the *New York Herald Tribune*, called it a 'paper thin and exceedingly odd decision … Marciano won, but it was a gift.'

'The public craved a rematch and the IBC envisioned a tremendous gate. Norris argued for it. Rocky wanted it for the big money involved and to prove he could knock LaStarza out. But, in a rare stance against the wishes of the IBC, Weill would have no part of it. It wasn't only Weill's pride that made him balk. Roland was an excellent boxer who had waged a tough, intelligent battle against Rocky. But now Marciano was undefeated and LaStarza was not. Rocky was at full steam, bucking the stormy seas that led to the heavyweight championship. Another fight with LaStarza would prove nothing and, to Weill's cautious mind, could be disastrous. Weill was never a man who risked millions to make thousands.'[38]

When the time was right, Al Weill would let Rocky fight LaStarza again. But only when the time was right …

---

36 INS *Chester Times* Pa.

37 Russell Sullivan *Rocky Marciano: The Rock of His Times* 2002

38 Everett M. Skehan *Rocky Marciano: Biography of a First Son* 1977

6

MARRIAGE – AL SAYS 'YES!'

BARBARA MAE Cousins met Rocco Francis Marchegiano at a local dance in the spring of 1947 and by the spring of 1948 she had a shiny engagement ring on the third finger of her left hand. When her girlfriends admired the ring, they always asked when the wedding was going to be. Barbara kept asking Rocco the same question. When Rocco, now the heavyweight prizefighter Rocky Marciano, kept asking his manager Al Weill, Al kept saying, 'Take it easy. You're just learning. When I think you're ready to get married, I'll tell you.' So Rocky kept explaining to Barbara why Al kept saying no, because he was a great manager and a great disciplinarian.

'I could understand a little better than she could,' Rocky would say, 'and she'd get mad at him and mad at me. One night she got so mad she picked up the phone and called Al. She was going to get real tough with him, but he said, "Barbara, I've been a manager all my life and I know best. You're a smart girl. You're doing the right thing. Rocky will be proud of you. You wait and see. Later on you're going to appreciate this period, because it will be the right time and you'll be able to enjoy the future. I'll make a lot of money for Rocky. As soon as the right time comes, I want you kids to get married."'[39]

Waiting for the right time, Rocky went back to Providence, to the Rhode Island Auditorium, where he was matched with Eldridge Eatman, a black fighter from Norwalk, Connecticut, with a 14-17-3 record.

---

[39] *Saturday Evening Post* September 1956

Eatman had seven pounds on Rocky at the weigh-in but had nothing on him when they got into the ring. A left hook to the body in the second round sent Eatman down for a nine count and he was down again in round three from a right to the head. The referee started to count, then ordered the fighter to get up and fight. He later explained, 'I thought Eatman tripped and fell to the canvas and that's why I stopped the count and ordered him to get up and resume fighting.' Eldridge got up and faced Rocky, who hit him with a right hand to the jaw and it was all over. A month later and Rocky was in Boston to fight Gino Buonvino at Braves Field. From Bari, Italy, Gino had won 15 of 19 fights since arriving in the United States, but his three defeats had all been inside the distance and when Rocky dropped him with a left hook in the first round the fans headed for the exits. But the Italian hung in there until the tenth and final round when the referee called a halt due to Buonvino's cut eye.

'The night Marciano fought Buonvino at Braves Field in Boston proved to be a surreal experience for all involved, because the fight took place amid a steady drizzle, under poor lighting, and within a ring that was antique and dilapidated. "I'll never forget that night," a bemused Marciano would say two years later. "It was raining and they put the fight on early. And what a ring. It was really small and tilted. I felt like I was fighting uphill all night." Arthur Siegel of the *Boston Traveller* was unimpressed by Marciano's tenth-round TKO victory. He wrote that the heavyweight field must be "a stinker if Marciano was a leading contender, because the Brockton heavyweight was nothing more than a good club fighter."'[40]

In September 1950, Rocky and Baltimore giant Johnny Shkor drew a near capacity crowd of 6,072 paying $12,081 to the Providence arena. Shkor stood 6ft 5ins and weighed 30 pounds more than Marciano. 'So Shkor's manager, Johnny Buckley, calls me up,' recalled Weill, 'and he says "Why should we put this on in Providence, where we're lucky to get a $16,000 draw? We can put it into Boston and do $40,000." Sure, we coulda made more money in Boston, but I had one thing in mind. In Boston, if he gets cut they might stop the fight and he suffers his first defeat. But I know that they know Rocky in Providence and how good he can punch. So in Providence they're liable to let the fight go just a

---

40 *BoxRec*

little longer than they would in Boston and if he's in trouble, he's gonna bomb this guy out quick.'

Weill's prognosis was spot on. Shkor had his moments in the early going as he cut Rocky's left eyelid in the first round, and re-opened the wound with a butt in the third round. The blood covering the left side of Marciano's face only spurred him on and in round five a short left hook dropped the big fellow for a nine count. The bell saved him for round six, when a looping right put him back on the canvas and again the count reached nine before he got up. The right was working well and Rocky dumped Shkor for another nine count before bringing one up from the canvas and Johnny was ready for home.

When two guys make a good fight, a rematch is not always a good idea. It was that way when Marciano fought Ted 'Tiger' Lowry a second time, in November 1950, a year after their first bout, which Rocky won over ten rounds. The standing-room only crowd of 7,155, who paid a record Rhode Island gate of $15,463, were sadly disappointed. Rocky won seven of the ten rounds, losing the fourth for a low blow, but at least Lowry won his place in boxing history by being the only fighter to go the distance twice with Rocky Marciano. 'I think Lowry would have gone the distance if we had fought 100 times,' Rocky said later. 'I could never get used to his style of fighting.' It had been a lousy fight, Rocky's 30th straight win, but he felt better when Weill told him that 'maybe one more fight and then you can get married'.

'Boy, was I happy,' recalled Rocky. 'I couldn't hardly wait the month until the next fight. It was against Bill Wilson. When the bell rang, all I had in my mind was Al saying, "If you look good against this guy I'll let you know." I belted Wilson out in one round. The guy didn't even lay a glove on me. I wanted to be sure that if Weill let me get married, I wouldn't have a mark on my face for the ceremony. And I didn't, not a scratch.' Barbara was ringside for the fight and she was a bit worried at Wilson being some 40 pounds heavier than her fiancé, but she needn't have worried. A whistling left hook brought blood streaming from a gash over Wilson's left eye and referee Dolly Searle stopped it halfway through round one. Rocky and Barbara were delighted, Bill Wilson not so.

'Two days after the fight,' said Rocky, 'I picked up my share of the purse in Weill's office and he told me OK, we had his permission. Right away, I called Barbara and Al took the phone out of my hand to speak to her. "Congratulations, honey," he said. "I want you to be the first to know it's OK for you to get married. I promised you, didn't I? And I kept my promise. You can have ten days for a honeymoon, but you got to promise me you won't bother my fighter. Now, Barbara, no distractions, remember!" My wife had to remember. Al wouldn't let her forget.' Just what Al had in mind about 'distractions,' god only knows.

On New Year's Eve, 31 December 1950, Rocco Francis Marchegiano and Barbara Mae Cousins were married at St Colman's Church in Brockton by Rev. Leroy V. Cooney. When the priest asked, 'Who gives this man and woman to be married to each other?' you could visualise Al Weill speaking up to say, 'Yeah, I do. It's OK they get married now.'

'It was quite an affair,' recalled Rocky. 'We sent out 650 invitations and about 800 showed up. Afterwards we all went to Cappy's restaurant about three miles away. I was really duded up, coat with tails, winged collar, striped pants and a tie like you see Englishmen wear at the races. It was the first time Al had been to Brockton, Charley Goldman was with him and he made a nice speech about how I was an easy-going kind of guy who did what he was told and would make a good husband.

'Then Weill grabbed the mike and said, "Remember, Barbara, Rocky's boxing future comes first. This marriage has to play second fiddle because he'll have to pay strict attention to me. I don't want you to be bossy and you got to understand we got a big job to do. So, Barbara, honey, here's a toast to you. Rocky will be the next champion. I promise you."'

The happy couple went to Miami Beach for the honeymoon. 'We checked in at the Dempsey-Vanderbilt Hotel,' Rocky would recall. 'Al called three times asking when we were coming back. The third time, after a week, he told me to come back to New York. "You got to be there, Ezzard Charles is fighting Lee Oma and I want you to take a bow." I did that and asked what about the rest of the honeymoon. "You can forget about that," he said. "I got you booked with Keene Simmons in Providence in two weeks. Stay here and get your sparring. I'll talk to Barbara." We went back to his office and he said, "Barbara, this fight is necessary. Already booked, can't cancel for an extra week. You go home and wait until after the fight." Then he said, "Did you have a nice time in

Florida? Didn't I tell you you could get married? Didn't I keep my word? Now, remember, Barbara, you promised me you wouldn't interfere with me and Rocky." What could we say? I stayed in New York and she went home from her honeymoon all by herself. And I didn't see her again until after the Simmons fight.'[41]

The sound of wedding bells had barely died away when the timekeeper's bell was calling Rocky back to work. Twenty-nine days into 1951 and he was back at his old stamping ground, the Rhode Island Auditorium in Providence, where he would fight 28 of his 49 career bouts. In the opposite corner stood Keene Simmons, up from Bayonne, New Jersey, bringing a so-so record 8-7-1 but with names like Roland LaStarza and Cesar Brion among his dance partners. He had come to fight, as Rocky discovered in the second round when a vicious right cross stopped Marciano in his tracks. By round three, Rocky was bleeding from a cut over his left eye and Allie was telling his pal to step it up. Rocky came out for the fourth round with both guns blazing and Simmons was soon having difficulty seeing as both eyes were swollen shut and after 2.54 of round eight, referee Sharkey Buonanno signalled the finish. Marciano, the battling bridegroom, was back in business.

What about the blushing bride, waiting at home for Rocky to come home? 'Barbara didn't mind my fighting at first,' Rocky said. 'She didn't like me being away so much.' The Stacy Adams shoe factory in Brockton, where Pop laboured over his machine all those years, would send a new pair of boxing shoes for Rocky before his big fights. Barbara would take the shoes to the priests at St Colman's Church in Brockton and get one of them to bless the shoes. Then she would mail them to Rocky. There were three priests there and they took turns.

Rocky would recall, 'One would bless my shoes and I knocked the guy out in one round. The next fight, another priest would bless and it would take me two rounds. Then the third would do it and it might take three or four rounds. We always said we wanted the one-round priest to bless the shoes.'

The other woman in Rocky's life was his beloved mother, Pasqualena. All the time he was fighting, she never went to a fight, listened on the radio or watched on TV. She would stay in her room and pray or a family

---

41 *Saturday Evening Post* September 1956

friend would take her for a car ride until it was over. Every now and then, she would go over to Fall River to get St Jude's oil from St Anne's Church there. It was believed to protect you from injury, and she would rub it on his hands and sometimes on his chin. For a time, Rocky did have trouble with his hands, but he never had any trouble with his chin, so maybe St Jude had something there.

After his narrow win over LaStarza, Weill and Goldman figured he still needed more experience, so it was back to Providence for seven fights, with one each in Boston and Hartford. Nine fights, seven knockouts, with Ted Lowry sticking it out for ten rounds the second time around. The other stubborn guy was Willis 'Red' Applegate, a tough trialhorse from Newark, New Jersey, with a 10-14-2 record. Red had lost his previous three fights so it came as something of a surprise when he defied Rocky for ten rounds, actually winning the third round. Rocky won eight rounds and the decision and as he came out of the ring it was announced that he would fight Duilio Spagnolo for the New England heavyweight title at the Boston Garden on 14 May. But the Italian retired two months earlier and the fight never happened.

After the Applegate fight on 30 April 1951, Rocky went into training camp at Greenwood Lake, situated in the Ramapo Mountains of New York State. He was matched with Rex Layne of Lewiston, Utah, a big, strong puncher who had shocked New York fight fans in November of 1950 by hammering out a bloody ten-round decision over Jersey Joe Walcott. Manager Marv Jensen would cause an even bigger shock seven years later when he brought Gene Fullmer in from Utah to rip the middleweight title away from Sugar Ray Robinson at the Garden.

But back in 1951, Marv was dealing in heavyweights and Rex Layne looked headed for the world title. He was back in the Garden ring to hammer out a split decision over Cesar Brion and stop Chicago puncher Bob Satterfield in eight rounds. Now he was going in with Rocky Marciano and the smart money was making him favourite over the New Englander.

Garden boss Jim Norris was interested in Layne and told matchmaker Weill to put him in with Rocky. Al didn't want the match but Norris gave Marciano a purse of 30 per cent, with Layne having to settle for 25 per cent. Actually, Charley Goldman had been in Brion's corner when

Layne beat the South American and he had figured a way to beat him. He saw that Layne didn't like body shots and instructed Rocky, telling him, 'You can slow this guy down by going to the midsection. Cesar couldn't do it, but you're stronger. I want you to get inside and pound his gut until he's ready to be taken.'

'Boxing is on the decline. Who hasn't heard that one?' wrote Nat Loubet in *Ring* magazine. 'Some maintained that all the game needed was an outstanding heavyweight, a two-fisted knockerouter who would remind us of the old days. We maintained that as the heavyweights go, so goes boxing. The heavyweights were going, and none were coming in. Then it happened! 12,565 fans paid $73,190 to see it happen … A two-fisted mayhem, bent, block busting Marciano, blasted the third-ranking Layne to an inert mass. The 26-year-old Rocker racked up his 36th win and 31st knockout at the expense of his 23-year-old rival from Lewiston, Utah. The early rounds saw two savages out to devour each other. In close, banging away, with Layne trying for the body with that right, Marciano was trying to throw that long left hook which, according to pre-fight predictions, was to be his chief weapon.

'Rex punched and tied up the Rock. The Brockton Belter bobbed, weaved, threw uppercuts, hooks and sharp rights that earned for him every round of the fight … In the second round Marciano opened a gash over Layne's left eye that bled throughout the entire fight. He bullied the pudgy Layne with mounting fury. Touted for his left hook, Marciano had dynamite in his right as well. As early as the second round, a right flush on the mouth slowed Rex down and caused him to shake his head. In each succeeding round the Utah heavy was on the receiving end of those rights and it was a right, not a left, that was the clincher … In the fifth the fighting moved to longer range as Layne stayed away from Marciano. Until he walked into another right chop to the whiskers, Rex was on his way to having a good round. That right hand buckled him at the knees and he almost went down.

'In the sixth, Layne still showed the effects of those rights. He received a right and left to the body and then the knockout blow, a blasting right to the jaw that took about 15 seconds to seep in. Then Layne swayed from the hips, pitched to his knees, then to his side, rolled over and curled up like a sleeping babe while referee Mark Conn tolled off the ten. Though anything but a good boxer, the ability to take it and the colourful manner in which Marciano throws his bombs with either hand remind one of the Jack Dempsey school when fans thronged to the arenas to witness the Manassa Mauler beat the brains out of his opponents with a right to the body and a left hook to the chin. Marciano uses a similar technique. He bores in and blasts to the body and then puts 'em away with a solid jolt to the chin.

'Marciano scored a notable victory over Layne, whipping him all the way and placing himself in line for a fight with the Charles–Walcott winner, when he KO'd Layne in 35 seconds of the sixth round. Charles probably would defeat Marciano with left hooks and tie up his right. Walcott with his ring sanguinity would stand a good chance. But we must not forget that when a man with knockout drops in either hand goes into the ring, anything can happen.'[42]

'A few days before the fight, a contractual suit brought by Gene Caggiano against Marciano was decided in favour of the defendant. This gave Rocky a psychological lift. Following instructions perfectly, he crowded the favoured Layne, backed him up, wore him out. In the sixth Layne went down. Until then, acceptance of Marciano had been grudging. Some of this traced to Weill. Ruthless, shrewd, ideally equipped for the no-holds-barred business he was in, he had made many enemies among managers. It grated on them when he was named IBC matchmaker and could subject them to his arrogant terms. They complained of the stiffs Weill had fed his fighter. But after Rocky KO'd Layne, they quieted down, somewhat. Now the favourable destiny discerned occasionally in Marciano's corner really got busy. In the upset of 1951, Jersey Joe Walcott knocked out Charles for the championship. He also knocked a Louis-Marciano fight into Weill's lap. Sidetracked until after a Walcott-Charles return, as far as a title chance was concerned, the venerable Bomber now had to grab the best payday available. That was Marciano.'[43]

---

42 Nat Loubet *Ring* September 1951

43 Tim Cohane *Look* magazine November 1951

7

END OF AN ERA

'I REMEMBER one time,' recalled Rocky, 'Joe Louis was in Providence in exhibition with Bill Weinberg. All of a sudden Mom said, "I think I'll take a look at this." I stayed home but waited till she got back. She came into my room and said, "Rocco, I don't care who you fight. Now that you're a fighter I suppose you got to fight everybody. But promise me one thing, Rocco. Promise me you'll never fight this Joe Louis. He's a big, strong man. He's like a big monster. His hands were going like machines in the shoe shops. Promise, *figlio mio?*"'[44]

If Rocco did promise his mother that day, he must have had his fingers crossed behind his back. Otherwise, Pasqualena Marchegiano would have beaten Al Weill on that one. Actually, Weill had barred Rocky from going in with Louis when Joe was on an exhibition tour around New England. The Brockton heavyweight had been offered $2,000 to share the ring with Louis. 'More money than I ever saw,' he recalled. Weill put a quick stop to that, saying, 'Rocky isn't ready for Louis. I don't want him to fight Louis yet.'

Al thought Rocky was ready for a shopworn Freddie Beshore, who had gone into the 14th round against Ezzard Charles for the National Boxing Association heavyweight title a year before he climbed into the Boston Garden ring to swap leather with Marciano. The once-durable Beshore had lost 13 of his 44 fights but had never been off his feet in a ten-year career. That changed at the 50-second mark of round four,

---

44 *Saturday Evening Post* September 1956

when a two-fisted attack by Rocky laid Freddie out like a rug. He was still unconscious when referee Johnny Martin reached the ten count, giving Marciano his 32nd knockout in an unbeaten streak of 37 bouts.

Al Weill was convinced. Rocky was ready for Joe Louis.

'Take the Louis fight,' wrote Tim Cohane, sports editor of *Look* magazine. 'Of the 60 per cent of the gate which went to the fighters, Louis got 45 per cent, Marciano only 15 per cent. Louis insisted on 45 per cent largely because of a personal dislike for Weill. This traced to Weill's behaviour at the Sugar Ray Robinson-Jake LaMotta middleweight championship fight at Chicago on 14 February 1951. Robinson won by a knockout. Weill, an inveterate gambler on fights, rooted openly for LaMotta from a seat in the press section. Maybe he had money riding on him. Considering his position as IBC matchmaker, Weill's display was injudicious. It seemed even worse than that to Louis, who was a close friend of Robinson's. So when the day came to make a Louis-Marciano match, Louis was of a mind to drive a hard bargain. He maintained his stand for 45 per cent, despite repeated beseeching visits by Weill. "No, sir," said old Joe. "I'll take 45. Furthermore," he added, "I'll knock your boy into your lap." When an impasse threatened, Norris called Marciano into his office. 'Would you like to fight Louis?" Norris asked. The Rock was all eagerness. "Well," said Norris, "the only way I can make the match is if you'll agree to take 15 per cent." Marciano realised that the price was inequitable. "Gee, Mr Norris, I ought to get at least 20 per cent," said Rocky. "You better take a walk around the corner," said Norris, "and think it over." The Rock took the walk and the 15 per cent. The IBC made out cheques for $94,281 to Louis and $49,605 to Marciano.'[45]

As if getting the short end of the purse wasn't bad enough, Joe went and upset Rocky even more with his remarks about the forthcoming contest. Marciano was shown a newspaper at his training camp at Greenwood Lake, New York. The story quoted Louis as calling Marciano 'a stubby-armed, made-to-order opponent.' 'That's what Rex Layne said before I flattened him,' said the undefeated Brockton Blockbuster. 'Let Joe keep on talking and I hope I catch him with his mouth open. He'll swallow his words.'

---

45 Tim Cohane *Look* magazine October 1956

One person impressed with Rocky was chairman Robert K. Christenberry of the New York State Boxing Commission, who took his first look at Marciano in training, saying afterwards, 'He certainly lives up to his advance advertising. He appears to be a fine young athlete.' Rocky worked six hard rounds against three sparmates. He drew blood from the mouth of big Ray Wilding, a British heavyweight. Then he went to work on Keene Simmons for two rounds and followed up with two rounds against Dave Davies of Tacoma, Washington.

'All Lowell seems to be buzzing about the coming Joe Louis-Rocky Marciano bout in New York late this month,' wrote George McGuane in the *Lowell Sun* on 3 October. 'And the talk was a little more feverish than ever after publication in last night's *Sun* of Lawton Carver's syndicated story concerning the change-over from the Polo Grounds to Madison Square Garden, on Friday 26 October. Carver said he thinks Marciano will win … This writer admits he's prejudiced in this one. We're all for Marciano. After seeing his start in the Golden Gloves and watching him come along, it's hard not to be rooting for his corner even though physical statistics of the two favour the Brown Bomber in every department but age and the calf of their physiographies.

'Yes sir, Rocky's 27 while Joe's 37, while Joe's measurements are bigger in every part of the anatomy, but the calf. Now we don't see how Rocky's 14¾ inch calf to Joe's 14¼ inch can have much to do with the fight, but we're certain the ages can. We think age will be the telling factor. As Freddie Beshore said down in Boston after being knocked out by Marciano, "Louis is still a good jabber and you can't discount his experience. I look to Louis to control the early rounds but I feel Rocky will wear him down and win towards the end of the fight."

'If you're interested, the IBC reports Louis weighing 210 at present to Rocky's 184. And the thing that caught our eye as we thought about a jabbing Joe was the relative reach of each. Louis has a reach of 76 inches against only 67 for Marciano … that's a lot of extra arm to have in a fight. And, of course, Louis goes 6ft 2ins against Rocky's 5ft 11ins.'

A report out of New York by the Associated Press stated that, 'Seven television manufacturers have joined with the Gillette Safety Razor Company to foot the bill for rights to put the Joe Louis-Rocky Marciano boxing bout on 26 October on home television, it has been disclosed. It marks the second time that set makers have joined forces to assure home viewers of seeing a top sports event which might otherwise have been seen exclusively on theatre TV, as has happened on a number of recent major bouts. The first time was for the Ezzard Charles-Joe Walcott fight. The Louis-Marciano fight will be telecast live coast to coast over the National Broadcasting Company network, the first time for both fighters'[46]

If confidence was everything, Rocky Marciano was home and dry. Reporting from Greenwood Lake, *United Press* sportswriter Jack Cuddy quoted the man from Brockton, '"Don't think I'm bragging, but it's not just a question of Louis in particular. I believe I can beat him because I believe I can beat any man in the world." Without bluster, without hint of pride, the curly-haired slugger explained, "I've had 37 professional fights and I won them all, but that's not important. None of my opponents hurt me. None of them had me on the canvas even once. And any man who would stand up and fight with me I knocked out. I had trouble with some cuties who wouldn't fight. But Louis is no cutie. He'll fight and I expect to take him, probably by a knockout." The 27-year-old mauler said Louis still was a good fighter at 37, but no longer the great one of the pre-war days.'[47]

A couple of days later, reporter Cuddy found a buoyant Louis camp at Pompton Lakes, New Jersey. 'Confidence in a knockout victory was running at a new high in the Joe Louis camp today as the former world's heavyweight king ended his "heavy" training for Friday night's bout against Rocky Marciano. An extremely impressive showing in his last sparring session yesterday – featuring a display of the old time Brown Bomber power – convinced Louis and his handlers that he will whip the young and eager Marciano. Right now, wagering men are inclined to agree with Louis to the extent of making him a 6½ to 5 choice for the bout that may gain him a 1952 shot at the title or end his title hopes forever.

'The form showed by the 37-year-old ex-champion in his final ring drill should keep the odds from falling much lower. Highlight of the workout was a ripping left hook to the chin that floored spar mate Holly

---

46 *Bedford Gazette* Pa. 20 October 1951

47 Jack Cuddy *Statesville Daily Record* Nth Carolina 23 October 1951

Smith of Bermuda, a booming knockdown like the kind always seen in the training camp of the "old Joe Louis". And the Louis right was also shown to be in fine working order. Since he lost to Ezzard Charles in September 1950, Joe has depended more and more upon his right for some unknown reason, and that was landing just as effectively as his left yesterday. He used right uppercuts and left hooks in a "lifting attack" which is designed to straighten Marciano up and give Joe a target for those booming hooks. The lifting attack was a success against spar mate Elkins Brothers. Louis emerged from the drill, which ended his rounds of sparring here in camp at 92 since 18 September, in high good humour.

'He was asked whether he considered Marciano's looping rights more dangerous than straight rights like those thrown by Cesar Brion of Argentina, whom he twice defeated on the comeback trail. With a broad smile, Joe answered, "I get hit by all kinds of rights. Even my little daughter hits me with rights." Somebody asked him what the "old Louis" of ten years ago would have done to Marciano. "What I'm worried about is what the old Joe Louis is going to do Friday night," quipped Joe.'

The old Joe Louis did not have much faith in the younger generation of heavyweights moving up, especially Marciano and Rex Layne. When movies of Marciano's sixth-round knockout of Layne were run off at Pompton Lakes, Louis walked out after two rounds. 'Don't you want to see the finish?' asked the amazed tub thumper, Harry Mendel. 'That's enough,' grunted Louis. 'He can't fight.'

Veteran sportswriter Bill Corum commented two days before the fight, 'It's good to have a Joe Louis around. Even an old Joe Louis. I was forcibly reminded of this during my vacation in Florida. There was a surprise interest in Friday night's fight between Louis and Rocky Marciano. Time and again, people, both men and women, said to me, in effect, "I'm scared for Joe Louis this time. I'm afraid that whatever-his-name-is will knock him out, but I hope not. I'd sure like to see the old champ win this one." The majority seems to feel that Joe is washed up, and the worst that they can be is partially right. Yet in the public mind his name, in the important sense of honesty of effort and performance, appears to be as the name of sterling on silver.'[48]

---

48 Bill Corum *Defiance Crescent News* Ohio 24 October 1951

It was that feeling among sports fans that sent Louis into the Garden ring a 6½ to 5 favourite, the lowest-ever odds in one of his fights, and it was that feeling that brought a near-capacity crowd of 17,241, paying $152,845, into the Eighth Avenue arena that October night in 1951. Among them were thousands of New Englanders ready to bet everything they had on their boy Rocky. He had never lost and neither had they. And they never would.

At the noon weigh-in, Louis had rocked the scale at a solid 213¾ pounds against Marciano's 184, a whopping advantage of nearly 30 pounds. But the best thing Rocky had going for him was his age; he was ten years younger and each of his 27-year-old fists carried dynamite. Would it be enough? The judges appointed by the New York Commission were Joe Agnello and Harold Barnes, the referee Ruby Goldstein. Ruby almost didn't make it, as he recalled in his 1959 autobiography.

'Everywhere I went, I was asked, in one form or another, "Didn't you find it difficult to give a decision against your friend?" My answer always was the same because it is the only true one. Joe Louis was my friend before the fight, and when it was over. While he was fighting, he was just a fellow who was fighting Jersey Joe Walcott. I thought he lost the fight, and said so. It wasn't difficult at all. There was a repercussion from the Louis camp, although not from Joe himself, nearly four years later. It was Louis himself who, by expressing his confidence in me, relieved a tension mounting about me on the night of his fight with Rocky Marciano.

'This was on 26 October 1951 and Louis, engaged in a comeback from the retirement of two years before, was in his dressing room in the Garden and I was in my seat at the ringside as knockdown timekeeper for the semi-final bout, when a deputy commissioner hurried to my side and whispered, "You're slated for the main bout but you may not get it. Marshall Miles is in there screaming that he won't stand for you. He says there is no question about your loyalty but if you're the referee it might upset Joe because you gave the decision against him in the Walcott fight."

'I was understandably disturbed. It was the first, and only, time my fitness had been questioned by a manager on any grounds. "Take it easy," the deputy said. "I know it will come out all right. I'm going back there now and I'll keep you posted." "Does the Commissioner know about it?" I asked. Robert Christenberry, chairman of the New York Commission, was seated at his regular first row seat on the other side of the ring. "They're telling him now," he said. I looked across and saw him talking to another deputy. He seemed to be snapping his words. The one he was talking to went on the double toward the dressing room. The one who had been telling me what was going on followed him. In a few minutes he was back. He was quite excited.

"I wish you'd been there!" he whispered. "Charlie (the other deputy) told Miles, 'The Commissioner says to tell you Goldstein is the referee. If you are unwilling to accept him without further delay, he will have an announcement made from the ring that the fight is off and the money will be refunded.' Before Miles could say anything, Joe said, 'Leave Ruby referee, like I told you before. Anyway, I'll knock Marciano out.'"

'So I was the referee, but Louis couldn't knock Marciano out.'[49]

Next day, all the papers had the story. Arthur Daley of the *New York Times* lamented, 'The moment everyone had been dreading finally arrived last night … It had to happen sometime and it happened last night.' Daley mused that perhaps he should be writing about the fighter with the future (Marciano) instead of the fighter with the past (Louis). 'But this reporter has been carrying the torch for Joe for much too long to start any new flirtations. It's still love. In this corner, Louis losing is more important than Marciano winning.'

'It was a bitter end for a great champion,' headed Oscar Fraley's column for *United Press*. 'Joe Louis lay under the ropes, his head lolling over the apron of the ring, and the most remarkable career in ring history was finished by the black oblivion of a right hand to the jaw … They told him his right hand had regained the murderous efficiency which 25 times defended the heavyweight championship of the world … But the king was dead at 2.36 of the eighth round at Madison Square Garden last night. His hopes and his dreams were slain by the flailing fists of a rugged young Italian named Rocky Marciano, proving once again that they never come back.'[50]

'Joe Louis is through,' wrote Murray Rose. 'Boxing has a new idol today in Rocky Marciano. It's the old story of the ring. Youth must be served … Today 27-year-old Rocky, a one-time soldier, shoeworker and

<hr>

49 Ruby Goldstein *Third Man in the Ring* 1959
50 Oscar Fraley *Lowell Sun* 27 October 1951

ditchdigger with little more than three years of professional fighting behind him, is the man of the hour … He'll be offered a shot at Ezzard Charles, the ex-champion, for February or March, and a possible shot with Jersey Joe Walcott next summer. Thirty-eight fights, thirty-eight victories, 33 knockouts, almost a carbon copy of the string hung up by the once-magnificent Brown Bomber. And Rocky tore a page out of Louis' book in writing a finish to it. Make way for Marciano, the new golden boy of boxing.'[51]

Veteran scribe Bill Corum painted a vivid word picture of the passing of the torch. 'The big coffee-with-cream man came to his feet at the count of eight and tried to punch at the bouncy little fellow in front of him. One of these stuttering punches hit the smaller man in the face and for just a fleeting moment, he was checked and moved back a bit. Then he leaped in again with another winging left and the giant that he was bringing down swayed and half-stumbled along the ropes. This was the last ten seconds of an era of boxing. Time, which had caught up with him, as it does with all men, was running out on Joe Louis and this was the final tableau. This was the end of a long road along which for 17 years almost every signpost had read, "victory this way."

'Here then was how the story of a fighter, whose name already was a legend, was ending in the ring where he had known so many triumphs and no defeats. For Joe had never been beaten in Madison Square Garden before. Again the little man fired and landed that left, this time a half uppercut, and then he swung his right at the unprotected chin of the helpless giant, and Joe Louis went through the ropes and out, flat on his back on the apron of the ring. Quickly Ruby Goldstein spread his arms in token of the end. They go that way. The great and the small. All of them. They must. For Joe, as everybody knew except Joe, had been walking for a long time on a street looking for a house that had no number.'[52]

In his report for the *New York Times*, Joseph C. Nichols wrote, 'In the dressing room Louis was in good enough condition, considering, and expressed the opinion that "the best man won". As a matter of fact, the best man didn't have to be too good against the Louis of last night. His

---

51 Murray Rose *Albuquerque Tribune* 27 October 1951
52 Bill Corum *Troy Times Record* 27 October 1951

armament was best described by Edmond Rostand when, in speaking of Cyrano, he lamented that he was "shod with marble and gloved with lead". Obviously the lead in Joe's instance was not calculated to aid the Bomber in administering punishment to his foe.'[53]

A. J. Liebling, the brilliant essayist for the *New Yorker* magazine, was in the Garden that night, writing, 'Near the end of the first round of the fight, Marciano threw one of those rights and it landed, it seemed to me, just under Louis's left ear … This was the kind of punch that addles a man's brains, and if it had happened 30 seconds earlier and Marciano had pressed his advantage, he might have knocked Louis out in the first round. I think that punch was the one that made Joe feel old.'[54]

'That boy took me out with three punches,' Joe said in the dressing room. 'It took Schmeling a hundred. Of course I was 22 then, but this Marciano is tough enough to beat anybody.' When a reporter said that the KO had come as a surprise to the onlookers, Joe said ruefully, 'It came as a surprise to me, too.'

Shortly after the fight, Rocky would recall, 'I got even more of a kick out of what Joe told me than I did out of winning the fight. "Man," he said, "you really pour it on in the ring." He asked me if I ever was a southpaw. "I've never been anything but a right-hander, Joe," I said. "Everybody always said all I got is a right hand." "They told me that, too, Rock," Joe said, "and they don't know how wrong they all was. You did all the hurting with that left hand of yours." Maybe it isn't important to Joe Louis that he taught me dignity. But I think it is.

'Louis hit me good once, with a left,' said Rocky, 'that I don't even remember. But they tell me it was a left. That was about the best Joe had, and I took it and came back. When I knocked Joe down, he took a count and then came back to me, not like guys usually do, not covering up. Joe's got guts. He came back fighting and that's why I was able to knock him out. I was sorry I had to do it to Joe, but that was the one I had to win.'

'Perhaps the end of dignity in the press section,' wrote Barney Nagler in *Ring* magazine, 'was signalled by the behaviour of Rocky Marciano's mob the night the Brockton Blockbuster saddened the world by finishing off Joe Louis in eight rounds in the old Garden. When Marciano put

---

53   Joseph C. Nichols *New York Times* 27 October 1951
54   A. J. Liebling *The Sweet Science* 1987

Louis down for the first time, his followers from Massachusetts began inching toward the ring from their ringside seats. Then, when Louis got up, Marciano hit him with two hooks, which set up the erstwhile Brown Bomber for a conclusive right smash to the chin. The Bay State horde climbed over the shoulders of the sportswriters, kicked them under the typewriter tables, stamped on their typewriters and got into the ring to shake hands with Rocky. Joe Nichols, the *Times* man, lost his syntax in the onslaught. This moved Al Weill, Marciano's manager and a noted literary figure, to say, "I'm a sport. I'll spend a few dollars to keep Nichols happy." He replaced Nichols' typewriter with a new one.'[55]

Al could afford to be generous. His boy Rocky was on his way to the title. Even little Charley Goldman was smiling. 'I knew I had the champion the night he fought Joe Louis,' he said.

'The first thing I felt was the thrill of winning,' Rocky would recall. 'But then I turned around and looked at Louis again and I was remembering that this was the great Joe Louis, the guy I used to hear about and read about and he was all through. It wasn't until I got into the dressing room that I began to think what this fight meant to me instead of what it meant to him.'

---

55 Barney Nagler *Ring* June 1983

8

THE CONTENDER

IT WAS a Wednesday night in October 1940 and New York's leading sportswriters were in their ringside seats at Madison Square Garden to see light-heavyweight champion Billy Conn box the main event, with young Brooklyn heavyweight Henry Cooper subbing for Steve Dudas. The Pittsburgh stylist was making his run at the world heavyweight title and had stopped Gus Dorazio in Philadelphia, but on the evidence of the Cooper fight he was light years away from Joe Louis. Cooper was no match for Billy the Kid, something that was glaringly obvious to New York fight fans, who stayed away from the Garden in droves. A reported attendance of 5,658 paying $14,400 was the lowest for Conn's Garden fights.

Dan Parker, the *New York Daily Mirror* columnist wrote, 'The card wasn't a sheer waste of time … The semi-final bout introduced in the person of a Norwegian-American gent named Lee Savold, the best-looking heavyweight prospect that has turned up hereabouts since last Groundhog Day … If they're really looking for a formidable opponent for Joe Louis, Lee shapes up as a good prospect.' After seeing Savold stop big Jim Robinson in three rounds, Jack Mahon of the *New York Daily News* commented, 'Savold, who may not be quite ready, is definitely on his way.'

Veteran scribe Hype Igoe of the *New York Journal-American,* reported, 'The other night in Madison Square Garden, Lee Savold, a one-time bartender in St Paul, Minnesota, came to show us what he could do with his fists … Savold's advent against Robinson was his first New York bow. They'll see more of him from here on, as the fellow has a nice presence, a punch and a style which is easy on the eye.' Top columnist Bill Corum liked the new boy also, writing in the *New York Journal-American,* 'There was one blond newcomer out of Des Moines, Iowa, who did his best to rid the evening of lethargy. His name was Lee Savold … he can punch. He gave his opponent, Jim Robinson, something like 35 pounds on the scales and before Jim Robinson could say Jim Robinson, he had one of his eyes closed and was wobbling down Queer Street without a cane. The referee put an end to it about the fourth, with James sitting on his little stool … wishing he was back in Philadelphia. A man is badly hurt when he wishes he was back in Philadelphia.'

Savold got his shot at Joe Louis but it was 11 years later and Joe was no longer champion of the heavyweights, and Lee was no longer the darling of the New York press. He was 36, with 140 bouts against the best of the division, but he hadn't fought in a year and Louis, at 37, still had enough left to score a knockout in round six. And Al Weill figured Lee Savold still had enough stuff left to go a few rounds with Rocky Marciano. The fight was made for 13 February 1952, 10 rounds at Philadelphia's Convention Hall.

A few weeks after retiring Joe Louis, Rocky retired another old man – his father Pierino. 'Pop was a sickly man until I sort of gave him a new interest in life. All his life in this country he worked at a shoe machine called a Number 7 bed laster. He never made any money and he never had any fun. He was only existing. He was always tired at night. All of a sudden people started talking to him with new interest. He became a big man wherever he went. I was winning fights and Pop became the expert. He was having a big time and enjoying it, and who could blame him? He even got to telling me he was a tough guy with his fists when he was younger and he tried to make me remember a time when I wasn't more than six when he belted out a man at a picnic.'[56]

One man sorry to see Pierino Marchegiano leave the shoe shops was his supervisor. 'Your whole life, your friends are in this shop, Petey,' his boss reminded him. 'You are a part of this shop.' But Pierino's mind was made up. 'My son, the future world's champion, wants me to go with

---

56 *Saturday Evening Post* September 1956

him so I'm gonna retire.' He did go back occasionally to visit his friends, and whenever he did, someone would measure his feet and he would get a new pair of shoes.

When the Marciano-Savold fight was given to the press, 'everyone asked, why? Marciano was entitled to a breather as he resumed his march to the title, but why Lee Savold? A year or two before he would have made a worthy opponent, but now he was plainly washed up. The public ridicule and cynicism of the impending fight even forced a bizarre public relations move from the Pennsylvania State Athletic Commission, the sanctioning body for the bout. A week before the fight, when both fighters checked in at the commission's office, one of the commissioners, the rotund John "Ox" Da Grosa, told them, "People are asking me why you two are fighting. You've got to show them why. And it's got to be a good fight, or I'll hold up your purses."'[57]

It wasn't a good fight. It was a lousy fight, one of the worst of Rocky's career. Rocky had been training at Greenwood Lake and was in excellent condition. Then, about a week before the fight, he began to get sluggish in his workouts. He lost his appetite. A few days later he was in bed with a virus that raised his temperature to more than a hundred degrees. But he wouldn't hear of any talk of putting the fight off. 'They've got the TV and everything all committed,' he said. 'There's no way we can call it off now, so don't even talk about it.'

Rocky wasn't feeling good when he entered the ring that night. He complained of having chills and being nauseous. 'You got a fever,' Goldman said. 'You probably have the flu. Maybe we should call it off.' 'No, I'm going through with it,' Rocky muttered.

From ringside, an *Associated Press* reporter observed, 'A fighter should have his annuities paid up before going against Rocky Marciano. Marciano, the hard-punching heavyweight from Brockton, Mass., not only beats his opponents into bloody submission, but he sends them scurrying for a rocking chair and retirement. Like last night when to all intents and purposes he ended the career of the veteran Lee Savold. It is no exaggeration to say that Marciano slaughtered Savold. The 35-year-old Englewood, New Jersey fighter was a blood-soaked hulk when his manager, Bill Daly, asked referee Pete Tomasco to stop the uneven match

---

57 Russell Sullivan *Rocky Marciano: The Rock of His Times* 2002

at the end of the sixth round. "The will was there but not the body," said Daly. "I'm going to advise Lee to retire from the ring tomorrow." Pennsylvania Commissioner John "Ox"Da Grosa said he was going to suspend Savold indefinitely and ask him to retire. "He looks all done," said the commissioner.

'Savold never had a chance. The unbeaten Marciano charged across the ring from the first bell, smashed two tremendous left hooks into Savold's face and then unmercifully cut down his bigger opponent. Marciano weighed 186½ pounds and Savold 200 for the televised scheduled 10-rounder. The announced attendance was 9,243 and the gate a disappointing $61,386. Despite his easy victory, the Rock was far from satisfied. "I wasn't sharp at all. I need to fight oftener. A four-month layoff is too much." He thought the beating he gave Savold was the worst he had ever administered to any opponent. "I hit him with everything I had, but he wouldn't go down."'[58]

Savold looked bad during the fight and he looked even worse at the end of round six when Daly pulled him out. In the first round, Marciano brought the crimson stuff to Savold's oft-battered nose. In the second he opened a cut inside Savold's mouth and in the sixth he opened cuts over both eyes. It was the worst beating of Savold's 17-year career. 'I just couldn't get started,' the veteran said when he came out of the ring. And now he was finished.

With the Savold fiasco out of the way, Weill figured Rocky should go back to school and shipped him back to Providence, where Manny Almeida promptly scheduled two fights aimed at getting his man back in the popularity business. The tough Italian heavyweight Gino Buonvino had taken Rocky into the tenth round when they clashed in July 1950 in Boston, having survived a first-round knockdown until a cut eye ended the fight in the dying seconds of the final round. Now he was getting a chance to improve on his 24-14-8 pro record.

Actually, Marciano didn't give the Italian a chance to do much of anything. At 1.35 of the second round, Gino and the ring canvas were closer than the hands of a clock at 3.15. 'We told him to box as he did in the first fight,' said the guy in Buonvino's corner, 'but he slugged it out and paid the price.' Buonvino tried for a KO in the opening round,

---

58 *Reno Evening Gazette* 14 February 1952

slamming a terrific right cross into Rocky's startled face. 'He hurt me with that right,' said the Rock when he came out of the ring, 'I walked into it, but that was the only dangerous one.' There wouldn't be any more from 29-year-old Gino. He hung up his gloves and went back home to the Bronx, where he had lived since leaving Italy in the spring of 1947.

Three weeks later, Rocky was back for what would be his final showing at the Rhode Island Auditorium, ten rounds with Bernie Reynolds of Fairfield, Connecticut, sometime holder of the New England heavyweight title. Bernie brought a pro record of 51-9-1 to the ring and actually won the first round. Rocky hadn't lost a round in his last 20 Providence bouts, according to an *Associated Press* reporter. Round two saw Rocky in control as he scored with heavy shots to the body and looping rights to the head. One of those murderous rights in the third round sent Bernie back to the showers, a knockout victim at 2.21 of the round. 'Marciano can beat anyone with his punch,' said Bernie's manager, the veteran Joe Vella. 'It takes a real punch to finish my boy.' Charley Goldman later recalled, 'Reynolds actually floated through the air in a horizontal position and his shoulder blades and the back of his heels hit the deck simultaneously.'

That punch gave Rocky his 36th knockout victory in 41 pro bouts, still undefeated and looking for the champ. He would have to wait. For one thing, the day after putting Reynolds away, his licence was suspended for 30 days, courtesy of the Maine Boxing Commission. Weill had told Rocky an exhibition tour in Maine would be a great idea. 'They're looking at you as a real contender. Walcott was there recently and the fans would like to see you.' Weill advised Rocky to find a sparmate. 'Nobody gives a damn who he is. They just want to see you.'

'Rocky asked Allie Colombo to get a suitable sparring partner and Allie suggested Peter Fuller, an amateur heavyweight, well known in New England because his father happened to be former Governor Alvan T. Fuller of Massachusetts. Allie was so sure Fuller would do it that when he couldn't contact him, he phoned Weill and told him Fuller would be on the tour. But when Fuller found out, he said he couldn't do it as he was going out for the 1952 Olympic squad and didn't want to hurt his amateur standing. So when Rocky arrived in Waterville for the start of the tour, he found his younger brother Louis, known as Sonny, climbing into the opposite corner. A rugged 17-year-old, Sonny had often sparred with his brother and they put on a good show. As Weill had said, the people wanted to see Rocky. Sonny was advertised as Peter Fuller for the first bout but when they showed in half a dozen other towns he was advertised as Louis Marchegiano. Everyone was happy, except the Maine Boxing Commission, which promptly slapped a 30-day suspension on the fighter licensed as Rocky Marciano.

'Unfortunately, there were repercussions for Sonny. He lost his amateur standing and could not participate in the baseball and football programme at Brockton High. Two colleges – Holy Cross and Boston College – which had offered Sonny scholarships, withdrew their offers. Rocky always felt bad about this happening because he believed Sonny was a better all-around athlete than him and could have had a great collegiate career in sports.'[59]

'It was a serious setback for Sonny, who was eager to impress the major league scouts,' said Everett M. Skehan in *Rocky Marciano: Biography of a First Son*, published in 1977. 'He was forced to miss the first two games while further deliberations were being made. "What the hell's the matter with them?" Rocky said. "You didn't get paid. Tell them you were just doing something for your brother."

'Fortunately, Sonny was reinstated and finished out the season at third base. He had a very good year and received offers from several league teams.'[60]

In June 1952, old man Jersey Joe Walcott defended the world heavyweight title against former champion Ezzard Charles. Joe had taken the title from Charles with a stunning knockout the year before to become, at 37, the oldest fighter ever to win the title up to that time. This time Charles was still on his feet at the end of a dull 15 rounds that saw Walcott given the unanimous decision, although many in the ringside press disputed the verdict. One man happy with the result was Rocky Marciano, the undefeated number one contender. He wasn't really bothered who won just as long as he got the next crack at the championship. But some people had a different agenda. People like Jack Hurley, veteran fight manager … people like Jim Norris, boss of the

---

59 Michael N. Varveris: *Rocky Marciano The 13th Candle* 2000

60 Everett M. Skehan *Rocky Marciano: Biography of a First Son* 1977

International Boxing Club … people like Frankie Carbo, underworld boss of the fight game.

'There are two honest managers in boxing,' wrote Damon Runyon. 'The one is Jack Hurley, and I can't remember the name of the other.' Hurley liked to work with one fighter at a time and before he got Harry Matthews the best he had was a lightweight named Billy Petrolle, who beat the top guys around New York in the 1920s through the 1930s. When Hurley got Harry 'Kid' Matthews, he was no longer a kid. He was 28 with 70 fights in the book but he was broke and thinking of quitting the ring, as he had once before. His wife, Jo, and a Seattle tailor named Sammy Casmir persuaded Harry to give boxing another chance. Casmir took Harry to see Jack Hurley, who was hustling in Chicago at the time. Hurley put Matthews in with George Sherman. He won over ten rounds but Hurley was less than enthusiastic, telling the fighter, 'If you fought like that in a street, they wouldn't even arrest you. But maybe three months, six months, a year, I can make a fighter out of you.' The only way Matthews could get into Madison Square Garden was to buy a ticket.

Eighteen months and 16 fights later, Jack Hurley brought his new fighter into the Garden to fight Irish Bob Murphy and after ten rounds Murphy and the sceptical East Coast found out about Harry Matthews. 'He's terrific,' said Murphy in his dressing room. 'It's like being hit by a freight train.'

'It's a knack, a matter of leverage,' said Hurley as sportswriters jammed the dressing room. 'I had to make Harry forget everything he ever learned, then teach him separately how to use his feet, arms and body. When he put 'em together, he had the proper leverage, the knack.'

Tim Cohane, sports editor of *Look* magazine, ran the story in a 1951 issue, asking 'Can Hurley Make Matthews Champion? The Professor, as Jack Hurley likes to refer to himself, merely sells his fighter, a light-heavyweight turned heavyweight named Harry "Kid" Matthews. "The Athlete" – his favourite name for Matthews – "is not what you would call a really great fighter," says Hurley. "But he is the best heavyweight around. The best box office bet today is The Athlete against that Rocky Marciano. Don't it stagger you just to think about it?" Even after Matthews beat Murphy, the International Boxing Club gave Murphy the light-heavyweight title shot at Joey Maxim, and clever Joey gave him a boxing lesson. With logic, Hurley hollered, "Why didn't Matthews get the shot?" He was heard by Senators Warren G. Magnuson and Harry Cain of Washington, and Herman Welker of Idaho. They requested Congress to investigate. Recently, the Federal Government instituted a suit against the IBC as a monopoly.'[61]

Jim Norris and the IBC, feeling the pressure, asked Jack 'Doc' Kearns, manager of Joey Maxim, if he would let Maxim defend the title against Matthews. Doc sent a telegram to Senator Cain offering to match his tiger with Hurley's 'athlete' for the world light-heavyweight championship. 'It is rare in boxing,' Kearns telegraphed the Senator, 'for the champion to appear in the role of a virtual challenger, and I go back to the days of the incomparable Jack Dempsey, whom I had the delightful pleasure to manage.' When word of Kearns's offer was relayed to Hurley by Senator Cain, Matthews's manager rejected the match. Senator Cain was outraged and announced publicly that he had changed his mind about asking the Senate to investigate the IBC.

Now Hurley was in a spot. So were Norris and the International Boxing Club. Senator Cain's outcry against the IBC had set in motion a federal grand jury investigation. The effects of this inquiry were pinpointed in the reaction of the sponsors of the IBC televised bouts. They didn't like it, and nobody knew this better than Norris. He sought an easy way out and hit upon a simple plan: why couldn't Matthews be matched to fight Marciano? 'Let's put Marciano in with Matthews,' Norris suggested to Weill. 'Not me. I don't want it,' said Weill. 'We need the match, Al, because it's one way to get Hurley out of our hair. He's causing us all kinds of congressional pressure. Let's put the guy on the spot and find out if Matthews can fight.' 'Get somebody else,' Weill said sneeringly.

'Norris persisted in his request. He talked to Weill many times, but each conversation produced the same reaction ... Finally, Norris took a course he had taken before and would take frequently in the future: he appealed to Frankie Carbo for help. "Talk to Al," he told Carbo, "and see what you can do." Carbo exercised his sway over Weill. A few days later, Norris's matchmaker came into the promoter's office and said, "I'll take the match. If I hadn't talked to certain people, I would never have taken

---

61 Tim Cohane *Look* magazine 1951

that match for you." "Certain people" meant Carbo.'[62] Carbo, whose real name was Paul John Carbo, boasted a number of aliases, including Jimmy the Wop, the Ambassador, the Superintendent, Mr Fury and Mr Gray. He also boasted a long criminal record filled with assorted bad deeds and transgressions … As trigger man for Murder Inc., he was allegedly the man behind the 1933 murders of Max Greenberg and Max Hassel, two beer racketeers from New Jersey. Carbo was also allegedly the man responsible for the infamous shooting of Murder Inc. refugee Harry Greenberg in Hollywood on Thanksgiving Eve 1939. Carbo was indicted for the Greenberg murder but wriggled away when his first trial resulted in a hung jury and his second trial went south after the key witness fell, or was pushed, to his death from a hotel room window … His lifetime record: nearly 20 arrests, five of them for murder.

'As he moved into middle age, Carbo turned his attention from murder to boxing. Carbo was a passionate fight fan, he also saw boxing as a way to make money. As early as the mid-1930s, Carbo started to acquire pieces of fighters, including a string of middleweight champions (Babe Risko, Al Hostak and Solly Krieger). He also fell in with Mike Jacobs, exercising influence within the formal corridors of the Twentieth Century Sporting Club. By the close of World War II, Frankie Carbo could boast of a number of substantial interests in a variety of boxers and managers. Then he got serious. Under Carbo's leadership from the late 1940s until the late 1950s, the Mob infiltrated boxing as never before … Eventually, Jim Norris and Frankie Carbo found each other. Although they had known each other for years from racetracks and other sporting circles, they deepened their relationship considerably in the early 1950s … Carbo thus became a major player in the IBC power structure. Norris would use him to keep a recalcitrant manager or promoter in line.[63]

'People used to ask me if Frankie Carbo had a piece of me,' Rocky told writers Al Hirshberg and Milton Gross, who were putting his memoirs together for a six-part series which ran in the *Saturday Evening Post* in September–October 1956. 'As far as I know, he didn't. I met Carbo only twice in my life. One day I was coming out of Stillman's Gym with Allie Colombo and Chick Wergeles, who worked for Al. It was only

62 Barney Nagler *James Norris and the Decline of Boxing* 1964
63 Russell Sullivan *Rocky Marciano: The Rock of His Times* 2002

about the second time I was ever in Stillman's. A couple of guys were on the sidewalk and one yelled to Wergeles. They talked for a minute and then Chick turned around and says, "Rocky, come over here. I want you to meet somebody." I went over and Chick says, "This is Frankie." I shook hands and the guy asked me my name, and I said "Rocky Marciano". And he says, "You're another Italian boy, aren't you? Kid, make us proud of you." Later Allie asked me who he was and Wergeles told us it was Carbo. The only other time I met this guy was in a restaurant. I was with Al Weill and Allie and a few other guys. Weill pointed out Carbo and said to me, "Go ahead over there and say hello to Frankie and all his friends. Make him feel good." So I did.'[64]

So while Rocky went to sleep at night dreaming of fighting Jersey Joe Walcott for the world heavyweight championship, the wishes of certain people were being granted – Jack Hurley had hustled his fighter into the big fight that summer of 1952, Jim Norris had got the big fight he wanted, Marciano vs Matthews, thanks to his pal Frankie Carbo, and Al Weill had got the message. Rocky Marciano's next fight would be against Harry 'Kid' Matthews.

'Marciano was furious when he learned he was to fight Matthews, not Walcott. It enraged him even more that Weill had told him nothing until the fight was agreed upon and it was too late for Rocky to enter the discussion. He was convinced that no light-heavyweight, regardless of his boxing skills, stood a chance of going the distance against him. But it meant he had to wait again. It meant Norris and Weill were "screwing" him to solve their own problems … A few weeks before the fight, the word in the fight crowd was that Hurley had nurtured Matthews with a steady diet of stiffs, and that Marciano would take him apart. Hurley himself feared it. He argued for a direct shot at Walcott, insisting to Norris that he wanted no part of Marciano. But Norris had Hurley exactly where he wanted him. Rocky was the number one contender. He could not be expected to wait around while Matthews had a shot at Walcott. So Hurley was trapped. But it was worth taking the chance.'[65]

---

64 *Saturday Evening Post* October 1956
65 Everett M. Skehan *Rocky Marciano: Biography of a First Son 1977*

9

ROCKY AND THE KID

IN THAT summer of 1952, Italy's former heavyweight boxing champion of the world, the gigantic Primo Carnera, was back in the ring as a wrestler, aged 46. He had quit boxing in 1946 with little money and only one kidney. Now free of the racketeers, he got to keep some of the money he was earning throwing his not-inconsiderable bulk around the wrestling circuit and on this hot July day he was in Albuquerque, New Mexico, cooling off in the local Ice Arena. You could see his match with Hardy Kruscamp for $1.50 ringside, with tickets available from Cook's Sporting Goods store.

Across the other side of the globe, in Helsinki, Finland, the Games of the XV Olympiad was packing them in. The United States team would top the leader board with 40 gold medals, five of which were won in the boxing ring at the Messuhalli. Star of the American team was a 17-year-old black kid from Brooklyn, Floyd Patterson, and he dazzled everyone with his flashing fists on the way to taking the gold at middleweight. Red Smith, the *New York Herald Tribune's* syndicated columnist, wrote from ringside, 'He has faster paws than a subway pickpocket and they cause more suffering.' Four years later, Floyd Patterson was heavyweight champion of the world, knocking out Archie Moore to take the title vacated by Rocky Marciano.

To get that title, Rocky had to fight Harry 'Kid' Matthews for the chance at the crown worn by the veteran Jersey Joe Walcott. Scheduled for 28 July at Yankee Stadium, the fight was being promoted by the

International Boxing Club but was rapidly becoming a Jack Hurley production. 'Hurley won every pre-battle decision,' wrote Harry Grayson. 'First he landed the match, giving Matthews the right to fight for a crack at Jersey Joe Walcott's heavyweight championship. He got an equal split of 30 per cent. He threw out radio and television, and finally even theatre TV. There is no return bout clause in the contract. Matthews is not tied up by the International Boxing Club. Al Weill, speaking for Marciano, at first demanded that the fight go 15 rounds, offered to compromise on 12, but Hurley stuck out for ten. Many schooled observers believe Matthews, the much more seasoned and scientific, has a big advantage there, but not Charley Goldman, the little man who developed, trains and seconds Marciano. "Most heavy punchers tire easily," says the bantamweight veteran of more than 400 fights. "They punch themselves out throwing so many free-swinging and sometimes wild blows. We are sure Rocky can catch up with Matthews in ten rounds, so why take a chance on making him go beyond that point."[66]

Forced to accept the fight with Marciano when he had hoped to get Matthews a straight shot at Walcott, Hurley had told IBC boss Jim Norris, 'No television. You've ruined the game with TV, now you want to ruin my fighter with it. We'll draw half a million dollars without it.' When Norris disagreed, Hurley said, 'I tell you if we don't have TV we'll draw 5,000 people from Seattle alone.' There was no television. In fact, there was no anything.

From New York on 16 July, INS sportswriter Lawton Carver gave out the news. 'You would think that all the brainwork, money and manual skills that went into the perfection of television and radio would inspire only unstinted appreciation from our promoters, such as the International Boxing Club. To the contrary, the IBC does not care a hang about the world progress along said lines and wishes it known that there will be no local or general television, no theatre television, no local or national radio and no short wave radio on the Rocky Marciano-Harry Matthews bout. Briefly, there will be nothing on this heavyweight clash at Yankee Stadium on 28 July in the way of communication, except what you read in your favourite newspaper.

---

66 Harry Grayson *Pittsfield Berkshire Evening Eagle* 22 July 1952

'The managers of the worthy gladiators feel the same way about it, only more so. Officials of the IBC revealed that a figure in the region of $100,000 was turned down for a theatre television set-up around the country. Harry Markson, IBC managing director, said the general feeling was that the fight would draw more money without being on the air than could be made up by selling air rights. This was the original idea of Jack Hurley, Matthews' manager, and the rest went along with it.'[67]

A few days later, Hurley was at it again, suggesting to chairman Bob Christenberry of the New York State Athletic Commission that the automatic eight-count knockdown and the three-knockdown rule be waived for the Yankee Stadium fight with Marciano. 'I have no opinion until I confer with my fellow commissioners,' said Christenberry. 'And I would not ask them unless I received a similar request from the other fighter.'

Rocky welcomed Hurley's suggestion to waive the eight-count knockdown and the three-knockdown rule just so long as they had a referee who could count to ten. Manager Marty Weill, however, refused to go along with the request from the Matthews camp, saying, 'We're not going to request any change in the rules.'

Charley Goldman was not underestimating Matthews. 'They ask you who he ever fought,' said the man in charge of the Marciano muscles. 'They asked the same thing about Jack Dempsey and Joe Louis. They don't ask who licked him. You take my word for it that Matthews is no myth. He has lost only three times in 105 fights and hasn't been beaten in 70 through 6½ solid years. That would be good if he were fighting Frank Sinatra. And he belted all the fight out of an ambitious, tough and left-handed Irish Bob Murphy, easily handled Danny Nardico and had Rex Layne on the deck.'[68]

In the Pacific edition of the *Stars and Stripes* newspaper, B. E. Lindeman painted the picture. 'The highway is just wide enough for two cars going in opposite directions and a white line between. There is one quiet sign that says "Long Pond Inn Directly Ahead" and makes mention of steaks and dinner. Suddenly the concrete rises and veers to the left. The Inn is a white stucco structure just off the highway. It perches on

---

67 Lawton Carver *Newark Advocate* Ohio 16 July 1952
68 Harry Grayson *Pittsfield Berkshire Evening Eagle* 22 July 1952

a small hill that drops to Greenwood Lake in the back. Talking about the place one summer afternoon two years ago, a newspaper man said, "It's not too nice but if it was too nice a lot of people wouldn't go there." As it is, Eddie McDonald's "Long Pond Inn" isn't too nice and a lot of people go there. A lot of people will go there next week because right now trainer Charley Goldman is getting Rocky Marciano ready at Long Pond to fight Harry Matthews on 28 July.

'On a level with the highway, in the left wing of this odd structure is the small but adequate gymnasium. Its incongruous interior decoration features a small ring in the centre of the room and pine panelled walls. The room lacks the toughness that people demand of boxing shops but fighters like Long Pond. Rocky Graziano always trained for the big ones at Long Pond.'[69]

From Greenwood Lake, the *Associated Press* reported on 1 July, 'Rocky Marciano, Brockton, Mass., heavyweight, opened his camp Tuesday for his 28 July Yankee Stadium bout with Harry Matthews of Seattle. Marciano went two fast rounds with Al Winn of New York. The Brockton belter said he weighed 194 pounds and that he had been doing ten miles in roadwork a day for the past three weeks and had been strengthening his arms by throwing heavy stones and rocks … Wednesday Rocky took a one-hour workout on the light and heavy bags, chest machine and rope skipping after boxing three rounds with Al Winn. Watching proudly were Rocky's mother and father, celebrating their 30th wedding anniversary … Thursday Rocky stepped up the pace as he boxed four rounds with Jimmy Cerello of Hoboken, NJ., and Al Winn, both are light-heavyweights.'[70]

Some 2,400 miles away in Seattle, 'Harry "Kid" Matthews did light roadwork, to follow with gym work Wednesday and Thursday and then more hill climbing, tree chopping and hiking on the neighbouring terrain. Matthews will continue that schedule, alternating road and gym work until leaving for New York on 11 July. There he will work out in a Catholic Youth Organisation gymnasium in keeping with manager Jack Hurley's announced dislike for the hurly-burly of training camps.'[71]

---

69 B. E. Lindeman *Pacific Stars and Stripes* 20 July 1952

70 *Phoenix Arizona Republic* 1–3 July 1952

71 *Union Bulletin* Washington 2 July 1952

When he arrived in New York that first week of July, Jack Hurley told reporters, 'The IBC wanted me to take Matthews to a training camp in the country. Offered me all expenses and half the gate. I never had a fighter in a training camp, I'm not starting now. I've got The Athlete, that's Matthews, believing this is just another fight, and if he went to a training camp he'd look around and begin to think it's important. So I'm taking him to the same stuffy gym where he trained for the Bob Murphy fight. Why, a training camp would be comparable to putting a man in the death house. He'd be up there thinking of what was going to happen, and that's not good.'[72]

When Hurley headed east for New York to see to fight details, Harry remained behind to await the arrival of his third child. A dark-haired daughter weighed in at 7lbs 5oz Sunday noon to join a family where girls already were in the majority. Harry and Jo Matthews have two older daughters. The newcomer 'probably', (said Harry after a consultation with Jo), 'will be named Carol Lynn.'

From Seattle on 11 July, 'Harry "Kid" Matthews, his western training schedule completed, heads East today for his bout with Marciano. Matthews ended training here for the critical ten-rounder on a high note yesterday. He went several fast rounds with assorted sparring partners and almost KO'd one of them – Mexican heavyweight Ray Aguilar – with a stiff left jolt. Matthews was to board a train for New York this afternoon.'[73]

Meanwhile, in the big city, Hurley was enjoying himself talking to the press, 'We wondered out loud what Matthews thought of the fight,' wrote Whitney Martin for the *Associated Press*. 'Hurley's eyebrows raised, and he gave up a bland, surprised look. "Why?" he said, "What's he got to do with it? He knew about it when he read it in the papers. Somebody mentioned the fight to him, and he said, 'Yeah, I read about it.' 'How do you feel about it?' the guy asked. 'I don't know, you'll have to ask Hurley,' The Athlete said. Why should he have anything to do with it, I'm his manager, aren't I?"

'We mentioned that a lot of supposedly ring-wise folks thought he was leading Harry the Kid to slaughter. "Did I ever put a fighter in over his head?" Jack asked. "I put Billy Petrolle in with Jimmy McLarnin when

---

72 *Phoenix Arizona Republic* 12 July 1952
73 *Newport Daily News* 11 July 1952

McLarnin was a ten or 15 to 1 favourite, and they said the commission should be arrested for sanctioning the match. Petrolle beat him badly, and then lost two decisions because McLarnin ran like a thief. In this fight, there is doubt that either man can fight. Or the fans doubt it. I know Matthews can fight. I think Marciano is green. He'll get hit long before the Athlete gets hit. Let's see if he can take it.'"[74]

Both the Professor and The Athlete got a kick out of the news item from Greenwood Lake. 'SPARMATE FLOORS MARCIANO for 1st TIME IN CAREER', it read. 'Heavyweight contender Rocky Marciano was floored for the first time in his career today while training for his challengers' fight with Harry Matthews at Yankee Stadium on 28 July. Unbeaten Marciano was hit on the chin by an overhand right thrown by sparmate Jimmy Cerello of Hoboken, N.J. Marciano was driven to one knee for what would have been a count of three had there been an official in the ring. A light-heavyweight, Cerello landed the knockdown punch when Marciano was off balance after missing a hook to the head.

'Rocky insisted he had not been knocked down, that he had merely slipped. But trainer Charley Goldman said, "Quit kiddin', Rocky – it was a definite knockdown." Marciano sparred five rounds, three with Cerello and two with Al Winn, a New York light-heavyweight.'[75]

'Harry Matthews, a boy from the wide open spaces, sweated it out in the 90 degree heat of the CYO gym on West 17th Street in Manhattan. A salty breeze from the Maritime Union across the street filtered through an open window. It was Matthews' first New York workout for the Marciano fight and some observers were impressed with the speed of his hands and his quick counters. In the distance, you could see the Hudson River through a heavy haze. Up close, you could see heat waves steaming off the backs of Matthews and his sparring partner, Keene Simmons. "The Athlete is not a good gym fighter," warned Jack Hurley. "He's not in here to make an impression. He's just working on timing and judging distance. He used to try to prove he could lick his sparring partners. That was before I got him. He knows all the moves. He's a pro. No use getting banged up in the gym."'[76]

<hr>

74 Whitney Martin *Morning Herald* Maryland 12 July 1952

75 *Independent* Long Beach Ca. 10 July 1952

76 *Greeley Daily Tribune* Colorado 17 July 1952

From his training camp in Ogden, Utah, 'Rex Layne, only man who has fought both Rocky Marciano and Harry Matthews, said that "Matthews will counterpunch Marciano silly," when the two men meet in New York. "Matthews is sure to beat him. He's too fast and clever for Rocky. Matthews is the hardest man to hit I've ever fought."'[77]

As the date of the fight neared, more fighters weighed in with their opinions. 'If Matthews can still move like he did against me and doesn't tire in four or five rounds,' said Irish Bob Murphy, 'Marciano is going to be in for a rough night.' Light-heavyweight champion Joey Maxim watched Rocky go four rounds in the gym and told reporters, 'He may look crude, but he'll wear him down. He gets his punching power from leverage like Jack Dempsey.'

'Other fighters have sat in on Marciano,' wrote Grayson, 'and the ones I've talked to are unanimous in picking him to repel the darling of the big potato belt. Joe Louis has no doubt but that he would take Marciano. "Rocky will improve a lot as he gains more experience, but right now he has several weaknesses." Yet Louis likes Marciano over Matthews because he doesn't believe most of the talk he has heard about the latter. Jake LaMotta asks the familiar question, "Who did Matthews ever fight?" Billy Graham has been the constant companion of Marciano in training, indoors and at roadwork over the hills flanking Greenwood Lake. "Rocky will beat Matthews and go on to win the title," says the welterweight contender. "He's awkwardly clever, a style which is likely to bother a stylish boxer like Matthews. Marciano is a fellow who hits you with a lot of punches, and you feel them all. He's two years younger than Matthews, has been subjected to 11 years less wear and tear. He's the fresher fighter."'[78]

'"There was a driver unloading a truck across the street when I first met Matthews," recollects Hurley. "You think that fellow has a hard job tossing those boxes and bales around," I said to The Athlete. "Well, it isn't half as tough as that of a good fighter, and he couldn't possibly do it on less than three meals a day."

'Matthews went on the truck driver's diet and something of his schedule. Matthews rises at 6.30, breakfast at 7 just like the teamster –

<hr>

77 *Lethbridge Evening Herald* Alberta 19 July 1952
78 Harry Grayson *Naugatuck Daily News* Conn. 6 July 1952

orange juice, cereal, bacon and eggs, toast and coffee. There is a quart of water in him by the time he starts no more than two miles of roadwork at 10. At 12 he has the truck driver's luncheon – green salad, double lamb chops, rolls, cup custard or bread pudding and milk. There is no rope skipping, shadow boxing or bag punching at 3. "That's for guys who are learning," scoffs Hurley. Boxing is limited to four rounds. "And I don't care how capable the sparring partners are," explains The Professor. "All the Athlete is doing is perfecting his timing and judging. I could have him ready in three days."

'At 6 o'clock, Matthews gets the teamster's dinner – steak, baked potato and two other vegetables, crisp hard rolls, ice cream and tea. Before retiring at 9.30 or 10, he has his choice of milk toast, a milk shake or ice cream. Like Billy Petrolle, Matthews has never had a rubdown. "Rubbers rub all the fight out of a fighter," says Hurley. "A good fighter doesn't need a rubdown and a bad fighter doesn't deserve one."

'If Harry "Kid" Matthews was eating like a truck driver, it could help him when he gets in there with Marciano. A lot of guys who have been in with Rocky say he hits like a runaway truck going down a hill. Since arriving in New York, Matthews had trained at the CYO gym on West 17th Street, where he boxed no more than four rounds daily.'[79]

'Harry Matthews has the fight mob puzzled,' wrote Jack Hand. 'The boys ride the subway down to 17th Street and climb two flights to watch him work every afternoon. They stand and wait. Nothing happens. Jack Hurley's protégé glides through a couple of rounds with husky Keene Simmons of Bayonne, New Jersey, and calls it a day. They have been waiting for him to cut loose. So far he hasn't. "He's ready now," says Hurley, "He was ready when he came east from Seattle."

'Over in a corner, two veteran trainers sat side by side. They have been daily visitors to the gym. "Who do you like?" somebody asked. "I got to go with Marciano," came the answer. "This guy ain't showed nothing yet." "Don't take this boy too light," said Johnny Attell, the promoter. "Do you think Marciano would have taken a match with Bob Murphy a year ago? Murphy was the hottest guy around until Matthews cooled him off. If Marciano is another Dempsey, Matthews is a new

---

79 Harry Grayson *Beatrice Daily Sun,* Nebraska 20 July 1952

Tunney. He's a smart fighter who knows all the moves. I think Matthews is a clinch."'[80]

Support for that theory came in the current issue of *Sport* magazine from renowned trainer of champions, Ray Arcel. 'I know a champ when I see one and Rocky Marciano isn't ready to become one yet. If I put a timetable on Marciano it would say he's a year away. If he gets his big chance before that, he'll be beaten. He'll take a beating and all the spirit may go out of him. I know I always say I like fighters who have a little kioodle in them – fear, I mean. I don't think Marciano has got even a little kioodle in him …'[81]

From Greenwood Lake, the *Associated Press* reported, 'The old timers, who rave about the fighters of the past, have tagged Rocky Marciano as an old school heavyweight. "This is a fighter who would have been good in any period," declared Charley Goldman, Marciano's trainer. "The modern fighter doesn't want to work. This guy loves it and loves to fight. He walks ten miles a day. Most modern guys don't walk ten miles in a month. This fellow wants to be a real fighter. That's half the fight. He picks up stones – heavy ones – and throws them just to strengthen his arms. He works and acts like a fighter. I'm not saying he's your next heavyweight champion or that he'll even beat Matthews at this early stage in his conditioning, but I will say that he is a highly underrated fighter. Don't sell Rocky short."

'Jack "Doc" Kearns, who managed Jack Dempsey and has never seen beyond the Manassa Mauler before, is all praise for Marciano. "He hits as hard as Dempsey, if not harder," says Doc. "He's what I call a hurting fighter – he hurts you with every punch. You don't see fighters like him around any more. I only wish Joey Maxim [Doc's light-heavy champ] had one-tenth his punch."'[82]

Six days before the fight, Rocky disregarded orders by manager Marty Weill and boxed. 'I want to be used to the heat,' he said. He went two rounds with 205-pound Dave Davey and one with light-heavyweight Tommy Harrison. As Goldman pulled the gloves off, Rocky let off steam. 'They tell me some guy said that if I was a Dempsey, then Matthews is

---

80 Jack Hand *Pacific Stars and Stripes* 25 July 1952
81 Russ Davies *Elyria Chronicle Telegram* Ohio 2 July 1952
82 *Pittsfield Berkshire Eagle* 11 July 1952

a better Tunney. In the first place I never said or thought I was another Dempsey. In my opinion there was only one Dempsey, just as there was only one Joe Louis. But I can punch pretty good with either hand. I'm a young fighter and have good legs. I can catch up with Matthews no matter how he back pedals. If he fights that way, I have the punch to knock him out.'

The Matthews camp was equally confident. 'Harry will take Marciano easily enough,' said Jack Hurley. 'I'm not worried about that. What I'm afraid of is that somebody will get in my room and steal all my papers. I buy 400 copies of every paper that has a story about us and send them air mail to sports editors all over the country. It's working me to death. If somebody stole them I'd be out of business.' 'Hurley may buy more copies than a small paper can sell in a month', quipped one writer.

Arthur Daley wrote in his *New York Times* column on 20 July, 'The circulation of this newspaper will go up an extra 300 or 400 copies today because the indefatigable Hurley will mail copies of this essay to sportswriters all over the country. "I spend more buying newspapers and postage stamps," confessed The Professor, "than most managers make in a year, five or six thousand bucks. But it pays off. The name of Harry Matthews is in at least one newspaper in these United States every day in the year."'[83]

One man getting tired of all the ballyhoo was Charley Goldman, Rocky's trainer. Taking off his derby, he scratched his head and asked reporters, 'Who are we fighting, Matthews or Hurley?'

'The Marciano-Matthews meeting stacks up as a corking fight which should draw well,' wrote Whitney Martin, 'but the timing was a little unfortunate. The Democrats and the Olympic committee never should have scheduled their shows in competition with this colossal battle of the unknown quantities.'[84]

---

83 Arthur Daley *New York Times* 20 July 1952
84 Whitney Martin *Reno Evening Gazette* 24 July 1952

10

THE WINNER GETS WALCOTT

A WEEK before the fight, Hurley was having another rant against the IBC, claiming that managing director Harry Markson and matchmaker Al Weill had 'stole up to Marciano's camp at Greenwood Lake like thieves in the night and they propositioned Rocky about fighting Walcott on 8 September, but he said he wanted to wait until 22 September.'

'They told reporters that they had tried to talk to me about a September fight, but that I wouldn't discuss it until after the 28 July bout. That's an outright lie … They've ignored any mention of a fight with Walcott. They'll force me to make a private agreement with Walcott and his manager Felix Bocchicchio. I mean an agreement for a September title bout in which the IBC will be left outside completely.'[85]

'Jersey Joe Walcott is ready to defend his heavyweight title 8 September against the winner of the Rocky Marciano-Harry Matthews fight at Yankee Stadium on 28 July,' wrote Jack Hand for the *Associated Press*. 'Felix Bocchicchio, manager of the 38-year-old champ, made it definite Tuesday as Marciano and Matthews signed contracts for their ten-round elimination battle. "We're ready to fight the winner," said Felix. "We can't sign because we don't know where it will be. If Marciano wins, the match belongs in the east. If Matthews wins, it belongs in the west. Maybe San Francisco, Los Angeles or even Seattle, his home town. But we'll insist on the champion's share – 45 per cent. New York would be okay with me, if I could get a licence to manage my

---

85 Jack Cuddy *Cedar Rapids Gazette* Iowa 20 July 1952

fighter." Bocchicchio has no licence to manage in New York State and Bob Christenberry, chairman of the State Athletic Commission, has indicated in past statements he would not be welcome. "We'll cross that bridge when we come to it," Christenberry said yesterday. "At the present time, Bocchicchio has no application pending in New York State."[86]

'Felix Bocchicchio was a well-known figure around New Jersey and Philadelphia,' wrote James Curl in his biography of Walcott. 'He was also a well-known underworld criminal, gambler and gangster. In fact, Felix was described by writer Bill Kelly as "being so crooked that he had to screw his socks on". As a young man Felix worked in a pharmacy but soon became involved in a sordid life of crime. His first arrest was reported in 1925. His rap sheet grew from there to include such acts as larceny, hold-ups, assault and battery, state liquor violation, white slave trafficking, and prison breaking. His list of known accomplices included such gangsters as Angelo Bruno, Dominick Pollino and the legendary mobster Charlie "Lucky" Luciano, the father of modern organised crime.

'By 1930 Felix was incarcerated in Pennsylvania. Upon his release he made his way to New Jersey, where he continued his criminal activities. By 1934 Felix was a suspect in the murder of Camden police detective William Feitz; he was also a suspect in several break-ins around the Camden area. By the summer of 1936 Bocchicchio had moved to Mount Ephraim, New Jersey. It was here that he met Vic Marsello. Felix and Vic started promoting fights around this time, as Felix more or less became a somewhat respectable businessman.'[87]

But to boxing commissioner Robert K. Christenberry in the summer of 1952, Felix was still a felon. In New Jersey, where he picked Walcott off the fistic scrap heap in 1944, Bocchicchio brought in a local café owner, Joe Webster, as manager of record and got Nick Florio to train Joe. The comeback was on track.

In July 1952, Marty Weill was the manager of record of Rocky Marciano, but as New York sportswriter Gayle Talbot put it in his column, '…there are quite a few boxing writers and conductors of daily sports columns in this locality who are not convinced that Al actually deeded Marciano to his stepson, Marty Weill. These doubters continue

---

86   Jack Hand *Charleston Daily Mail* W. Va. 15 July 1952
87   James Curl *Jersey Joe Walcott: A Boxing Biography* 2012

to insist that Al, who is a powerful figure in the industry, only pretended to give up his tiger when he joined the IBC and that he has, in reality, gone right on guiding Rocky's lumbering footsteps right up to this happy moment ... Had he, we asked, read the latest blast at his reputed absentee ownership, a vivid article which asserted that Marty Weill had not yet even located Rocky's training camp? "I saw it but I didn't read it," he said. "Just so they mention the fight, that's all I care about. It's like I've told you all the time – when I had to give up Marciano, what was more natural than to give him to my son Marty? There's nothing wrong with that, is there?"

'We assured him there wasn't and asked if we could expect to see Rocky's present proprieter in his corner on Monday night. "You bet Marty will be there," Al replied. "That stuff about him not being around is all the bunk. He was here last week and now he's here again to direct Rocky's training." The world somehow seemed brighter after talking with Al Weill.'[88]

Veteran columnist Grantland Rice gave his view of the coming battle, writing, 'What boxing needs more than anything else today along its own highway is a ring man who can punch. This means punching with authority. For this reason Rocky Marciano seems to be the one who fits the roles on the day of his heavyweight meeting with Harry Matthews ... the one who wins the coming engagement will be in a juicy spot. He will be a young fighter facing a fading heavyweight champion – a champion who staggered safely through his last test against an opponent who refused to step out and pick up the crown. His name was Ezzard Charles. I doubt that either Marciano or Matthews will lug such timidity into the September ring. Both have been aggressive enough so far – Marciano especially ... A shot at the heavyweight title should be more than enough to bring out the best in each challenger.'[89]

One writer who was in no doubt as to the outcome of the fight was W. C. (Bill) Heinz, a good friend of Jack Hurley. 'The Marciano fight was one I never wanted for Jack, and I tried to talk him out of it. Putting Matthews against Marciano was like sending an armoured jeep against a tank, but by the time Jack had sold the press and the public on Matthews

---

88   Gayle Talbot *Raleigh Register* W.Va. 23 July 1952
89   Grantland Rice *Newport Daily News* 28 July 1952

he had also sold himself. "I've been watching Charley Goldman working with Marciano," I told Jack. "Charley's really making a fighter out of him," I said. "He's got him moving inside now and punching to the body, and you know he can sock." "Ah," Jack said. "You know what you do with those body-punchers? You belt them right back in the body, and that puts an end to that." "But this guy is too strong for your guy," I said. "You can't hurt him."

"Ah," said Jack, and there came that look, as if he had just bitten into another lemon. "Matthews will do to that Marciano just what he did to that Murphy. It'll be the same kind of fight." Jack really believed it, and he had a $10,000 bet on Matthews.'[90]

The afternoon of the fight, the double life of Al Weill came to an end. Boxing writer Barney Nagler recalled the tale in his book *James Norris and the Decline of Boxing*. 'The weigh-in for the bout was held at noon on 28 July 1952 in the lobby of Madison Square Garden. Marciano arrived early and was quickly ready to step on the scales. Matthews was late. "Where's Matthews?" Christenberry asked Weill. "How should I know. All I know is my fighter's here." It was a slip of the lip, Weill had openly confessed to the chairman of the New York State Athletic Commission that he was the *de facto* if not the *de jure* manager of Marciano. Some minutes later, Matthews arrived at the Garden for the weigh-in, which went off without further hitch. The weights announced and hastily scribbled down by the boys with the pencils were Marciano 187½ and Matthews 179.

'That afternoon Harry Markson was summoned to Christenberry's office. "Harry, I'm telling you this straight. I'm giving Norris 24 hours to get a new matchmaker. Weill must go. The masquerade is over. If you don't have his resignation by tomorrow at this time I will lift the IBC's licence." Markson rushed back to the Garden and informed Norris of the ultimatum. "He's got to go," Norris said, not without a measure of pleasure. By now he was tired of Weill, who had too much cheek for him. "Call him in." The next day, Weill was through as Norris's matchmaker.[91]

---

90   W.C. Heinz *Once They Heard the Cheers* 1979

91   Barney Nagler *James Norris and the Decline of Boxing* 1964

Those New York fight fans who were lucky enough to beat Jack Hurley to their local news-stand and pick up their favourite sports page that Monday morning of 28 July could read all about the big fight between Rocky Marciano and Harry 'Kid' Matthews, and on that sizzling hot night they joined a crowd numbered at 31,118 making their way to the Bronx for the bout at Yankee Stadium. The Broadway sharpies had Rocky pegged at a solid 2-1 favourite and there was plenty of New England money in town. It was estimated that at least 5,000 people from Brockton alone were in the big city with hundreds from Lowell, Boston, Providence and Worcester on hand to cheer their boy.

'I work hard for every bout,' Rocky was saying on a recent afternoon at Greenwood Lake, 'but this time I really sweated it out. Because of Matthews's speed and experience I feel I'll almost have to knock him out. It means I've got to go out winging from the opening bell and try to force him to slug it out with me. If he does that I think I can knock him out.'

He was a long way from home, but Harry the Kid lacked nothing in confidence as he faced his big test. 'I expect to fight Rocky the same way I have fought my last 35 opponents since I joined forces with Jack Hurley,' he told the press. 'It is a tough, dangerous fight but I expect to make it a winning one. It would not surprise me if I won by a knockout. Anybody I tag right goes down. Marciano to me is no different than the others I have fought. Frankly, I think I might knock him out with either hand.'

While tickets were priced at $5 to $25 ringside, the day before the fight some rush seats were announced for three bucks and long before fight time at least 8,000 were taken. This grand stadium suffered a minor quake during the second preliminary bout as the crowd rose to its feet and whistles filled the air. The cause of the thunderous roar was TV's celebrated 'Dagmar' appearing at her beautiful best. Governor Tom Dewey made an entrance at 9.20pm. He sat in the press section while New York's mayor, Vincent R. Impellitteri, sat in the first row of the heavily priced seats. General Doug McArthur made an auspicious entrance and sat at ringside. The biggest cheer went up from the crowd when heavyweight champ Jersey Joe Walcott made an appearance shortly after McArthur, while Sugar Ray Robinson, in a flashy white suit, almost went unobserved. Jake LaMotta's blonde wife even made Dagmar sit up and take a look.

The main bout was hurried along because of a last-minute threat of rain. The big drops, small in number, came down at 9.55pm at the conclusion of the fifth round of the Dave Davey-Charley Norkus scheduled six-rounder. So foreboding were the drops of rain that announcer Johnny Addie immediately requested the permission of commissioner Bob Christenberry to stop the prelim after five rounds and bring in the main boxers. Permission was granted and the fans were treated to the fastest pre-fight ceremonies in history. Matthews came rushing out and was in the ring before the crowd knew it. Things were going so fast that the national anthem was played before Marciano even arrived in the ring, an unprecedented thing in ring history.

That night, when referee Ray Miller got them away, The Athlete pleased The Professor with his performance. Round one as reported by *United Press*: 'Marciano flicked a light left jab to the face and followed with a left hook to the face. Matthews stepped in with a mean right to the jaw and pumped two short lefts to the stomach. Matthews, in a clinch, shoved two left uppercuts to the stomach. Matthews jabbed three light lefts, and landed a terrific right to the chin. Matthews shoved a right to the ribs and jabbed a light left to the face and Marciano missed with a wild right aimed at the chin. Matthews landed a left flush in the face. Matthews hooked with a right to the jaw. Marciano landed a solid left hook to the jaw and then another one. Marciano had a bruise over his left eye and Matthews' nose was bleeding. Matthews' round.

'Round two – Matthews ducked a wild left hook. Marciano jabbed two light lefts to the face and connected a left hook to the button. Marciano went in with a left hook aimed at the stomach but missed. Marciano missed a wild roundhouse left. Matthews bounced a left to the head. Marciano was on the offensive. Marciano landed three straight left hooks to Matthews' jaw and floored him. Matthews rolled over trying to get up but was counted out before he regained his feet.'[92] Time of the knockout 2.04 round two.

George McGuane reported, 'The first round started out all in Matthews' favour. He looked cooler as his longer reach jabbed Marciano effectively several times. What's more, he belted Rocky with hard rights several times while the Brockton Bomber was groping for a chance to

---

92 *United Press* 29 July 1952

throw. Then, in the middle of the first round, the tide turned. Marciano, who had missed his lefts and rights earlier, began to find flesh. He caught Matthews solidly with his left twice. He hit him hard to the body with a right. And just before the round ended he belted Matthews a terrific left that brought blood to Matthews' left nostril. When the bell sounded, Harry turned and started [to walk] to the wrong corner.

'The second round started like the first. Matthews jabbed well and and hit Marciano solidly with a right. It appeared that Matthews, the lighter of the two at 179 pounds, wanted to mix it with his heavier opponent at 187½. This was his crowning mistake. Told by trainer Charley Goldman at the end of the first round to quit swinging his left but to change his tactics to one of jabbing and then following through with a right and left, Marciano did just that. He jabbed and then followed with a right. Midway in the round he swung a vicious right that would have killed Matthews had it landed fully. Only about 60 per cent of the punch landed to the left of Matthews' face. But it hurt. It was then that Rocky felt he could beat the rain and beat Harry the Kid all in one fell swoop. He threw a right that didn't get into Matthews as he backed towards his own corner. But then came that tremendous left that Rocky has developed. It landed solidly and Matthews' knees began to buckle. Then came another left just as fast as the first, and down Harry went in a heap. It was the kind of punch that seemed to take a delayed-bomb effect. Because Matthews seemed to stiffen in spasms from his head to his feet, he just couldn't shake off the effects and was unable to rise for the count of ten.'[93]

'I got tagged on the chin with a left hook,' blurted a broken-hearted Harry 'Kid' Matthews in his dressing room following the fight. As perspiration poured from his head, the still partially dazed Matthews said, 'It was one of the hardest punches I ever took in my life. Rocky can hit. There is no doubt about it. When I went down I was not out cold, I was muddled. I first heard the count at nine. I kept trying to clear my head. The punch that sent me down was the only one in the fight I really felt.' A downhearted Jack Hurley was back in a corner of the dressing room collecting his thoughts on the bout. When queried, he said, 'I have no excuse for my boy, aside from the fact that after ten years as a

---

93 George McGuane *Lowell Sun,* Mass. 29 July 1952

pro he suddenly turned amateur in the second round and pulled back. That's when he got walloped. If he stood up straight, Rocky wouldn't have come in.'[94]

'A jubilant, grinning Rocky Marciano said tonight he "didn't think it was gonna go the limit, after the first round." "He hit me with a few left hooks that I can still feel," he added. "You know, he's a pretty strong guy for a fellow who weighs only 179 pounds." Confirming that it was a left hook that knocked Matthews down and out in his corner, Marciano said he began planning a renewed attack as he went to a neutral corner. "I saw him lying there," explained Marciano, "and I wasn't sure whether he would get up or not. I know I hit him a few good ones – two rights that set him up and the left that put him away. But I was wondering what to do if he got up again."'[95]

Champion Jersey Joe Walcott, who was a ringsider during the brief bout, said 'Marciano is going to be a terrible, tough opponent.'

Wrote George McGuane in the *Lowell Sun* on 30 July, 'The International Boxing Club must feel mighty good over the outcome of Monday night's abbreviated brawl between Rocky Marciano and Helpless Harry. The IBC had shunned Matthews for so long after his victory over Irish Bob Murphy that a great hue and cry went up demanding something be done. Senators and Congressmen were demanding an investigation of the IBC monopoly in boxing. The clever manager Hurley was putting the big New York mitt club on the spot. Writers everywhere demanded the Kid be given recognition.

'Well, you all know the rest of the story. It was unfolded in approximately four minutes and four seconds of actual fighting in the centre of "The House That Ruth Built", Yankee Stadium. In busting the Matthews bubble to smithereens, Marciano not only won himself the coveted shot at the world championship crown, now held by the aged Jersey Joe Walcott, but he salvaged the IBC from a mighty embarrassing "hot seat," built and kept perpetually burning by the wily manager Hurley. Marciano took the IBC off the spot and judging from the party thrown in the Hampshire House up in the vicinity of Central Park immediately after the fight, James D. Norris and his matchmaker Al

---

94   Ed Harrington *Lowell Sun* 29 July 1952

95   Jack Cuddy *Independent Long Beach* 29 July 1952

Weill were certainly grateful. It was one of the biggest blow-outs we've ever attended and right in the middle of it all were the IBC bigwigs mentioned above … After all the bigwigs had their pictures taken with him, Rocky wouldn't let the photographers leave until they took a picture of him with his two coloured sparring partners, Al Winn and Ricardo King. "These boys I can't forget," said Rocky, "they helped me a lot." This little show of appreciation to two young coloured lads who never expected to be remembered at such a big moment in Rocky's life just goes to show the high type of fellow he is. That little deed was big stuff in our book and makes him a champ long before he cools off Old Jersey Joe this early fall.'

11

THE FINAL HURDLE

THERE WERE 23 fighters named 'Rocky something-or-other' active in American rings in 1952. The best one was Rocky Marciano, 28-year-old son of an Italian shoemaker from Brockton, Massachusetts. What made Marciano the best was his professional fight record. As August 1952 rolled up on the calendar, Rocky was looking forward to his next fight, challenging Jersey Joe Walcott for the heavyweight championship of the world. He was unbeaten in 42 bouts and in 37 of those he had the other guy thinking alternative employment – bomb disposal or mountain climbing, something prosaic. In the fight ring, he was unstoppable. He would not be beaten.

Officially back in the driving seat was manager Al Weill. Not so fortunate was Walcott's manager Felix Bocchicchio, who had no manager's licence in New York State. In 1949, Bocchicchio's application for a manager's licence, complete with pardons from two Pennsylvania governors, John Fisher and James Duff, for crimes committed in Pennsylvania, was held for three months and returned by the New York State Athletic Commission, then headed by Eddie Eagan. In 1952, Uncle Felix was still *persona non grata* in the Empire State. He had already announced that if he was unable to work Joe's corner in the big fight, he wouldn't let Walcott defend the title in New York.

That statement was welcomed by a syndicate of big-money men in Boston. According to a *United Press* bulletin on 1 August, 'A $400,000 offer was made to world's champion Jersey Joe Walcott today to defend his heavyweight title against Rocky Marciano at Braves Field here on 29 September. The sum was guaranteed by a group of businessmen. Promoting the bout would be Sam Silverman, who was authorised to make the offer ... Ben Kaufman, who said several hotel owners and other businessmen were in the combine, pledged to deposit the cash at the Union Savings Bank here, to be paid Walcott on fulfilment of the contract. Silverman estimated the bout would draw at least $600,000 at the gate and that television, radio and movie rights would bring in another $500,000. General manager John Quinn of the Braves said his park could seat 50,000 spectators for the bout.'

The big fight belonged in the big town, New York City. But for that to happen, the New York State Athletic Commission would have to rubber-stamp a manager's licence in the name of Felix Bocchicchio and chairman Bob Christenberry was adamant that was not about to happen. Governor Thomas E. Dewey, a former prosecuting attorney whose successful racket-busting career had sent him to Albany, was in his third term and chose not to step into the arena and fight for those tax dollars that now looked headed for Philadelphia.

Author Russell Sullivan wrote in his Marciano biography, 'Walcott-Marciano almost didn't happen. Instead, for the better part of three weeks Felix Bocchicchio, Al Weill and the IBC squabbled over dates, sites and purses. By early August, talks had broken off, and Bocchicchio was threatening to take Walcott to England to fight. Several weeks later, with time running out on scheduling an outdoor fight, the IBC was set to abandon the bout. Then everyone came to their senses and realised they were leaving too much money on the table. They finally agreed on the date (23 September), the site (Philadelphia) and the money (a 40 per cent cut for Walcott, 20 per cent for Marciano). On 20 August 1952, amid much fanfare at City Hall in downtown Philadelphia, Walcott and Marciano finally signed contracts for the title fight.'[96]

Of course, with these guys involved, nothing was that simple, with columnist Harry Grayson writing, 'Optimistic Felix Bocchicchio must believe that Jersey Joe Walcott is going on forever. Manager Bocchicchio insisted on a 90-day return clause in his 38-year-old tiger's contract for the defence of the heavyweight championship against Rocky Marciano

---

96 Russell Sullivan *Rocky Marciano: The Rock of His Times* 2002

in Philadelphia on 23 September. Bocchicchio could be right, of course. They've been trying to get rid of Walcott since he came out of retirement eight years ago. He's been running longer than *South Pacific.* The old pappy guy made Joe Louis an ancient … Unless a lot of people are as wrong as they were on Truman in 1948, a second edition between Walcott and Marciano will be totally unnecessary, if not impossible.'[97]

With the fighters finally settled into their respective training camps, with champion Walcott at Atlantic City, New Jersey, and challenger Marciano at Grossinger's in New York State, their managers were still going hammer and tongs over that return bout contract. An *Associated Press* report from Rocky's camp stated, 'What was expected to be a routine physical examination of Rocky Marciano by the Pennsylvania State Athletic Commission turned into a noisy rhubarb today regarding a return bout contract. Dr Joseph Bartone, who arrived at Marciano's camp with George Jones, chairman of the commission, pronounced the challenger in "very good condition". Dr Bartone earlier today examined Walcott in the first leg of the aerial training camp safari at Jersey Joe's camp in Atlantic City. He and another doctor found Joe in excellent condition. The rhubarb developed when Al Weill, Marciano's manager, objected to signing a return bout contract on a Pennsylvania commission form. Walcott's manager, Felix Bocchicchio, had insisted that it be used. Commissioner Jones said the two managers would have to get together and iron out the matter.'[98]

Bocchicchio's idea of compromise was to threaten to call the fight off if Weill didn't sign the new contract by the time of the official weigh-in, claiming the original document contained provisions that kept Walcott bound to the IBC. Weill had already signed a return bout contract on a lawyer's form and posted a $5,000 forfeit with the Pennsylvania commission in the event that Marciano won the title, giving Walcott a return within 90 days at 30 per cent each. A reporter told Bocchicchio that Al Weill had announced that if Bocchicchio pulled out of the fight he would claim the title for Marciano. 'Let him claim the title,' the champion's manager retorted. 'Walcott won it in the ring and that's the only place he can lose it.' Five days before fight time, promoter Jim Norris

---

97   Harry Grayson *Ogden Standard Examiner* 24 August 1952
98   *Bradford Era* Pa. 17 September 1952

was being called upon to settle the rhubarb. The baton was passed to Harry Markson, a director of the IBC, and a report out of Atlantic City a couple of days later stated that Walcott's manager said that an amicable agreement had been reached in his meeting with Markson. Bocchicchio was to meet Norris that weekend to iron out any discrepancies in the contract. 'I'm sure that everything will be satisfactory,' the manager said.

One man happy to hear that statement was Herman 'Mugsy' Taylor, the veteran Philadelphia promoter who was working with the IBC. He started as a floor sweeper at the old National A.C. for promoter Jack McGuigan in 1901 and was soon driving a horse-drawn cart through the cobbled streets of Philadelphia, advertising the latest boxing show at the National, while clanging a huge cow bell and pointing to the fight posters that adorned the sides of the wagon. By 1912, Taylor was promoting his own shows and purchased the old Broadway A.C. He was an immediate success as a promoter and by 1916, with Bobby Gunnis, was bringing such fighters as Harry Greb, Jack Britton, Johnny Dundee, Sam Langford and Lew Tendler to his shows.

In 1952 Taylor was still in the fight business and on Monday 1 September he put more than a million dollars' worth of tickets on sale for the Walcott-Marciano fight and said 'he hoped to sell 'em all'. Taylor, optimistically, had 68,577 reserved seat tickets printed with a face value of $1,152,170, ranging from $40 ringside to $10, with general admission at $5. When he opened for business, Taylor said his mail had been swamped for a week with applications from all over the country. One request came from Los Angeles, with the guy flying in on the day and returning immediately after the fight. His plane trip would cost him between $200 and $300, his order was for two $10 seats – the lowest priced reserved seats. Philadelphia's first, last and only million-dollar gate was for the 1926 Dempsey-Tunney title fight in Municipal Stadium.

'Heavyweight champion Jersey Joe Walcott begins boxing drills at Bader Field here tomorrow,' reported *United Press* from Atlantic City on 25 August, 'for defence of his title at Philadelphia against Rocky Marciano on 23 September. The champion moved here yesterday from a farm at Hawkinsville, N.J., where he had been roughing it for three weeks. Manager Felix Bocchicchio said Walcott is in "excellent physical condition". Walcott will spar tomorrow, lay off Thursday and box again on Friday, Saturday and Sunday. His schedule from then on will be to box five days a week, passing up Tuesdays and Thursdays. Bocchicchio said Walcott and trainer Dan Florio talked him out of a plan for night training, which Walcott said would upset his routine.'[99]

'As soon as I heard that Rocky had been made with Jersey Joe,' wrote A. J. 'Joe' Liebling, 'I went in quest of Weill to hear how his fighter's education was getting on. "He come a long way since you seen him," he said. "You wouldn't know him. I got him up at Grossinger's." Grossinger's is a legendary and dietary resort hotel in the Catskills. With its attached golf courses and airfield, it is only slightly inferior in area to the King's Ranch in Texas. A prizefighter training for a big match is one of the attractions at Grossinger's. It was a mark of Rocky's advancement that in the course of one year he had come to be considered an attraction of Grossinger's magnitude.

'I flew up to Grossinger's on the Tuesday just two weeks before the fight, in a plane chartered by the IBC and freighted mainly with photographers going to take pictures of the challenger posing with Jack Dempsey, the old heavyweight champion and restaurateur, who was scheduled to watch him spar and then make the customary Delphic prediction. I found Rocky and Charley Goldman and the rest of the camp, including Rocky's father, sprawled on cots in the sun in front of the training quarters, which were on the rim of the airfield, a couple of miles from the hotel. The fighter and his faction had a rather large cottage and an annex to live in, and an old airplane hangar had been fitted up as a gymnasium, with benches for spectators who paid a dollar a head to watch workouts. The workout in the hangar that day was not spectacular. Marciano boxed two rounds with a coloured light-heavyweight from California named Tommy Harrison, a fast, shifty fellow who kept stabbing and going away while Rocky slid along after him. It was logical to expect evasive action from Walcott, a celebrated cutie who had never, as far as anyone could remember, made a standup fight with any opponent.

'Then Marciano did two rounds with Keene Simmons, a coloured heavyweight every bit as big and rugged as Walcott, and much younger. His imitation of Walcott was good — he would throw quick sneak

99 *Lebanon Daily News* 25 August 1952

punches, some of them right-hand leads, and slide away. He even did the kind of jig-step shuffle Walcott uses to disconcert his opponents. Marciano, I noticed, wasn't throwing as many long, looping punches as he threw the previous year. He couldn't afford to be caught off balance by a sharpshooter like Walcott, who could move in fast on any mistake. While waiting for an automobile to pick me up – the plane had long since gone back to New York with the photographers and their undeveloped plates – I stood on the lawn with Charley Goldman. "The shoe factory that laid him off sends him a new pair of boxing shoes before every bout," he said. "They done it for his last ten bouts and every pair has his name inside. Everybody rides with a winner."'[100]

One guy looking to defeat the challenger was champion Walcott. From his training camp he vowed that Marciano 'won't hit me with those roundhouse swings. They tell me Rocky used to be a baseball catcher. Well, when he delivers a punch he still looks as if he is throwing to second. I can see the punches from the stands.'

Joe's quote was picked up by Rocky. From Grossinger's, the *Associated Press* reported, 'Challenger Rocky Marciano said yesterday he hoped heavyweight champion Jersey Joe Walcott wasn't fooling when he said he planned to open up in their title fight. "Joe was quoted as saying he would pitch and I would catch when we meet for his title," said Rocky. "I hope he doesn't lose his nerve. I hope he really means to make an aggressive fight. If he does, he'll be playing my game. Let him pitch one of his wild throws my way and I'll knock his head off pegging back to second."'[101]

'Rocky celebrated his 29th birthday 1 September with his hardest workout since beginning training for his title bout with Walcott. He hammered away at three sparmates for a total of six rounds, two each with Tommy Harrison, Keene Simmons and Lolly Smith of Bermuda. Despite a persistent rain and a howling wind outside his training quarters, Rocky went through a brisk workout concentrating his attack to the mid-section. Charley Goldman, Marciano's trainer, said the challenger is in tip-top condition, despite the fact the bout is still three weeks distant. "Rocky weighs 191 pounds now," Goldman said, "and he

---

100 A. J. Liebling *The Sweet Science* 1987
101 *Charleroi Mail* Penn. 29 August 1952

should go into the ring at about 187. He has sparred 34 rounds already and he keeps learning something new each day."'[102]

From Atlantic City, champ Walcott indicated he would be looking for an early knockout, which would make sense as a distance fight – they were scheduled for 15 rounds – would go harder on the older man. Joe's listed age was 38, he was born on 31 January 1914, although his age was always a talking point with boxing men. One of those men was former light-heavyweight champion 'Slapsie' Maxie Rosenbloom. In July 1952, Maxie was interviewed in Columbus, Ohio, saying he was 45 and Jersey Joe was a year older then he was. 'He was fighting when I was,' recalled Maxie, 'and I've been through since I gave up the title in 1931.' When Joe Louis took a decision from Jersey Joe on 5 December 1947, Walcott was listed as being five years older than the Bomber. They are the same age today. Louis aged fast after his Rocky Marciano match, but not that fast. 'At this rate,' said Rosenbloom, 'Walcott will be 37 next year – the same as Jack Benny.'[103]

'Walcott looked so good in a Sunday workout that a reporter wondered out loud how long Joe intended to keep fighting. "So long as the good Lord blesses me with health and strength, I may go on until I'm 50," said Walcott. Another reporter murmured, "That leaves him about three months." Someone else told Joe that Sophie Tucker only got started after she was 50. "And she's doing pretty good now," said Walcott with a big grin.'[104]

Joe Louis was 38, born on 13 May 1914, and he was in New York in August to announce plans for a movie on his life, *The Joe Louis Story*. 'It's not a boxing documentary,' Stirling Silliphant, a representative of the producers, explained. 'It's the story of this man's life. It'll be a story of his triumphs and frustrations.' The Bomber, who looked happier and younger than he had in years, had a unique role in the production. He would play a stand-in – in the fight scenes – for the character picked to play Joe Louis. (That role would go to heavyweight boxer Coley Wallace, who held a controversial decision over Marciano in their amateur days). When details of the forthcoming film had been exhausted, Louis turned his attention to the Walcott-Marciano fight. 'Rocky may be heavyweight champion some

102 Milton Richman *Pacific Stars and Stripes* 3 September 1952
103 *Brainerd Daily Dispatch* 9 July 1952
104 *Albuquerque Journal* 16 September 1952

day,' the Bomber said. 'But not this year. Walcott has too much savvy for him. Old pappy is too smart and tricky. He'll run Marciano crazy moving in and out and don't forget, he's got a mean right hand. It's quick and it'll pulverise you. Besides, I don't think Marciano is the best heavyweight around. Personally, I think Ezzard Charles is. And the best heavyweight prospect – I'd say Clarence Henry, out in Los Angeles.'[105]

They threw a bash in New York for Al Weill on the occasion of his standing down as IBC matchmaker, with host Toots Shor remarking that he hadn't seen so many thieves in one gathering since his last visit to Alcatraz. Weill was presented with a watch by president Jim Norris of the IBC as a reward for his faithful services over the past three and a half years.

'You've been hearing this stuff about whether I was pushed or shoved,' Al said with a proper note of scorn. 'All I've got to say is that I feel that I have done my duty and that I would be crazy if I didn't stop doing it to manage the boy who is going to be the next heavyweight champion of the world. I love you all,' Al concluded.[106]

One guy who was not too happy about Al Weill resuming his old role as manager was the 'boy who was going to be the next heavyweight champion of the world'. His name was Rocky Marciano and he talked it over with his pal Allie Colombo one day at Grossinger's, where he was training for his big fight with Walcott. At odd times when Weill had worked his corner, Rocky and Allie were not happy. 'Allie told Rocky later that Weill was "giggling and laughing and sort of hysterical. He made everybody nervous". Rocky said he would ask Al if he wouldn't be in the corner for the title fight. As expected, Weill blew a gasket, saying, "This is what I have worked for. You think the most important fight of my life I'm not going to be in your corner? Why, I'll be valuable to you in that corner. I can think faster than those two guys. What does Colombo know? Nothing! Goldman, he's getting old. I'll be the key in that corner. Don't you ever say that again, Rocky. That's not funny." "Well, Al, there's nothing else I can say, is there?" "Absolutely not," he said. I never mentioned it again and he was in my corner for all my fights after that.'[107]

---

105 *Titusville Herald* Penn. 21 August 1952

106 Gayle Talbot *Carroll Daily Times Record* Iowa 30 August 1952

107 *Saturday Evening Post* October 1956

Joe Louis wasn't the only former champ to pick Walcott to retain his title. Jack Dempsey had visited both training camps, with *United Press* reporting from Atlantic City, 'Manassa Jack, usually a severe critic of the IBC, which is co-promoting the Philadelphia fight with Herman Taylor, consented to help boost the million-dollar fight because of his friendship for Al Weill. He watched Marciano box at the Grossinger's Country Club on Tuesday, and then came to Atlantic City yesterday with the expectation he would pick Marciano to win. However, during the night his praises of Walcott's skill and punch convinced most hearers that he was leaning almost to the point of falling for Walcott.'

Columnist Harry Grayson wrote, 'Rocky Marciano may be the people's choice against Jersey Joe Walcott but the Old Guard is taking the short end. Having seen Marciano flounder around on television, chasing a fleeing Lee Savold for six rounds, Billy Roche has to see the Brockton Blockbuster in the flesh to believe he is as good as they say … Roche, a living legend, back on Broadway from California at 84, points out that Walcott is one of the comparatively handful of fighters around today who thoroughly knows the trade … "If Savold could render Marciano's attack almost totally ineffective, what do you suppose the more mobile and skilful and harder-hitting Walcott will do? The Marciano I saw on TV had two left feet and was nearly always off balance." Lew Tendler, one of Philadelphia's greatest fighters, who twice fought lightweight champion Benny Leonard before record crowds and gates, said, "Walcott steps around like a lightweight. He will knock out Marciano inside six rounds."'[108]

After listening with due respect to the old-timers, columnist Grayson was not convinced they were backing the right horse. 'Rocky Marciano should knock out Jersey Joe Walcott,' he wrote. 'The way I see it, the 38-year-old Walcott's only chance is to flatten the determined Marciano in an early round … At 187 pounds, Marciano is big enough, possesses the artillery, is dead game, has sufficient speed and made every sacrifice to win the title. It's tough to beat a heavyweight like that, let alone spot him anything, and Jersey Joe Walcott is conceding a lot. You've got to string along with the younger and hungrier Rocky Marciano.'[109]

----

108 Harry Grayson *Ogden Standard Examiner* 17 September 1952
109 Harry Grayson *Chester Times* 18 September 1952

12

THE KING IS DEAD …
LONG LIVE THE KING!

ON THE night of Friday, 5 December 1947, heavyweight fighter Jersey Joe Walcott climbed into the ring at Madison Square Garden and over the next hour proceeded to make fools of the bookies, the boxing experts and world champion Joe Louis, the legendary Brown Bomber. At the end of 15 dramatic rounds, referee Ruby Goldstein marked his card for Walcott, but he was outvoted by two myopic judges, who marked their cards for Louis, making him the winner and still heavyweight champion of the world.

The following Friday, Jersey Joe was back at the Garden, standing in line for a ticket, just another Joe. Jack Fried, *Philadelphia Bulletin* fight expert, reported, 'It cost Jersey Joe Walcott $12 and some change to get into the Garden for Friday's Ike Williams-Tony Pellone tussle.' The item was picked up by sports pages across the country, with columnist Hugh Fullerton Jnr. commenting, 'If that's correct, then was when Jersey Joe really was robbed.'[110]

At the end of the Louis fight, the 18,194 fans who had paid $216,497 erupted with thunderous booing. They thought Walcott was robbed. Of 42 sportswriters around the ring, Walcott had it by 26-16. They thought Walcott was robbed. Walcott's trainer, Dan Florio, was disgusted, saying, 'He won the fight. If he didn't I don't know anything about fighting.' Felix Bocchicchio and manager Joe Webster confronted New

---

110 Hugh Fullerton Jnr. *Wisconsin Rapids Daily Tribune* 18 December 1947

York commission chairman Eddie Eagan at ringside and demanded justice. In the summer of 1948, Walcott got justice with a return fight and Joe Louis did what he always did in return bouts; he knocked the guy out. Jersey Joe lasted into round 11 before the Bomber closed the show.

Fast forward four years and Jersey Joe Walcott was heavyweight champion of the world, taking the title from Ezzard Charles on Joe's fifth attempt. Charles had become champion after Louis retired and had beaten Walcott twice before running into Joe's left hook. Walcott couldn't land the left hook when they fought again and the champ had to settle for a 15-round decision after a dismal contest that many observers thought could have gone to Charles. Sports editor Harry Grayson was one of those, writing, 'Everybody who saw the heavyweight champion against Ezzard Charles in the same ring, 5 June, knows that the phenomenon that is Walcott is very near the end of the line, as it figures to be after 22 years. While he won a highly debatable 15-round decision, the old pappy guy had nothing after the eighth round, was utterly feeble after the tenth. Timid and shell-shy Ezzard the Gizzard only had to walk in and belt him to regain the crown.'[111]

From Grossinger's, columnist Red Smith wrote, 'The way you've got to figure the J. J. Walcott-Rocky Marciano fist fight, you've got to figure Jersey Joe will run and jab and shuffle and feint and duck and throw that sneak right, trying not to get hurt in 15 rounds. You figure he'd never dare, unless he got cornered and desperate, to dig in, flat footed, and try to punch for keeps the way he did in Pittsburgh when he won the heavyweight championship from Ezzard Charles. He knocked out Charles that way, but he won't be in there with Charles in Philadelphia next Tuesday night. He'll be in there with a young, rough, rugged young fellow who can take a good punch and throw a better one, and if old Joe were to slug with him, why – bong! There'd go his title, and his intellect along with it.'[112]

For *United Press*, Oscar Fraley forecast, 'The first good punch of the fight – no matter who lands it – figures in this corner today to make Rocky Marciano the new heavyweight champion of the world tomorrow

---

111 Harry Grayson *Independent Record* Helena, Montana 21 September 1952
112 Red Smith *New York Herald Tribune* 21 September 1952

night. If Marciano lands that first lethal wallop, it may well make an old man out of champion Jersey Joe Walcott, the marvellously conditioned ancient who laughs at the years. And if Walcott hammers it home, that first good one, the realisation that Marciano is practically impossible to stow in the hold could well change sunny autumn into bleak winter for the mauling man time forgot.'[113]

In a *United Press* poll of writers who would cover the 15-round fight, 28 selected Marciano and only seven picked Walcott. Twenty-three forecast a Marciano knockout victory and five picked him just to win. Lance McCurley of the *Philadelphia Daily News* was the bravest of the lot. He picked Walcott to win on a knockout. Meanwhile, the challenger was still favoured at 7½ to 5 in very heavy betting.

'New England will be blacked out from theatre television, which goes to 50 theatres in 31 cities from coast to coast. The Philadelphia area and Atlantic City also will be blacked out. There will be no home television nor broadcast on this continent.'[114]

So the only way to see this fight was to buy a ticket and get there early. By fight time on the night of 23 September 1952, a noisy crowd of 40,379 was gathered around the brightly lit ring in Philadelphia's sprawling Municipal Stadium. It was 26 years to the day that a record crowd of 120,757 sat in pouring rain in this same arena, then called the Sesquicentennial Stadium, and watched as Gene Tunney outboxed and outfought a ring-rusty Jack Dempsey to win the world heavyweight title in a shocking upset. On this chilly autumn evening, Tunney was in a ringside seat to see another challenger go for the big title.

On this night, Rocky Marciano was the favourite to beat the old man of the ring, three weeks past his 29th birthday with Walcott on the wrong side of 38. He was the first challenger to go in as favourite since Joe Louis fought and beat Jim Braddock in 1937. But as usual there were the big-fight rumours of a fix and the people around Rocky were concerned. His pal Allie Columbo warned Rocky as they were setting off for the stadium, 'You got to get this one over with quick. It don't look good to me from what I've seen. I don't think you're going to get the best of it if it goes to a decision.' Walking to the ring, Rocky's bodyguard said

---

113 Oscar Fraley *Ogden Standard Examiner* 22 September 1952

114 *Evening Observer* Dunkirk New York 22 September 1952

to him, 'I don't like the smell of this whole thing, Rock. The price has been coming down fast all week. Be ready for anything.'

'I never concern myself with odds,' recalled Rocky later. 'I don't bet, but I hear the talk. By fight time I was no better than 8 to 5. A load of Walcott money was coming in from Camden, New Jersey, and Philly, which were Walcott's and Bocchicchio's home towns. I guess the only thing that kept Walcott from becoming the favourite was that my gang from Brockton came into Philly ready to mortgage everything they owned to back me. I didn't intend to let them down.'[115]

Rocky had won every one of his 42 professional fights, all but five by knockout, but if Walcott was still on his feet at the end of 15 rounds, the Pennsylvania State Athletic Commission had appointed Pete Tomasco and Zach Clayton as judges, with referee Charley Daggert keeping everything under control inside the ring. Rocky was confident his two fists would render the judges' scores purely academic.

The challenger, at 184 pounds, from Brockton, Massachusetts – Rocky Marciano … The heavyweight champion of the world, at 196 pounds from Camden, New Jersey, Jersey Joe Walcott. Fifteen rounds of boxing to a decision.

At the bell the two boxers met in the centre of the ring after some untidy mauling, and Walcott was the first to make an impression, pouring punches at Marciano and staggering him with a right to the head before flooring him with a short left hook. It was the first time Marciano had been down in his career. He rose at 'two' but the referee counted to 'five' before waving on the action. Rocky, cut inside the mouth, fought back as they swapped punches.

'It seemed Walcott couldn't miss his swarthy short-armed target with the jarring left hook that won the championship from Ezzard Charles in July of 1951,' wrote Jack Hand. 'The hook almost ended matters in the very first round … when Walcott's left thudded on the Rock's chin he went down for a 'four' count … the huge crowd rose, expecting a quick ending, but it sat back when Marciano came up swinging only to run into another hook that wobbled him at the bell.'[116]

----

115 *Saturday Evening Post* October 1956

116 Jack Hand *Kingsport Times* Tennessee 24 September 1952

'Right away in that fight Walcott hit me a short left hook to the jaw,' recalled Rocky, 'and for the first time in my whole career I hit the deck … I let my guard down – my right-hand guard – and he hit me that hard left hook high on the head and it rocked me. I wasn't hurt. I wasn't even dazed … My fists were still clenched when I hit the deck, and I looked up at him and said to myself, "You S.O.B. I got to get you." I only took a count of four – some say three – because I was in good condition. I didn't need more rest. I wanted to start punching right away. I had him in the corner at the end of the round.'[117]

Widely reported as Rocky's first knockdown, it was actually the second. Sparmate Jimmy Cerello dropped him when training for Matthews and it was acknowledged by Charley Goldman, despite Rocky claiming a slip. (Chapter 9)

Round two and Marciano pursued Walcott at the start of the round. But it was Walcott who scored with a big right. Marciano was the shorter man and his head was often against Walcott's face during the infighting. Marciano continued to come forward and scored occasionally with body punches but Walcott replied firmly and hurt Marciano with a left hook followed by a right. Into round three and Walcott scored early with a left hook and continued on top, beating Marciano to the punch, although another left hook to the stomach was near the borderline. Marciano was not discouraged and scored with a right to the head. Both men were still punching at the bell and Marciano staggered Walcott with the final punch of the round. It was Marciano's best round to date.

Peter Wilson was ringside for the London *Daily Express* and he reported the fourth round, 'Suddenly you realised his tremendous strength. He absorbed a punch like a rock. He shoved the champion, 12 pounds the heavier, backwards. He accepted the correctly delivered blows and the fact that he was often made to look a gallumping lout – and he took the round on youth and aggression. In the fifth Walcott started to sweat, despite the night chill, and he winced from a punch under the heart. A little later a tell-tale pink stained his gumshield, but a right to the kidneys and a left to the head which buckled Walcott's knees made the round even.'[118]

---

117 *Saturday Evening Post* October 1956
118 Peter Wilson *Daily Express* London 25 September 1952

Round six and Marciano resumed his stalking but Walcott with his back to the ropes gave as good as he got. After another head collision Walcott started dabbing his left eye and was seen to be cut at the edge of the eye. Marciano threw punches at Walcott, who was again trapped on the ropes as the round ended. Marciano was cut on the head. Walcott tapped Marciano's chin at the bell but looked tired walking to his corner.

'By the end of the fifth I thought I was going to be able to get Walcott in another round or two,' recalled Rocky. 'I had him against the ropes and was banging him good in the belly. Then, in the sixth, we bumped heads and blood started streaming down my forehead and into my eyes. I was cut but I didn't know where. When we came out of that collision, which was an accident, Walcott's left eye was cut, too. I wanted to make that a target, but all of a sudden I couldn't see good. Both my eyes started to burn. I didn't know what the heck it was.'[119]

Seventh round and Walcott began with some substance covering the eye cut. Both men were slowing a little but Marciano exploded with a long, punishing right to Walcott's jaw. The blood from his own head wound started to pour down Marciano's face but he kept attacking. Walcott fought back with an overhand right as Marciano ducked low.

Marciano continued to force the champion in the eighth and kept trying to lure Walcott into the ropes. Walcott kept stabbing at Marciano's head but they were light blows. Marciano landed a light jab to the head and then blood started to show again from Marciano's forehead cut. After the eighth round Marciano complained to his manager that he couldn't see. Manager Weill protested that Walcott had some kind of medicine on his shoulder that was affecting Marciano's eyes.

Weill was chasing around the ring and yelling at the referee, but the referee chased him back to the corner and off the apron. Ox DaGrosa, the boxing commissioner, whose seat was near Rocky's corner, told Weill to shut up and sit down or he would have the police remove him. A few minutes later an officer came to Weill after DaGrosa spoke to him but Al talked him into giving him another chance. Then Weill told Rocky's bodyguard, who was sitting next to him, to yell his instructions, saying, 'I'll tell you what to say.' When the bodyguard started yelling Weill's instructions to Rocky, DaGrosa went over and told him to shut up. 'I'm

---

119 *Saturday Evening Post* October 1956

rooting for the guy, and nobody can tell me not to,' said the bodyguard, and the commissioner walked away. There were about 40,000 fans yelling their heads off and DaGrosa figured he couldn't tell them all to shut up, so he sat down to watch the fight.

'My corner was better prepared,' Rocky would say later, 'because they saw me blinking the whole seventh round. They had three big sponges soaking in ice water. Al Weill had picked up Freddie Brown for a cut man just before we left the dressing room, and Freddie was in the centre when I got back to my stool. Allie handed him one of those sponges. Freddie held my head back, squeezed the whole sponge into one eye, then handed it to Allie, who had another sponge ready for the other eye. They kept doing that until the bell ... In the ninth, my eyes seemed to be clearer. I started getting my confidence back. I was saying to myself, "Let them stay that way and I'll get to him."'[120]

Marty Weill would recall his father telling him, '"You go over by Walcott's corner and see if you can find out what's making Rocky blink like that." In Jersey Joe's corner I watched every move his handlers made. It wasn't until the bell sounded for the ninth that I found the trouble. When Walcott's handlers came down from the ring and sat beside me, I detected the acrid odour of liniment. I realised that in their excitement they had saturated Walcott with it to relax his old muscles, but then didn't wipe it all off. The leftover liniment made Marciano's eyes smart whenever he took a jab in the face, or rested his head on Walcott's shoulders ... I ran around the ring to the boxing commissioner and told him what had happened. At the end of the ninth he gave the information to Daggert, who turned in time to see Jersey Joe get another liniment bath. Daggert took a towel from Walcott's handlers and wiped all of the liniment from Walcott's gloves and body. He then warned them not to repeat the infraction, accidental or not. When the tenth began, Marciano's vision was clearing.'[121]

Round nine and Marciano's sight appeared to have cleared again as he advanced across the ring throwing long punches. Although many missed, Walcott tried to slow down the pace, fighting in bursts. Both landed with big punches to head and body. Just before the bell, Marciano

---

120 *Saturday Evening Post* October 1956
121 *Boxing & Wrestling* March June 1964

backed Walcott into a corner and scored with a solid short right to the chin. The effect of the punch forced the champion to drop his hands.

'In nine rounds,' wrote Joe Liebling, 'the lead changed hands three times – Walcott to Marciano in the third round, Marciano to Walcott in the seventh, Walcott to Marciano in the ninth. You don't see many fights like that. In the tenth, which was the hardest fought round of all, Marciano stayed on top. But somehow the calculations had gone awry; the old fellow looked further from collapse now than he had six rounds earlier. Then Walcott, as if bolstered by the certainty that he could last, came out for the 11th and had his best round of the fight, except for the opener, when he had floored Rocky. It was the fourth switch in the plot.'[122]

Round 11 and the younger Marciano looked fresher as he continued to make the running. Walcott grinned as Marciano missed and punished him with a right to the body, and another short left hook like the knockdown punch. He got in further rights and lefts as Marciano ducked and backed away. Marciano dabbed with his glove at a gash near his right eye and was forced to hang on as Walcott tried to finish him off.

'Walcott's right cheek was raw beef in the 11th,' wrote Peter Wilson, 'and his eye a red river when suddenly he came back with his greatest rally since the first round. Marciano was cut near the right eye. He was badly hurt, and only his great strength kept him going. In the next session both men were smothered in Vaseline and blood and looked ghastly. Marciano was chasing all the time but couldn't get within firing range. Walcott scored with a few jabs but took a left hook to the jaw which shook the blood and perspiration three rows outside the ring. Walcott was fighting in spurts, but they were effective spurts, and now he was further ahead than he had ever been in the fight.

'Then, like the car which you never see on the dark road … the shell which you never hear … shocking … irrevocable … heartbreaking … came that tremendous, horrifying right. It left Walcott looking down his own spine with eyes that could not see. He crumpled forward, clutching for a rope, black knees greyed by the resin dust. A brown paper bag burst by a thoughtless child. A headless, thoughtless, sightless, senseless, paralysed man. Rocky started a left hook which grazed the champion's

---

122 A. J. Liebling *The Sweet Science* 1987

… the ex-champion's … head as he crumpled. But the Rock pulled it back. It wasn't needed. Style, skill, pacing of the fight and good punching – all had availed nothing. Youth and strength are invincible. Add to them the ability to punch and take a punch, season with guts, and you've got a new heavyweight champion.'[123]

'With a devastating right to the jaw, Marciano ended the reign of the old champion after 43 seconds of the 13th round,' wrote James P. Dawson in the *New York Times*. 'Until that moment it was a bruising battle that thrilled 40,379 fans from all over America in Philadelphia's Municipal Stadium. The receipts were $504,645 … The knockout was the cue for a tremendous demonstration. Here was the new champion and nothing could halt the crowd in its eagerness to acclaim him. For a time, a wall of police about the working press rows checked the rush. Police climbed into the ring. A straggler broke through the cordon back of the press rows. Then another. Then it was a steady stream of humanity climbing and clambering over the backs of the writers. Then the crush became too much for the police. They gave up and let the demonstration run its course. Several telegraph instruments and typewriters at the ringside were kicked under the ring. A movie camera was broken.

'When Walcott had been counted out, his stricken handlers leaped through the ropes to the side of their fallen idol and carried him to his corner. It was several minutes before he could be revived sufficiently to leave the ring, with the assistance of trainer Dan Florio and his brother Nick, and his manager Felix Bocchicchio.

'Marciano, on the other hand, was virtually a prisoner in the ring, in more danger of injury at the hands of the crowd than he had been against Walcott through 12 bruising rounds of fighting. It was at least 15 minutes before the ring was cleared and order restored. Then Marciano was taken through the crowd under protection of a flying wedge of police and his handlers. Hundreds followed the conqueror to his dressing quarters, singing his praises, yelling themselves hoarse. Marciano pulled victory from imminent defeat with that one paralysing punch. He didn't know it, but the three bout officials all had Walcott in front on a rounds basis for the 12 completed rounds. Referee Daggert had Walcott leading, seven rounds to four, with one even. Zach Clayton, one of the judges,

---

123 Peter Wilson *Daily Express* London 25 September 1952

called it eight rounds for Walcott and four for Marciano. Pete Tomasco, the other judge, had Walcott leading seven rounds to five.'[124]

'Rocky Marciano, the cut, bruised and bleeding new heavyweight champion of the world,' wrote Ted Smits for the *Associated Press*, 'Tuesday night proudly proclaimed his willingness to defend his title and termed Jersey Joe Walcott, "a good, tough guy – a helluva fighter". His dressing room after the bruising, dramatic fight was a scene of utter confusion. Men shouted, glaring lights brought sweat to everyone's faces and in the midst of it all, the new titleholder looked small and subdued. Off in a corner of the dressing room, Rocky's father sat on a bench and wept. "I'm proud. I'm proud," he said over and over again.

'Finally Marciano was hoisted up on a bench and said in a low voice, "I hit him with a right up against the ropes. His head was at one side and I hooked with a left and he went down."

"For four rounds he couldn't even see," said Al Weill, his chubby manager. "We thought it was because of some stuff on Walcott's shoulder but we're not accusing anybody and we aren't saying that's what it was."'[125]

'A heartbroken Jersey Joe Walcott said Tuesday night he was taking his manager's advice and quitting the ring,' wrote Ralph Bernstein for the *Associated Press*. 'Surrounded by photographers, reporters and well-wishers, the 38-year-old veteran of the ring sat dejectedly on a dressing room table following his knockout defeat by Rocky Marciano. "I don't remember anything," said Walcott, as he was asked where the knockout punch landed. "He caught me open and that was it. I don't know if it was a right or left. I just don't remember anything." The Camden, N.J., jolter was taking the loss of his title very hard. He really didn't want to talk to anyone, but every bit the gentleman in defeat that he was in victory, Jersey Joe answered every one of the hundreds of questions tossed at him, either with a nod of his head or a quiet short half-murmured reply.'[126]

Rocky's wife, Barbara, had been sitting ringside watching him go for the title against Walcott but she was six months pregnant and she had to leave before it was all over. 'I didn't know about that until later,' said

124 James P. Dawson *New York Times* 24 September 1952

125 Ted Smits *Salt Lake Tribune* 23 September 1952

126 Ralph Bernstein *Salt Lake Tribune* 24 September 1952

Rocky. 'Frank Sinatra told me he sat in front of her and was so worried he kept turning around to watch her instead of watching the fight.'

Another lady worried about Marciano making his challenge was his mother, Lena Marchegiano. She had never seen Rocky fight; she always stayed home and prayed her son would be all right. That Tuesday morning in September 1952, Lena went to mass with her brother, John Picciuto, and his wife. Then she visited a hairdresser as she wanted to look her best for a television interview in Providence. On her way back home, she stopped at St Patrick's Church in Brockton to kneel in prayer. Then Lena went home to wait for the telephone call from her husband, Pierino, to tell her the, hopefully, good news, as he always did after his son's fights.

International News Service sportswriter James W. Bagley was in Brockton, writing, 'Mrs Marchegiano prayed all through the fight, fainted when she learned her son, former Brockton High school football player, had scored his greatest victory. In her home, crowded with neighbours and friends, she had shut herself in the kitchen and prayed with a picture of St Anthony clutched in her hand. She also had made Rocky put a picture of the Saint in the pocket of his robe before he climbed into the ring. Round by round returns on the fight were telephoned to the Marchegiano home, but the new champion's mother refused to listen. The returns were taken by his sisters, Mrs Camillo Cappiello and Mrs Lena Prosper.

'After the fight was over and she had recovered from her fainting spell, Mrs Marchegiano declared, "Rocky was always my champion. I'll have a big mass said for him. Then we'll go to Italy. He wanted me and his father to go last June. But I said, 'No, wait until you become champion.' Now I will tour Italy with the champion of the world. I don't care about the money. My boy Rocky is the champ."'

13

145 SECONDS!

PASQUALENA AND Pierino Marchegiano had their holiday in Italy in November, a couple of months after their son became heavyweight champion of the world, but Rocky wasn't with them and it spoiled the trip. Then they had to cut it short when Rocky's daughter, who would be called Mary Anne, was born on 6 December 1952 in Brockton Hospital. The champion was in California at the time and it was seven days before he was able to return home to see his wife and daughter. 'He would miss many other important weddings, birthdays, holidays, christenings and births. "Sometimes I think you're only the champ, not my son any more," Pasqualena said sadly. "Why don't you stay home? Spend more time with us."

"Gee, Ma, I've got to make a living," Rocky said. "You know I'd rather be here with you and the family." Rocky's brother Peter recalled, "He learned to handle Ma better than any of us ever could. She was very proud of him, and he knew just the right things to say to her. He always wanted to do things for Ma and Pa and make them happy, but he had to live his own life too." Rocky wanted to spend time with his wife and family in Brockton, but Al Weill had different plans. There was plenty of money to be made and Weill had the tours all scheduled. "The guy's ridiculous," Rocky said to his brother. "He tells me when to be in my room, who I'm going to see, when to come downstairs, when to go to bed. He never tells me where we're going or what I'm making. I think the guy's cheating me. I'm not putting up with it much longer."'[127]

---

127 Everett M. Skehan *Rocky Marciano Biography of a First Son* 1977

In his 1964 book, Barney Nagler would write, 'Now Marciano was the champion, apparently the master of his fate. In fact he was not. Walcott had a contract for a return bout and promoter Norris was eager to put it on because the first fight had been so exciting ... there was anticipation of a great profit from a second meeting. At this point, Frankie Carbo moved into focus. Marciano insisted that he did not know Carbo ... yet Carbo actually had a piece of Marciano. Or, to put it another way, he had a piece of Weill's piece ... and he was friendly with Walcott's manager, Felix Bocchiccio, who was like Carbo, a man with a wide and personal familiarity with the penal code in various jurisdictions.

'Together, Carbo and Bocchicchio put the squeeze on the promoter. They convinced Norris that the former champion would not fight Marciano again for less than $250,000, though he had received only $188,070 the night he lost to Marciano. Norris pledged Bocchicchio to secrecy because he did not want Weill to know of the enormous guarantee. Marciano, after all, was working for a percentage of the gate and radio and TV receipts. Then Norris went out and sold the television and radio rights to the bout to the Gillette Safety Razor Company for $300,000.'[128]

The return bout between champion Rocky Marciano and former champ Jersey Joe Walcott was scheduled for 10 April 1953, and since Walcott's manager Bocchicchio was still not flavour of the month in New York, Jim Norris put the fight on at Chicago Stadium. When the stock market crashed in 1929, real estate was depressed and was being offered at ten per cent of its value at bankruptcy sales. In association with Arthur Wirtz, old Jim Norris and son Jim acquired the Chicago Stadium, which in1935 had been a $6.5m 'white elephant' and was purchased in a bankruptcy proceeding at ten cents on the dollar. They had already bought the Detroit Olympia and there would be more additions to their property portfolio, including Madison Square Garden in New York City.

The fight would be postponed for a month because Rocky's nose was cut in sparring and he suffered a haemorrhage. He was training at Holland, Michigan, and reckoned that by fight time he had sparred

---

128 Barney Nagler *James Norris and the Decline of Boxing* 1964

225 rounds. 'As the fight gets closer I'm getting edgy again,' he said. 'Training camp is like that. After a while you get to hate all the guys around you. You get to hate the sight of their faces and the sound of their voices. But something happened which gave me a laugh, sort of … Allie and me were taking our usual walk in the dark after supper when something bumps me in the leg. First I can't see what it is. The next thing I hear is a growl, and I look down and there is this big boxer dog lunging at me. As I jumped away, frightened, the dog's teeth bit me behind my right knee, right in the muscle. The dog ran away and there I was bleeding six days before the fight.

'Allie was worried that I'd get rabies or something. I said to him, "Rabies? Don't that mean you go mad?" "Yeah," he says. I started laughing. "Is that bad for a fighter?" I said. Allie couldn't see the joke."I was just as close to that damn mutt as you were," he said. "Why did it have to be you? Why didn't he bite me? It's so close to the fight." We got back to the camp and called a doctor. He wanted to give me an injection, but I wouldn't let him. Once before, just before the Lee Savold fight in 1952, I had the virus and got an injection. It broke me up. I was terrible in that fight. I said I'd rather take my chances.'[129]

In Chicago to cover the fight for the *Lowell Sun* was George McGuane, who wrote, 'A recent rundown of opinion among top sportswriters from all corners of the country pick Marciano. All expound classy words as to the reasons why they like the Brockton Bomber, but we think the most honest pre-fight appraisal of the whole show came from a conductor on a West Madison Street trolley … In plain language, spoken as the electric trolley piled its way through the infamous "Skid Row" section of the Windy City, he said, "I wouldn't pay a dime to see the fight, never mind 50 bucks. What suckers people are! Here they're putting an old man of about 40 into the ring with a young brawler and they expect to see a fight. They must be crazy."

'Well, that's the way he looked at it. And in a way it must be a pretty good estimation of what the ordinary Chicago guy thinks of the title go tonight. Because Chicago, even though it will be blacked out on television, hasn't gone for the ducats the way the IBC had anticipated. It makes one realise that it was this poor sale of tickets and not a poor,

---

129 *Saturday Evening Post* October 1956

bleeding proboscis of Marciano's that caused the postponement last 10 April.'[130]

Manager Felix Bocchicchio was confident 'his old man of about 40' could do what he had done before, win the heavyweight title. 'I think Rocky figures to coast in on this one,' he told *United Press,* 'but he's going to have to tear into Walcott to win. He's got to fight to win the fight.' Bocchicchio indicated that one of their secret weapons would be a one-two combination punch 'which was used in only one battle previously, at Cleveland when we beat Jimmy Bivins and Walcott was a one-to-five underdog. We'll fight him round by round and I'm lucky to have a fighter who can change his plans from round to round. There aren't many that can do that.'[131] From Rocky's training camp at Holland, Michigan, 'He and his handlers were happy that he had finished the longest training grind in heavyweight history without any late injury. Not even a trickle of blood came from his nose during his final two rounds of sparring with Willie Wilson on Tuesday. "I'm confident of winning," Marciano told reporters, "and I expect the win to come midway in the fight. I've learned a lot this time and I don't believe he can show me anything new he didn't use last time, and I'm convinced Walcott can't hit hard enough to knock me out." Rocky even did roadwork during the time the fight was postponed, and he jogged four miles on the road here this morning.'[132]

The Chicago Stadium had a seating capacity of 20,000 but the promoters were expecting about 15,000 for the fight, which would be televised and broadcast on radio. For the *Lowell Sun,* George McGuane reported, 'They say the IBC officials were upset at the large number of turn-back tickets from Brockton. The folks from Marciano's home town, some 5,000, were reported to have sent back tickets, deciding to watch the show on TV instead of spending all the time and money in such a long trip out this way.'[133]

'Al Weill held court in the International Boxing Club's press headquarters to answer a barrage of questions. Needled about

130 George McGuane *Lowell Sun* 15 May 1953

131 *Oshkosh Daily Northwestern* 12 May 1953

132 *Montana Standard* Butte 14 May 1953

133 George McGuane *Lowell Sun* 15 May 1953

Bocchicchio's persistent claims that Rocky butted Jersey Joe in their first fight, Weill yelled, "No fighter of mine ever has lost a fight on a foul yet." Then he came up with a neat Weillism that would have done credit to Samuel Goldwyn. "This fight is going to be held in neutral territory," he said. "Favourable to both contestants. Marciano ought to win by a knockout … I hope he'll get him before the tenth. It would please me if it was the first or second."'[134]

It was a disappointing crowd of only 13,266 that paid a gross gate of $321,794, net $253,462. Rocky, the champion, was on 30 per cent of the net plus his share from TV and radio, which brought his end to $166,038. Jersey Joe was on a winner even if he lost with his quarter of a million dollar guarantee. 'Al Weill was furious when he heard of Walcott's windfall. "Norris did that to me," he charged. "He took advantage of me." The old professionals in boxing laughed. They had often seen Weill get the better of promoters when he was a manager and of managers when he was a matchmaker. Carbo laughed loudest of all. It was he who had set up the deal for Bocchicchio.'[135]

When referee Frank Sikora called them together in the centre of the ring, Jersey Joe was taller by just an inch but he looked bigger. At 197¾ pounds, he had 13 pounds on the champion. But Rocky had just turned 29 while Walcott had turned 29 some ten years earlier. The champ was rightly a 16-5 favourite.

In a press poll, 41 of 43 sportswriters selected Marciano to retain his title. This is what some of them shoved through their typewriters that night … Al Warden, sports editor of the *Ogden Standard Examiner* – 'Back in 1927 millions of Americans relived the famous "long count" of the Jack Dempsey-Gene Tunney world's heavyweight championship fight … The new theme now is the Rocky Marciano-Jersey Joe Walcott "short count" at Chicago Stadium. The writer had a fifth row press seat and the first-round knockdown was smack in front of my eyes. Marciano tossed a terrific left hook and followed with a smashing right hand and Walcott went down. In fact Walcott was sprawled flat on the canvas when the count started. Many of the writers, including this scribe, agreed with the majority in that Jersey Joe was glassy eyed and counted

<hr>

134 *Montana Standard* 14 May 1953

135 Barney Nagler *James Norris and the Decline of Boxing* 1964

The champ with beloved mother Pasqualena

The wedding on 30 December 1950. Al said it was OK to get married!

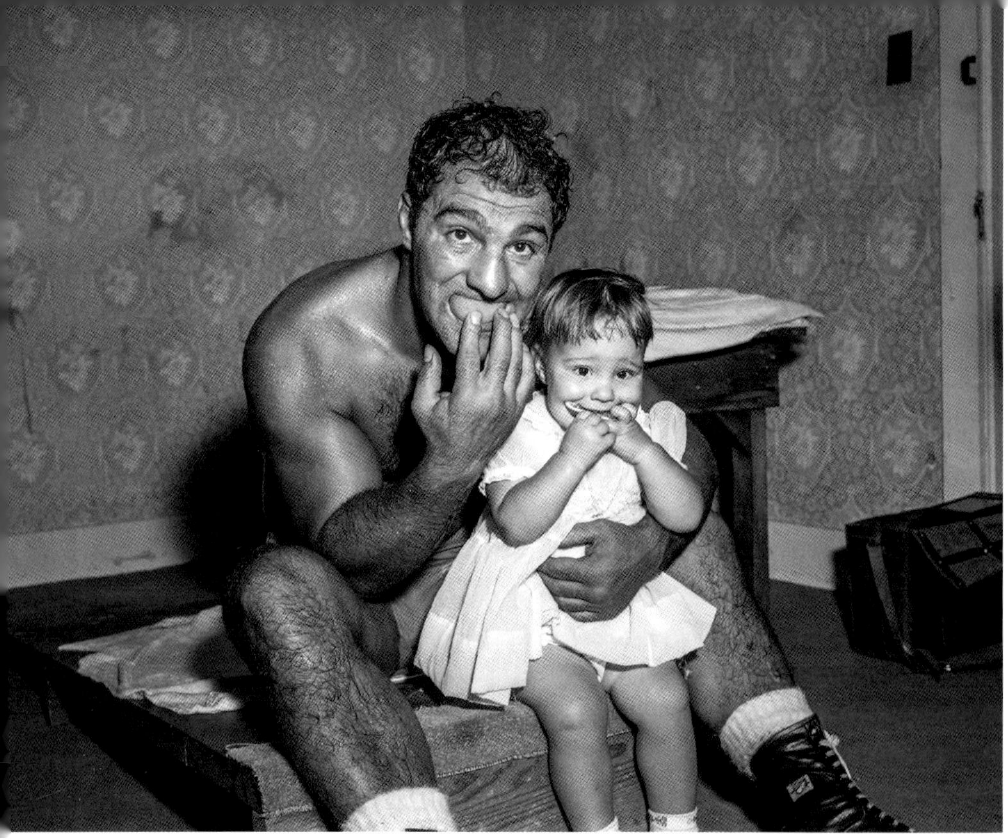

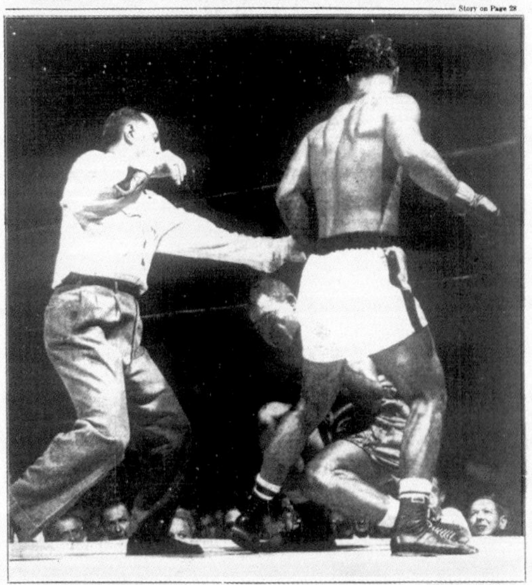

Rocky with his No. 1 girlfriend, daughter Mary Anne

FINAL

DAILY NEWS

Copr. 1951 by News Syndicate Co. Inc. NEW YORK'S PICTURE NEWSPAPER Trade Mark Reg. U. S. Pat. Off.

BROOKLYN QUEENS LONG ISLAND

32 New York 17, Saturday, October 27, 1951 3 Cents

MARCIANO KNOCKS LOUIS OUT OF RING IN 2:36 OF 8TH

Story on Page 28

(NEWS foto by Fred Morgan)

Crash of the Bomber. Practically paralyzed by Rocky Marciano's vicious right in the eighth round, the once-peerless Ol' Joe Louis falls back through the Garden ropes as referee Ruby Goldstein holds off his younger foe. Goldstein didn't even bother to count stiffened Brown Bomber out of his career. —*Story page 28; other pictures centerfold*

The front page of the New York Daily News *Marciano KOs Louis on 26 October 1951*

Harry 'Kid' Matthews ko'd by Rocky in two rounds on 28 July 1952

Marciano's first knockdown in a fight, versus Walcott in September 1952

Rocky KOs Jersey Joe Walcott in 13 rounds to become world heavyweight champion on 23 September 1952

Rocky has Roland LaStarza on the ropes for an 11th-round knockout on 24 September 1953

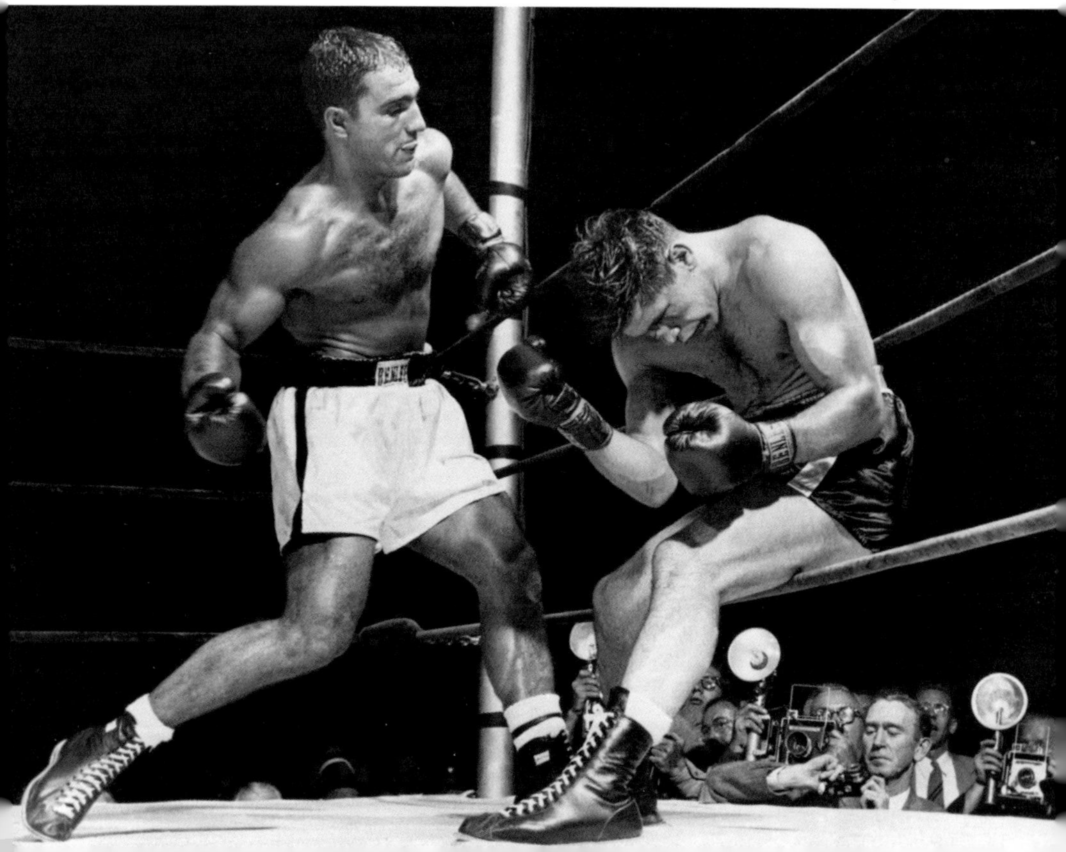

Charley Goldman makes a champ out of a chump

End of first Charles fight on 17 June 1954. Rocky is with manager Al Weill, in glasses, and bosom pal Allie Colombo

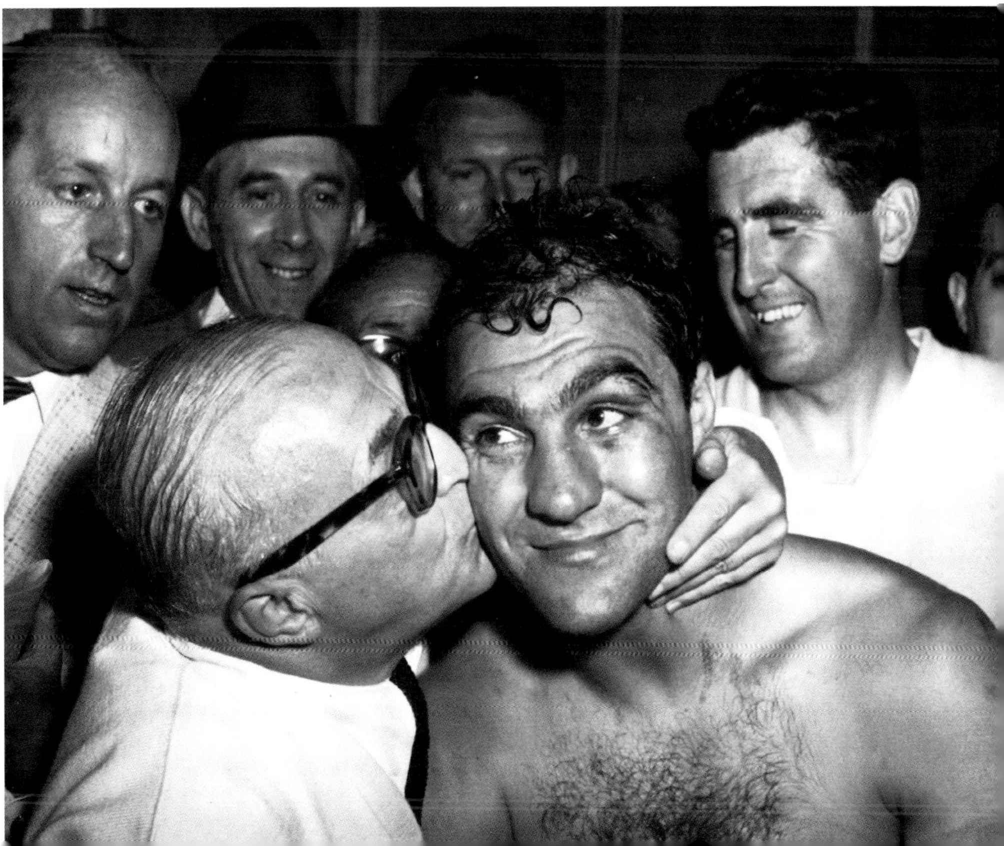

Rocky shows photo of nose injury in second Charles fight on 17 September 1954. He had to knock Charles out, and he did, in round eight, to remain champ

'Hair-raising' fight for British champion Don Cockell on 16 May 1955 as Rocky retained his title by ninth-round TKO

Ezzard Charles defied Rocky for 15 rounds in one of the greatest heavyweight title bouts on 17 June 1955, Marciano won by decision.

Light-heavyweight champ Archie Moore was battered to a ninth-round defeat in Rocky's last fight on 20 September 1955

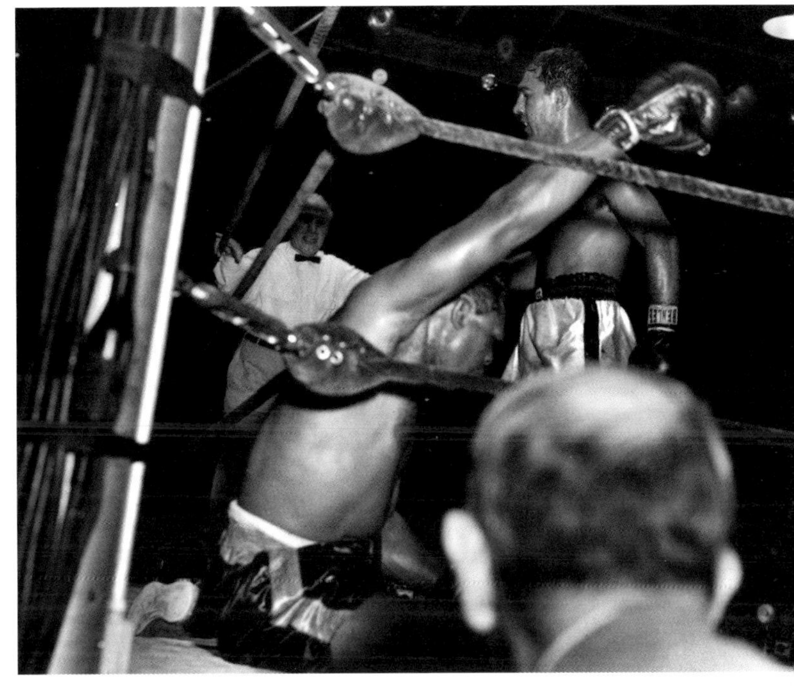

Rocky knocked down for only the second time, fighting Archie Moore in New York on 20 September 1955. He got up to KO Moore in the ninth round, his last fight.

Death of a champ. The wreckage of the Cessna 172 in which Rocky Marciano died on 31 August 1969, the eve of his 46th birthday

Rocky beats Cassius Clay/Muhammad Ali in the computerised 'SuperFight' of 20 January 1970

out … The ten count appeared to be legitimate in every sense of the word, in our opinion.'[136]

Harry McNamara, the *Chicago American* – 'Jersey Joe Walcott, who seemed bitter and bewildered rather than angry, described his stunning one-round knockout thusly. "It was the most ridiculous thing I have ever seen in the ring. I could have gotten up at the count of two. I wasn't hurt at any time. I didn't hear the referee count beyond seven or eight." Someone in Walcott's dressing room bellowed, "If you could have gotten up at two, why the hell didn't you?"'[137]

Sec Taylor, the *Des Moines Register* – 'Rocky Marciano trained for nine weeks for a job that took him only slightly more than two minutes to finish. The Brockton Blockbuster caught Walcott with a left hook to the jaw as the former king of the heavyweights started to throw a right hand, and like a flash followed with a right uppercut. It appeared that the left did the damage. Walcott slumped to the ring floor and lay there without moving perceptibly for what seemed to be an interminable period, as ringsiders wondered why he did not get to his feet. He did rise just as referee Frank Sikora tolled the fatal count of ten. Thus Jersey Joe, the 39-year-old ring relic, failed, as seven other former champions have done, to regain the coveted heavyweight crown.'[138]

Gene Kessler, *Chicago Sun Times* – 'The explosive right hand of heavyweight champion Rocky Marciano accomplished what Father Time's scythe could not do. With one terrific swing it wrote finish to the amazing ring career of Jersey Joe Walcott in 2.25 of the first round at Chicago Stadium.'[139]

Wilfrid Smith, the *Chicago Tribune* – 'Last night in Chicago Stadium, after an indifferent, cautious start, Marciano stunned Walcott with a left to the head and followed with a right uppercut. The second punch dropped the challenger in the champion's corner. Seated with his right hand grasping for the ropes, Walcott was almost motionless as referee Frank Sikora counted. His gaze directed toward his own frantic handlers seemed vacant. As Sikora shouted ten, Walcott vaguely attempted to rise.

---

136 Al Warden *Ogden Standard Examiner* 17 May 1953
137 Harry McNamara *Chicago American* 16 May 1953
138 Sec Taylor *Des Moines Register* 16 May 1953
139 Gene Kessler *Chicago Tribune* 16 May 1953

The bout ended even as Walcott moved. There was no question he had received the full count. The roar that signalled the knockdown ended as if a massive blanket had smothered ringside.'[140]

The *New York Herald Tribune* had two of its biggest guns at ringside, Red Smith and Jesse Abramson, and they let Walcott have both barrels. Abramson wrote, 'In two minutes 25 seconds in one of the shortest and most farcical heavyweight championship fights in the Queensberry era, Rocky Marciano retained his world title in Chicago Stadium Friday by dumping Jersey Joe Walcott, who sat and listened to a count of ten and then made a big show of being surprised that it was all over ... For a sitter, Walcott was well paid. Someone was had in this fistic production and it was the public and Jim Norris, the boss of the International Boxing Club which promoted the one-bounce fight.'

Larceny was on Smith's mind as he wrote under the heading, 'Jersey Joe Doesn't Look Like Jesse James, But...?' J. J.Walcott, the odd old gentleman from Jersey who has mocked the calendar for something like 40 years, made a mockery of the heavyweight championship of the world Friday night in two minutes 25 seconds. He also made a hooting, disgusted, short-changed gathering in Chicago Stadium understand why there has been so much confusion about his real age. He can't count his years, he can't even count to ten ... Walcott was guaranteed a quarter of a million dollars for this night's work. If its finish guarantees his departure from boxing, the price was not too great ... From the opening bell he backed away and grabbed as the champion moved in on him. Once, coming out of a clinch, he brought his right up to Marciano's face, once he dropped a looping punch that landed on the back of Rocky's head, and two or three times he pawed at the champion's celebrated nose with a long timid jab. Rocky threw a left hook which some observers thought was blocked, although Walcott said later that it landed. The uppercut followed and Walcott sprawled on his back, rocked to a sitting position and remained there. He sat in a kind of round-shouldered hunch, heels wide apart on the canvas, knees bent, the posture of a child playing jacks. He didn't stir until the referee had cried "nine" and he was not off the floor until well after "ten".

"I was robbed in New York the first time we boxed Joe Louis," Mr Bocchicchio announced with simple dignity in the dressing room, "but

---

140 Wilfrid Smith *Chicago Tribune* 16 May 1953

I never saw no robbery like this." He could, just possibly, have been thinking of that quarter of a million cold quid.'[141]

Return fights are rarely as good as the first encounters. The Walcott-Marciano fight of Philadelphia was one of boxing's unforgettable fights. The Marciano-Walcott fight of Chicago was one of the most forgettable fights in heavyweight history. In his report for the *New Yorker* magazine, Abbot Joseph 'Joe' Liebling used a theatrical analogy to open his piece entitled 'Long Toddle, Short Fight'.

'The spectator who goes twice to a play he likes is pretty sure of getting what he pays for on his second visit, especially if the cast is unchanged … This is not true of the form of entertainment that the Herodotus of the London prize ring denominated the Sweet Science. For one thing, a prize fight contains within itself the seeds of its own abrupt termination, a possibility of which the members of the fancy are well aware but which they push back into a neutral corner of their unconscious when they set out for the scene of the return match … It wasn't a crashing knockdown, the kind that leaves the recipient limp, like a wet hat, or jerky, like a new-caught flatfish. This appeared to be a sit-down-and-think-it-over knockdown, such as you might see in any barroom on a night of full moon.

'Jersey Joe must have begun the process of ratiocination right away. But the conclusion at which he was arriving was not instantly apparent. Like the drowning men in stories, he may have been reviewing his whole life, with a long pause on what had happened to him in Philadelphia. The dramatic significance of the fleeting seconds was lost upon the crowd, because everybody present, with the possible exception of Mr Walcott himself, took it for granted that he would get up within ten seconds. And maybe he thought so, too, for a while, but if he did, he dismissed the thought. Sprawled on the canvas floor covering, his right arm hooked over the middle strand of the ropes, he waited for the referee to count ten, and arose … The whole fight had lasted two minutes and 25 seconds. The Kentucky Derby this year lasted two minutes and two seconds, and nobody cried, "Stop thief!" But fight fans are accustomed to more protracted pleasures.'[142]

———
141 Jesse Abramson, Red Smith *New York Herald Tribune* 16 May 1953
142 A.J. Liebling *New Yorker* May 1953

The sudden ending came as a shock to Mr Walcott and to Mr Marciano. 'My plan was to hit him quick,' recalled Rocky, 'really hurt him with my first and second punches. I figured he'd remember the last time I hit him, and these would be good reminders. Well, I didn't get to hit him two hard punches. The first one did it – a right-hand uppercut. He was a moving target from the opening bell. He jabbed me a couple of times – I guess he was trying for the nose to test it out – but the jabs were high. I threw a left hook at him, which missed. I tried a right hand and he ducked. Then I threw another left and he blocked it, but as his head went down in defence, or maybe he was trying to go into a crouch, I let go with a right uppercut and caught him good on the side of the head with it.

'I put in almost five months training for this fight, and in two minutes and 25 seconds it was all over. At first I couldn't believe it. After he went down, he was sort of squatting on the canvas and I was waiting for him to get up. I had hit him with better punches in the first fight and he had stood up. I heard the count. I kept looking at Walcott, but he's not looking at the ref counting. He's looking straight ahead. When the count got to eight, it hit me. I said to myself, "This guy's *not* getting up." I was the most surprised guy in the house.'[143]

And still heavyweight champion of the world.

* * * *

Everybody in Brockton was a Rocky Marciano fan. Well, almost everybody. The new champion was presented with a Cadillac by his friends. Massachusetts governor Paul Dever bestowed a special licence plate with the letters 'KO'. During the celebrations, Rocky was introduced to an Italian patriarch. The old man inquired, 'What did you say your name was?'

'Rocky Marciano,' the champion replied. The old man shook his head and said, 'I don't follow baseball much.'

---

143 *Saturday Evening Post* October 1956

14

THE INQUEST
AND THE REMATCH

SO WHAT on earth happened in that Chicago ring the night of 15 May 1953? Look, the guy was 39, and while 39 is fine for a shoe salesman or a cab driver, it is not fine for a professional prizefighter going up against the undefeated heavyweight champion of the world, who is looking for his 39th knockout. Rocky Marciano throws rocks in his training camp and he throws rocks in the ring. The few rocks he threw that night in Chicago didn't look hard enough to render Walcott unconscious, and they didn't. Walcott wasn't knocked out, he was counted out.

Red Smith wrote in his ringside report, 'After 23 recorded years as a professional fist fighter, the former champion went out in a total disgrace which no excuses can relieve. If he was truly knocked out by the only real punch of the bout, then he didn't belong in the ring. If he was not knocked senseless and did hear the count of referee Frank Sikora, then it was a disgrace because it was apparent through the last several seconds that he was not going to get up, or even to try. If he did not hear the count, then he was befuddled by Marciano's blow or else his hearing is no better than might be expected at his age, for the toll of seconds was clearly audible in the press rows half the width of the ring away. By the time the count reached "eight", it was clear he would not get up before the toll was completed. He didn't stir until the referee had cried "nine" and he was not off the floor until well after "ten".'

Red Smith's colleague at the *New York Herald Tribune*, Jesse Abramson, rubbished the wild claims of Walcott and manager Bocchicchio that they had received a short count. 'There was no doubt at all in the minds of those watching the knockdown scene, hearing and seeing the knockdown timekeeper, Mike Murphy, and the referee counting ten in unison amid the sudden din that Walcott got the maximum count of ten.'[144]

Reporter Tom Branagan was in Walcott's dressing room to hear him say, 'I wasn't hurt at any time. I guess it was a left hook and a punch-push or something that knocked me down. I could have gotten up at the count of two.' Bocchicchio claimed, 'Joe knew what he was doing. He waited for me to tell him to get up, and when I told him to get up he was counted out.' Bocchicchio's words were literally spat at reporters as he ridiculed the manner in which referee Frank Sikora had counted out his 39-year-old protégé.'[145] The belief here is that Walcott's sit-down strike was orchestrated months previously, just after the first fight with Marciano, when Bocchicchio and his adviser, Uncle Frankie Carbo, convinced promoter Jim Norris that a return fight would sell like hot cakes, but as old Jersey Joe would be 40 next birthday, he couldn't possibly fight Marciano again for less than a $250,000 guarantee. They got it by using as a lever a $200,000 guarantee offered by Sam Silverman, who figured the fight would do good business in Boston. Norris went for the bait and the boys were halfway home. Joe would get the same pay packet if he fought just one round or the full 15, 'so why knock yourself out Joe, let Rocky do it for you, and sooner rather than later'. And that's the way Walcott's fight went, maybe a little too soon.

'Walcott had promised his wife Lydia and their six children that the rematch with Rocky would be his fistic finale, and with the biggest purse of his career some felt discretion was the better part of valour and Jersey Joe decided to sit this one out. "I think Walcott should have got up," said Rocky later. "I know I would have."'[146]

Chicago, Monday, 18 May 1953 – 'The Illinois Boxing Commission disallowed a protest by Jersey Joe Walcott's manager, Felix Bocchicchio, of his knockout loss to Rocky Marciano in Friday night's heavyweight

---

144 Red Smith, Jesse Abramson *New York Herald Tribune* 16 May 1953
145 Tom Branagan *Winnipeg Free Press* 16 May 1953
146 Rocky, a Tribute to Marciano *Boxing Illustrated* 1979

championship fight. Three dimensional moving pictures showed conclusively on Monday that Jersey Joe Walcott only stirred slightly at the count of ten, which gave Rocky Marciano an official knockout victory in Friday's heavyweight championship fight. Fight writers, representatives of the International Boxing Club, members of the State Athletic Commission, and Felix Bocchicchio, Walcott's manager, saw the films in a special showing. Four different angles were caught by the cameras. The knockout and the count by referee Frank Sikora were run in slow motion as well as conventional tempo.

'The pictures showed that Rocky landed a left hook which appeared to be not too hard and then followed with a right cross uppercut sort of blow that caught Walcott flush on the chin and sent him down on his haunches. The right which apparently did the damage did not appear as head-snapping as the terrific right cross Marciano used to KO the challenger in their first meeting in Philadelphia in September 1952 … Jersey Joe, sitting on the canvas with his right arm draped over a ring rope, appeared dazed at the beginning of the count and kept watching his corner and Bocchicchio. When the count reached five, Walcott appeared to be just sitting there and he was just ready to move one of his legs when the ten-count was clearly heard. "I still think it was a fast count," Bocchicchio said after viewing the movies, "and we are going ahead with our protests in the commission offices this afternoon."'[147]

Fight? Farce? Fiasco? Final words now to Pat Robinson, sportswriter for the *International News Service*. 'Now that the furore has died and tempers have cooled a bit, let's see if we can find out what made Jersey Joe Walcott quit to Rocky Marciano. Make no mistake about it. He quit cold … This was not a tank job as some have intimated. We say that because he and his ex-convict manager had too much to lose by not sticking around to make the picture worth a fortune. And if he were going to do a tank job, he would not have acted as he did. He would have stretched out cold, and then let himself be dragged to his corner, apparently in a coma.

'No, we think the reason he quit is because he was petrified with fear … Before their first fight Old Joe was disdainful of Marciano's fighting ability and he scoffed at Rocky's punching ability. But there

---

147 *Cedar Rapids Gazette* 18 May 1953

was a decided change before the last fight. He was not as physically fit as he had been, a fact which was obvious to any observing eye. As for his nerves, he plainly was shaken and unsure of himself even at the weigh-in for the fight. Now why should a man who has absorbed countless thousands of punches suddenly become afraid of another punch?

'Why should a man who has been knocked out often suddenly became fearful of the same thing happening again? We think his whole mental attitude had changed and that the old man was really afraid of his ability to make a decent showing more than he was of Marciano's punch.'[148]

It's on the record; Rocky Marciano wKO 1 Jersey Joe Walcott, Chicago, 24 September 1953.

* * * *

Time for trivia … 'Rocky's wife was being interviewed before the title fight in Chicago. "This baby you have," queried a reporter, "is how old?" "Five months," Mrs Marciano replied. "Do you want your baby to grow up to be a fighter?" was the next question. Mrs Marciano smiled and shook her head. "I guess not," she said. "You see, it's a girl."' *Cedar Rapids Gazette* 25 May 1953

* * * *

Back home in Brockton a week after the Walcott business, Rocky announced that the planned exhibition tour of Korea and the Philippines was off. 'We called off the tour because it would take too much time. It would be too close to the next fight.' Asked whether he'd rather fight Roland LaStarza or ex-champion Ezzard Charles, Rocky said, 'Well, I'm going to fight both of them eventually, but I think I'd rather fight LaStarza first.'[149]

The executive board of the National Boxing Association and Bob Christenberry, chairman of the New York State Athletic Commission, recommended that Charles and LaStarza fight it out for the title shot.

---

148 Pat Robinson *Morning Avalanche* TX 24 May 1953
149 *Camden News* 2 June 1953

But LaStarza, son of a Bronx butcher, declined the Charles fight, with manager Jimmy DeAngelo telling the press, 'Charles has had plenty of title fights. Now Roland wants his chance. He's waited three years for a promised return bout now. We want Marciano and nobody else.' The challenge to LaStarza was made by Charles's co-managers, Tom Tannas and Jake Mintz. 'We have sent forfeits to the NBA and the New York Commission as evidence of our good faith,' said the co-managers. 'If LaStarza thinks he is good enough to fight for the title, he can prove the same to Charles.' The *Stars and Stripes (Euro)* reported: 'Al Weill has been negotiating with promoter Jim Norris for Marciano's next title fight. Norris wants Marciano to fight either Charles or LaStarza in September. Weill said he hasn't made up his mind yet whether he'll permit the champion to fight in September.'[150]

From New York, Gayle Talbot reported for the *Associated Press*, 'The International Boxing Club will shortly announce plans for a heavyweight title fight here in September between Rocky Marciano and Roland LaStarza. This will come as bad news to the several managers of Ezzard Charles, but the IBC really has little choice. It wishes to hold the next big one in a local ball park for a number of reasons, and the men who run the cauliflower cartel regard Charles as a very poor draw in these parts … We believe Al Weill when he declares he has no choice between the two foremost challengers. He firmly believes that Rocky is good enough now to whip both of them on the same night.

'If anybody tells you the champion is ducking Charles, he simply doesn't know Rocky. Actually, if the Marciano forces are to be suspected of fearing either man, the more logical choice would be LaStarza. Back three years ago he gave Rocky the closest brush of his unbeaten career that went to Marciano on points only because he scored a knockdown in an early round. A majority of newsmen at ringside thought LaStarza won it. Where LaStarza is young (25) and at his physical peak, Charles has been putting on the years and there are those who seriously doubt the Cincinnati bull fiddle player would like Marciano's game.'[151]

Marciano versus LaStarza was announced 25 July. From New York, Harry Grayson wrote 'Al Weill finally stopped running from Roland

---

150 *Stars and Stripes (Euro)* 25 May 1953
151 Gayle Talbot *Raleigh Register* 29 May 1953

LaStarza after a three-and-a-half year chase. So Rocky Marciano, who would have fought LaStarza on a street corner the day after their controversial match of 42 months ago, now will take on the former City College of New York student in a joust scheduled for 15 rounds at the Polo Grounds on 24 September. Weill, then the Madison Square Garden matchmaker, carefully building Marciano on the side, and Jimmy DeAngelo, who handles LaStarza, were old friends, shook hands in agreeing that the winner of the first contest would give the loser a prompt return providing it was a good fight. It was an excellent battle to a highly debatable split decision.

'Quick to Weill meant three and a half years, however, or until he figured his tiger was just about ready to step in with anyone. Since then, Charley Goldman has nervously groomed and fretted over Marciano like a mother hen … LaStarza didn't look too bad and came from behind to beat Rex Layne. He couldn't get the finisher across despite flooring Dan Bucceroni five times. But LaStarza was fighting for ordinary money. This is a bit different. We don't look for him to win, but anticipate his putting up a rather well-executed and game stand. This one will be a fight while it lasts, not a sit-down strike.'[152]

'I've never made the big money before,' said Roland LaStarza. He was settled in his training camp at Greenwood Lake, New York, talking to newspapermen from around the globe, talking quietly, fluently. 'The biggest purse I ever got was when I fought Marciano before, that was three and a half years ago and I got $13,000. Out of that I had to pay my taxes and my manager's percentage, which is a third. For Thursday's fight, I'll get 17½ per cent of the gate. They say one way and another, it may come to half a million dollars. That would mean that my share would be about $87,000. I just can't begin to believe in that sort of money.'

About Marciano, LaStarza had definite views. 'Although Marciano had me on the deck, I've been worse hurt in other fights. There was a guy called Gene Gosney. Fighting him I'm like an elevator. One minute I'm up, the next I'm down – that was real punching.' Modestly, the New Yorker doesn't mention that he got off the deck to stop Gosney in the seventh. One of Roland's sparring partners is Johnny Neubauer, just out

152 Harry Grayson *Defiance Crescent-News* Ohio 25 July 1953

of the army and putting 210 pounds into his punches. But the world title challenger was in more danger running his five miles roadwork every morning. He had to wear calf-high army engineering boots because the vicinity of Greenwood Lake was infested with deadly snakes – rattlesnakes and copperheads, whose bites can kill a man in a matter of minutes.

Peter Wilson was in camp for the London *Daily Mirror* and he queried LaStarza's statement that 'the fight is probably over already, even though it doesn't take place until Thursday. Because every fight you have is won or lost during your heavy training. I've finished mine. There's nothing more I can do. I think I've done enough to win. So for good and all, it's over right now.' This was good news for sparring partners Jimmy De Lenge and Artie Lucido. 'I don't know how Roland feels,' both of them said, 'but we are sure glad that the heavy work is over. The last two days have been just too tough.'

'I think he will give Marciano as good as he's got as long as he's got anything,' Wilson said in his cabled report to London. 'I believe that this could be a really great heavyweight title bout, because when you've waited for something like three and a half years, and when your whole future depends on how you perform just one hour in your life, this could be your finest hour.'[153]

Billy Brown, who succeeded Al Weill as matchmaker for the IBC at Madison Square Garden, was bending Harry Grayson's ear as they watched LaStarza training. 'LaStarza went to Chicago with me for the Marciano-Jersey Joe Walcott return,' recalled Brown. 'All I heard to and from and while there was, "I can lick this guy, Bill." He even feared that Walcott might win and put his championship shot off another year. He's totally unafraid; a young fellow as well equipped as he is and weighing 188 pounds can be mighty dangerous. He is an excellent boxer, not easy to hit. In my opinion, this is by far Marciano's toughest fight.'[154]

That was also the considered opinion of former heavyweight champ Jimmy Braddock after watching Rocky spar four rounds at Grossinger's. 'Sure, Rocky's in great shape,' he said.

'But physical condition alone does not win fights. Marciano actually

153 Peter Wilson *Daily Mirror* London 22 May 1953
154 Harry Grayson *Chester Times* PA 19 August 1953

hasn't had a fight in almost a year.' Braddock observed that Rocky was being hit an 'unnecessarily lot of punches' in his workout against Jimmy Cerello of Jersey City, a fast light-heavyweight. 'LaStarza is fast and he can hit a lot harder than Cerello,' Braddock warned the young champion. 'I beat Max Baer, a puncher, and nobody gave me a chance before the fight,' Braddock went on. 'But I outboxed him. LaStarza can do the same against Marciano, if he's not careful. But it's not a cinch for Rocky,' he said with conviction.[155]

'Rocky Marciano is glad that he's putting the slug on a young guy for a change,' wrote sports editor Harry Grayson from Grossinger's. 'The condemned man this time is Roland LaStarza, aged 26. Marciano is tired of hearing that all he has licked are old men – Louis, Savold, Matthews and Walcott, twice.' "They completely overlooked the fact that Joe Louis was a much better heavyweight the night Rocky draped him over the ring apron than he was when he dropped the title to Ezzard Charles in 15 rounds," cut in Goldman, the grizzled little conditioner. "After losing to Charles, something he couldn't understand, Louis went back to work and had won eight straight fights when he tackled Rocky."

'For an old geezer of 37, Louis made it a remarkably good fight while it lasted,' said Grayson. "Indeed he did," said Marciano. "He jabbed mighty well. They didn't have to tell me it was close until I nailed him in the eighth.""[156]

In his column, sportswriter Joe Williams defended the champion against those who would call him a dirty fighter. 'Marciano is a rough fighter,' he wrote, 'rough without being dirty. Rough without design. It's the way he fights. Attack mostly is all he knows. Having started late and running more to power than finesse and obsessed with one single purpose – to crush the man as soon as possible – there are moments, to put it gently, that he is not always the perfect stylist.

'Lee Savold complained Marciano had carried his violence beyond proper bounds. Rex Layne protested the Brockton Rock was unseemly savage. But neither called him a deliberately foul or dirty fighter. LaStarza will get roughed up, too. Because Marciano is still a lunging

---

155 *Coshockton Tribune* Ohio 23 August 1953

156 Harry Grayson *Blytheville Courier News* Arkansas 10 August 1953

puncher and his footwork, although improving, often leaves him off balance. A miss or a slip doesn't stop Marciano; he keeps pressing forward, continues to punch, or to try to, and in the wild, undisciplined action that attends such determined fury he will at times land with a forearm or an elbow. If there is a crash of bodies, he's less liable to get hurt than the other fellow.

'To this extent, then, it may be correctly said that the champion is a rough fighter. But there is a wide difference between a rough fighter and a dirty fighter. Actually Marciano wouldn't know how to be a dirty fighter. For one thing, he's so inherently decent. For another, he hasn't the talent for it. Paradoxically, the foulest fighters are the most skilful. Unless they are clever, they can't get away with it. Any time an awkward fighter tries to give his opponent the lace or the elbow or thumb the eye, it's so obvious everybody in the house sees it. Marciano will never qualify.'[157]

'At the start of his sparring, LaStarza is working with a couple of big men,' reported Gayle Talbot from Greenwood Lake, 'Keene Simmons, 210, and Tony Carrion, 197. So far as we could detect in a single session, he isn't practising anything devious or sharpening any particular weapon. He's just laying into the hired hands with the big gloves until he sweats. Does he intend later on to import a few smaller and faster partners to improve his speed? "I can't say," he replied. "It's all up to Jimmy and my trainer Dan Florio. Whatever they say, that's what I do."'[158]

A couple of weeks later, it was revealed what Florio was saying and what LaStarza was doing. 'We're using mattresses under the ring canvas to stimulate Roland in attaining fast footwork,' Florio told the *DefianceCrescent-News*. 'When he shifts from this slow ring to the regulation speedier ring at the Polo Grounds, he'll be as fast as a tiger. And he'll have much more leg stamina.'

'This modernistic quest for speed features every department of LaStarza's grooming grind. For example, Roland's inflated striking bag is so small it looks like a toy, but it's lightning fast. And his jogs on the road in the morning are studded with all-out sprints and with bursts

---

157 Joe Williams *El Paso Herald Post* 27 August 1953
158 Gayle Talbot *Winona Republic Herald* 12 August 1953

of shadow boxing.' Sparmate Keene Simmons, who formerly worked with Marciano, declared today, "I'm really earning my money here with LaStarza. He's twice as fast as Marciano. He hits sharper, although not with as much power. He's got a great left jab, which Rocky hasn't. And he's much harder to nail than Rocky because of his speed. I wouldn't be surprised if he wins the title."

'Trainer Florio warned, "Rocky will get the surprise of his life this time. He'll meet a young, chained-lightning fighter – not an old man like Walcott, Joe Louis, Lee Savold or Harry Matthews. He'll meet a courageous athlete who won't die in his room the night before the bout."'[159]

* * * *

Reading the morning newspapers, Marciano took all the training camp gossip with a pinch of salt, but his swarthy face clouded over when he read an *Associated Press* bulletin from Greenwood Lake stating, 'Challenger Roland LaStarza expressed his admiration for Rocky Marciano but in an outspoken burst of oratory said that the heavyweight champion's slam-bang style of fighting is going to make Rocky "soft in the head".

"He's gonna get hurt," said Roland. "Maybe not by me. If I don't do it, somebody else will. He takes two, three or four punches to give one. If he keeps it up, he's gonna get soft in the head. That's no good. He respects only his power to take and give a punch." Only moments before, the handsome 26-year-old ex-GI had said of Rocky in an interview, "He's a great fighter. He's the champion." Then he came out with his explosive remarks.'[160]

Rocky would remember those ill-chosen words.

---

159 *Defiance Crescent-News* 22 August 1953
160 *Rocky Mount Evening Telegram* 31 August 1953

15

REMATCH FOR ROLLIE

WHILE TRAINING at Grossinger's for the LaStarza fight, Rocky had a visitor who told him he 'had some big news for him'. The guy was a Philadelphia policeman and when the workouts were finished for the day he joined Rocky and Allie on the porch. 'I made an arrest lately,' he said, 'and the person gave me the information I've been looking for.' The guy had watched Rocky knock Walcott out to win the title and had promised the new champion that if it took him his whole life he'd make an investigation to find out how Marciano was almost blinded for three rounds in the fight. At the time, it was believed that it was due to some medication used in Rocky's corner to stop the bleeding from a cut on his head that came from a butt.

'Well, here's the truth, as it was told to me by the policeman who found out,' recalled Rocky. 'I was blinded by capsicum Vaseline. According to the policeman, Walcott's manager, Felix Bocchiccho, rubbed it on Joe's gloves and on the upper part of his body. From the sixth round on through the eighth, every time Walcott jabbed me and his glove came in contact with my eyes, or every time I clinched with him and got my face against his body, my eyes would smart. I'm sure Jersey Joe himself had nothing to do with this. He was a helluva fighter that night, even without any extra help.

'But by the end of the sixth round my eyes were burning. They burnt so bad during the seventh and eighth rounds I could hardly hold them open. To see Walcott, I had to lift my head to look at him from under my lids. That way, I had to hold up my chin in the air. That way, I was a real easy target.

"Thank god, Walcott was tired then himself, and taking a breathing spell. For those three rounds I fought Walcott on instinct. That was his chance to knock me out. If I hadn't stopped him in the 13th, he would have got the decision and kept the title. The policeman says there were rumours around town that it was being rigged for Walcott to get the decision anyway – that I'd have to knock him out to win. A lot of smart money went for it – and the smart money lost when I hit Joe and put him out with the best punch I ever landed in my whole career.'

The policeman further explained to Rocky and Allie, 'I was told by this suspect in the course of my examination of him on another police matter that Blinky Palermo, the Philadelphia fight manager [Frank "Blinky" Palermo had a criminal record and was a bosom pal of Carbo and Bocchicchio], had come in possession of some capsicum Vaseline. It's a heat-producing medicine … It can be powdered, mixed in oil or used as a jelly. Somehow or other, this capsicum got to Bocchicchio. I don't know why that should be so complicated because anybody can buy the stuff in a drugstore. But my informant was afraid for his life if he told how it got to Bocchicchio.'

'Now the whole thing got clear to me,' recalled Rocky. 'It fit in with what happened that night and with my having to go to a doctor to get my eyes treated for eight weeks afterwards.'[161]

Frank Eck, news features sports editor for the *Associated Press,* was at Grossinger's a couple of weeks before the fight, talking to, or rather listening to, Al Weill, the champion's manager. Al was saying, 'Before he goes to bed each night, the last thing he does is pick up a chair. That's before he says his prayers. He picks up a chair and pushes it out in front of himself to strengthen his forearm muscles. It gives him good leverage and makes it difficult for a fighter to hold his right. I don't think there's anyone around today that Rocky has to worry about. I know Rocky doesn't worry. But the way he loves that title and the way he trains, they'll have to use machine guns to take away his title.'[162]

---

161 *Saturday Evening Post* October 1956
162 Frank Eck *Rocky Mount Telegram* 30 August 1953

Sportswriter Murray Rose was at Greenwood Lake listening to Roland LaStarza. 'I'm going to win,' said the broad-chested challenger. 'I beat him before and I know I can outbox him and I can outsmart him. He can be hit with a jab, a hook, a right and practically any kind of a punch. I may stop him or even knock him out. Probably stop him because he cuts easily and his eyes close up. Sure, I know he knocked me down with a right in the first fight, but I got up and was going after him at the end. In a few more rounds I would have stopped him.' 'Marciano, who rarely makes predictions, told several newsmen at the camp that he would win "within seven rounds". He now says he was misunderstood. But there's no doubt that the brawny-armed, heavy-fisted champ feels he can do it that quick. He has become a poised, assured fighter since he met Rollie last. He no longer relies on his looping right. He has learned to shorten up with his right and throw it in combination with crunching left hooks. His finishing punches against Rex Layne, Joe Louis, Harry Matthews and Jersey Joe Walcott were something to behold.

'The consensus of opinion is that "reluctant Rollie" – so named for his cautious fighting style – isn't a good enough boxer to keep Rocky off and not a hard enough hitter to stop the champion's ceaseless drives. The pick here is Marciano by a KO in five rounds.'[163]

The Stanley Theatre in Philadelphia was one of 44 movie houses in 33 cities from coast to coast that would project a televised view of the big fight. A reserved seat would cost $3.99 and the manager was looking to sell all 2,900 seats for a gross gate of $11,000. But he wasn't a happy fellow. The movie they were showing that week – *From Here To Eternity* – was doing capacity business all on its own and nothing was gained by showing the boxing match, even at an $11,000 gross. The guy was probably dreading a Rocky repeat of the Walcott fiasco, a one-round knockout, and 2,900 frustrated fight fans looking to let off steam in his nice movie theatre!

Breaking camp at Greenwood Lake for the journey into the city, the challenger told reporters, 'The guy who owns this place will be able to put up a sign saying "LaStarza, Champion, Trained Here!"' Manager Jimmy DeAngelo was saying, 'LaStarza is 26 while Marciano is 29 in the book and may be older. Roland is at his physical peak, he's two inches

---

163 Murray Rose *Chester Times* Pa. 21 September 1953

taller [5ft 10½] and heavier than he was in 1950. LaStarza's left hand will beat Marciano this time, just as it actually beat Rocky the first time.'

Marciano countered by saying, 'In our first fight, which was hard, tough and very close, too close for comfort, LaStarza showed me he had the ability to avoid punches and that he was in good condition. However, I wasn't impressed with his left hand, he used it mainly for jabbing and grabbing. He never hurt me that night. After knocking LaStarza down in the fourth round, I should have gone after him with everything I had in the fifth, but I didn't do it because I lacked experience. If I knock him down this time, I won't make the same mistake.'

When they boxed in 1950, LaStarza was a 6-5 favourite over Rocky. As they got ready to do it again in September 1953, Rocky was a solid 4-1 favourite. LaStarza was three and a half years older, Marciano was three and a half years better, he was the champion and had won 18 fights since that night in the Garden. The Bronx boy had lost two fights to light-heavyweights Dan Bucceroni and Rocky Jones, bringing his record to 53-3. He had avenged those defeats and was sure he could erase the other from his slate. 'I'll definitely beat Marciano this time because I'm smarter and faster. He can't improve his boxing because he's no boxer and never has been.' That was Roland LaStarza, whistling past the graveyard.

'This guy doesn't need a doctor,' said Dr Vincent Nardiello as he examined the champion at the weigh-in. 'He's in the finest condition of his career. Ice water, that's what he's got in his veins. He's the coolest thing you'd ever want to see.' The fighters were level on the scales, Rocky hitting 185 pounds, a quarter of a pound heavier than LaStarza.

A buzzing crowd of 44,562 filed into the Polo Grounds that night, with the IBC announcing a gross gate of $435,817. The New York State Athletic Commission appointed judges Harold Barnes and Arthur Susskind, referee Ruby Goldstein. Weights, Marciano 185 pounds, LaStarza 184¾. Brockton v the Bronx, slugger v boxer.

Covering for the London *Daily Mirror*, Peter Wilson drew a graphic picture. 'Inside a minute the left side of LaStarza's face looked as though it was covered with lipstick – although he was not bleeding – for Marciano's right fist had tattooed him red. But LaStarza boxed his man off crisply, reddening his nose and mouth, and at the bell there was nothing between them. From the second round onwards Marciano, that amiable, fleshy-nosed, happy, grinning character, disappeared and Rocky the Killer took over. Marciano fights rough. He caught LaStarza with a tremendous butt as he came in like a slow but indivertible torpedo. LaStarza fought back with fury spawned by rage. In a few seconds, there was a crimson thread stretching from the corner of LaStarza's right eye to his chiselled lips, and the Rock was pounding away at his jaw with the frenzied intensity of a pneumatic drill breaking up a concrete slab.[164]

Second round and Rollie met the champion in mid ring. They swapped short punches inside but as Rocky came in low his head butted LaStarza and the crowd booed. Referee Goldstein warned Rocky, then a few seconds later cautioned LaStarza for hitting on the break. Rocky was shoved into the ropes and took a right to the head. He tore back at his opponent with a vicious left and right and the crowd roared. Marciano landed a short right and left to bring another roar from the crowd. A right uppercut from the challenger found Rocky's chin but he seemed not to notice, came back slugging at the bell and Rollie was bleeding from the left eye as he went to his corner. Two of the officials saw Rocky take the round.

Round three was bitterly fought on the inside, with the challenger holding his ground, making Rocky miss with his wild swings. Referee Goldstein warned the champ for hitting on the break. As the bell ended the session, Rocky sent a long left to LaStarza's head and Goldstein again warned him as manager DeAngelo protested from the corner. All three votes were for the Bronx boy.

Coming out for work in the fourth, the champion drove a short left to the head and a sizzling right that just grazed Roland's chin. The challenger retaliated with a left and right to the head and a thumping right to the ribs, then another to the same spot. Rocky moved forward and hammered in left and right, taking two in return. Then the champion missed wildly with a big looping right and the fans whooped it up at that one. Rocky missed another right as he shoved Roland to the ropes, they clinched and wrestled back to mid ring. Marciano got home a short left to the head but LaStarza fired back with a right, left, then

---

164 Peter Wilson *Daily Mirror* London 26 September 1953

they both swapped body shots to the bell. Goldstein gave the round to Rocky but both judges saw it for the Bronx boy.

'In those early rounds,' noted Nat Fleischer, 'anyone seeing Marciano for the first time would have been justified in asking how he came to be the world heavyweight king. He was trying hard enough, but he looked like a raw novice as he missed and was bewildered every time he was tagged by LaStarza's left. So eager was he to connect in a hurry, to land the punch soporific, to prove his right to a place alongside Dempsey and Louis, that it was pathetic to see his blows land in mid air as Roland smartly stepped aside and countered with a straight, stinging jab.'[165]

Alternately stepping out of range of Marciano's wild lunges or moving inside to sting Rocky with fast combinations to the body, LaStarza swept the first four rounds on the card of judge Harold Barnes, won three out of four on the ballot of judge Arthur Susskind and was 2-2 in the eyes of referee Goldstein.

From his press seat, Joe Williams was writing, 'The black-haired, soulful-eyed challenger was out in front and long-shot players who had taken the 3-1 price he wouldn't last the 15 were encouraged that he'd not only go all the way but that maybe he'd win on points. LaStarza was getting the maximum out of his limited talents, and he was making the champion fight his kind of fight. He was jabbing and hooking well, stepping from side to side, feinting Marciano into aimless leads and waiting for him to commit himself before countering. In short, he was fighting the kind of fight best calculated to bedevil and befuddle an opponent who is essentially a slugger and his strategy was destroying whatever plan of action Marciano might have had, though the likelihood is he had none to speak of, beyond an overwhelming urge to obliterate the man in front of him with a punch.

'The fight hadn't gone very far when it was apparent the champion was becoming frustrated and annoyed by his futility; he was fighting under the stress of over-anxiety and he seemed to have forgotten all he had learned during his long scholarship under little Charley Goldman, who must have winced in the corner as he saw his million-dollar pupil flounder and fumble his chances away. Marciano was giving LaStarza a return match after three and a half years which had seen him the winner

---

165 Nat Fleischer *The Ring* December 1953

on a split decision [in the first fight] and a boxing writer who had seen that one was moved to comment scornfully, "He looks worse than he did then."'[166]

Round five and Rocky immediately moved in on LaStarza, who clinched. Rocky connected with a short right to the side of the head and Roland came back with a right of his own. Rocky hammered a right to the chin and the crowd roared, but it was not a solid punch. Rocky moved in again, missed a wild right, and then was held by LaStarza. Roland tried a left but Rocky thundered a right to the jaw and the punch shook the challenger to his toenails. The champion fired another big right but Rollie fought back fiercely. A terrific right to the body steadied LaStarza, who was bullied to the ropes. Roland had the better of some infighting just before the bell but it was Marciano's best round so far.

LaStarza fought out of his skin in the sixth round and returned punch for punch as Rocky followed him around the ring, getting home a good shot now and then, but the challenger was outfighting him and on his way to winning the round. If there were any doubts on that score, the champion handed it to Roland when he landed a low left hand and Goldstein warned him then took the round away at the bell. With six rounds in the can, judge Susskind had Roland leading 4-2, judge Barnes marked it 5-1, while Referee Goldstein had it 3-3.

'When the seventh round started,' continued Joe Williams, 'Rocky had lost much of his impetuosity and began to look more like the "new Marciano" the fight fans had been reading about. He began to shorten his punches, wait for the openings and hit in combinations. From then on, the champion was in control. The seventh round proved to be a big round for him in which he delivered more punishment than LaStarza had taken in all the previous rounds. But he had not yet gotten full control of himself and he let Roland escape a knockout, firing with wild, futile punches instead of taking dead aim at an open target.'

Barney Nagler reckoned Rocky's idea of a left hook to the midsection always was a vicious, full-powered thrust of his short arm. 'In the seventh round of his bout with LaStarza, he let one go. He had LaStarza backed into the ropes on the centrefield side of the Polo Grounds and he went into a crouch, bending to the right as if to unload that hand. Then he

---

166 Joe Williams *El Paso Herald Post* 25 September 1953

shifted and let the left go to the belt-line. LaStarza doubled up as if he had been shot. He fell into Marciano like a football player making a tackle. He has not been the same young man since.'

'I changed my style of fighting in the seventh round,' Rocky said afterwards. 'I had been going for the big punch – been throwing my overhand right. About the sixth round I felt I was behind and I said to myself I'd better get going. So instead of throwing my right so much, I concentrated on hooks and combination punches. That was the difference.'[167]

'Rocky stunned the brown-haired, broad-shouldered challenger with a left hook to the jaw in the seventh, and battered him from rope to rope and from corner to corner with a hooking attack to body and head. From then on, it was just a question of how long LaStarza could last. LaStarza suffered a terrific battering in the eighth, ninth and tenth sessions.'[168]

'The Rock came out for the eighth as though he meant to end it,' wrote Jack Hand, 'chasing LaStarza around the ring with steady fire while his corner yelled, "Keep on top of him" and "Bring it up." Early in the ninth, a smashing right to the jaw dazed LaStarza. A clubbing hook to the chin drove him into a neutral corner. Blood trickled from his mouth but he covered up and threw punches, trying to stave off the inevitable. LaStarza was still punching back in the tenth when Rocky appeared to be getting arm-weary from the continuous attack. There was a suspicion that LaStarza's nose might have been broken.

'Winging at full steam out of a crouch and later standing up straight to throw long punches, Marciano came out to end it in the 11th. A hook started Rollie on his way, then a terrific right to the head. The right-left-right combination dropped the dazed challenger on his back through the ropes. LaStarza's face was a gory mask as he got up and continued the struggle. The crowd yelled "Stop it, Stop it," but Goldstein let them mix again before he called an end.'[169] Time of round 11 was 1.31.

It was Rocky's 40th knockout in an unbeaten streak of 45 fights, but he took a beating himself from the critics. Veteran sportswriter Oscar Fraley noted, 'The "old" Dempsey still ranks today as the greatest

---

167 Will Grimsley *Lethbridge Herald* 25 September 1953
168 Jack Cuddy *Charleston Daily Mail* 25 September 1953
169 Jack Hand *Lethbridge Herald* 25 September 1953

fighting man in the history of the ring. Because Rocky Marciano, the man they have touted as the "new" Dempsey, wasn't even a fight carbon copy at the Polo Grounds Thursday night. It's true that he finally scored a bloody, brawling technical knockout over dead-game Roland LaStarza. But this was no "new" Dempsey. It was instead an awkward, lumbering man with tearing, damaging fists. He tried all the time, and kept boring in constantly, but it was a victory for a shambling bear over an ox with a cast iron chin.

'The old Dempsey instincts were there, the slashing, ever-throwing tactics which made the Manassa Mauler such a killer in the ring. But Marciano didn't do it with that savage Dempsey grace – nor even with the tactics of a true champion. He butted, hit on the break, and continually punched low – and he was a grotesque caricature of a heavyweight champion as he fell flat on his face in the tenth round throwing a roundhouse punch at a man who was standing shakily on the raw edge of his courageous instincts.'[170]

Bob Considine of the *International News Service* observed, 'Marciano missed so many punches that if their power had been harnessed it could have lighted Omaha, Nebraska for two years.' Columnist Jimmy Cannon of the *New York Post* proclaimed that his performance 'exposed the champion as an ignoramus at his trade'. A headline in the *New York World-Telegram and Sun* wrapped it up, 'Diamond in the Rough – Very Rough.'

'To Charley Goldman, Marciano was like another great but unorthodox athlete also in his prime in the early 1950s. "Maybe Rocky is not very fancy," he said. "Let's be honest, he's never going to be. But I see baseball and I see Yogi Berra and he isn't fancy either. He's never going to be. But he can throw the ball and swing that bat and he gets nice results, and that's what Rocky does too."'[171]

Maybe 'nice results' didn't describe what happened to Roland LaStarza in that ring at the Polo Grounds on a September evening in 1953. 'In his crowded, silent dressing room, Roland was saying, "The doctor says something happened to my left arm. I know I couldn't use it. That was in the second round." Dr Vincent Nardiello, physician of the New York State Athletic Commission, said the injury could be a

170 Oscar Fraley *Charleston Daily Mail* 25 September 1953
171 Russell Sullivan *Rocky Marciano: The Rock of His Times* 2002

dislocation. LaStarza's right eye was bleeding and swollen and his nose laced with a deep cut. Because of his injuries, LaStarza was sent from the Polo Grounds to St Clare's Hospital. Before going, the beaten challenger told pressmen, "Please don't think I'm trying to alibi. He's a great champion. He's definitely a better fighter than when I fought him before – 5,000 per cent.'"[172]

'Perhaps what happened to Roland LaStarza in that fight was the result of a remark attributed to him in his training camp at Greenwood Lake, where a reporter quoted him as saying, "He's gonna get hurt. Maybe not by me. If I don't do it, somebody else will. He takes one, two, three or four punches to give one. If he keeps it up, he's gonna get soft in the head. That's no good."

"This really burned Rocky up," Uncle Mike Piccento said. "It changed his whole attitude toward the fight. He forgot the strategy. He was bullshit."

"I'm not gonna knock this guy out, Mike," Rocky said. "I'm gonna punish him."

"They finally stopped the fight," Piccento said, "But I really think Rocky could have knocked LaStarza out any time."

"Just the sound of the word 'punchy' made Rocky cringe," Peter said of his brother. "Any time he saw a punch-drunk fighter he became upset. He never feared pain or injury or any man in the ring, but to see some guy walking on his heels made him sick to his stomach."'[173]

'When you have pride in your work, you appreciate it right away,' Marciano recalled later. 'When a fighter doesn't respect this, well, that's one of the reasons for me getting real mad a few times before fights. One time was the second fight with LaStarza. I kept my anger pretty hidden all through training and even in the ring. But after it ended in the 11th, I went over to Rollie right there in the ring. I asked him if it was true he had said I was getting punchy because I was taking too many punches on the head. I said "Rollie, did you really make that stupid remark up at camp about me being punchy?" "You know better than that, Rock," he said. "The writers put words in my mouth. I wouldn't talk about you that way."

—
172 Ted Smits *Lethbridge Herald* 25 September 1953

173 Everett M. Skehan *Rocky Marciano Biography of a First Son* 1977

"I thought you were a much smarter guy," I said. "You're a college fellow. If you ever said a thing like that, I really would be disturbed about it." Rocky later added, "LaStarza told me how much I'd improved between our first and second fights, and that really made me feel good."[174]

Whitney Martin reported for the *Associated Press,* 'There was the usual restless, milling crowd that is part of every weigh-in for a heavyweight championship fight, and the two little men standing side by side in this whirlpool of humanity were having their troubles. In the glare of floodlights, Rocky Marciano and Roland LaStarza were taking turns stepping on the scales as the cameramen recorded the scene, but the two little men couldn't see what was going on. They stood on tip-toe and shifted from one side to the other. But their only view was the shoulder blades of those in front of them.

'The two little men, one stocky and youthful looking, the other slim and bespectacled, glanced at each other, then turned away. It was obvious they weren't acquainted. "Hey, you two, look up here," a cameraman shouted. Out of curiosity the two little men turned, and blinked when a flash bulb popped. They couldn't figure out what it was all about. The two little men murmured something to each other, and then, as if slightly embarrassed, resumed their efforts to see over the shoulders blocking their view of the rival fighters. The two little men finally settled back on their heels, resigned to the fact they wouldn't be able to get even a glimpse of what was going on. The stocky fellow in the light grey suit swung his head around as if looking for a familiar face. He caught someone's eye and smiled shyly.

'Knowing who the two little men were, you couldn't help but wonder about the thoughts that might be racing through their minds. Maybe each was thinking of the nights he walked the floor cradling a colicky baby in his arms, or recalling that baby's first faltering steps, or the day a little tyke marched off to school for the first time, or a stalwart young man marched off to war. The two little men turned away from each other without speaking again, and mingled with the crowd, unnoticed. After all, Marco LaStarza and Pierro [Pierino] Marciano only were the fathers of the respective fighters.'[175]

---

174 *Saturday Evening Post* 20 October 1956
175 Whitney Martin *Jefferson City Daily Capital News* 25 September 1953

16

I'M NOT SUPERMAN

ROCKY MARCIANO was heavyweight champion of the world and when he wasn't pounding the highway during the early hours or making life miserable for his sparring partners in training camp, he attempted to cash in on his celebrity status by barnstorming. He boxed exhibitions, refereed wrestling matches, made personal appearances and gave speeches at banquets.

'Characteristically, he worked hard at honing his speaking ability,' noted Russell Sullivan in his fine Marciano biography. 'His speech sometimes began with a joke. "When I started in the fight game, I was very nervous at dinners like this. So I would say I wasn't much of a speaker but that I could lick anyone in the house. I don't say that any more. My manager tells me that when I fight I've got to make money." For some reason, the joke often brought down the house.

'Al Weill made sure that the champion was paid for every speech, every appearance and every moment. As Tim Cohane of *Look* noted, "Weill has industriously hustled him around the country to squeeze every possible dime out of the championship." Marciano's customary fee for an appearance was $3,000. In the beginning, he felt sheepish about collecting the money. "Three grand, three grand for the things I say," he would moan. The guiltless Weill would respond, "Don't be a big fish. They want to hear you, leave 'em pay to do so, you are the champeen." Marciano eventually lost his reluctance.'[176]

---

176 Russell Sullivan *Rocky Marciano: The Rock of His Times* 2002

A reporter once asked him if he ever thought that he might be beaten. 'I don't want to sound like a braggart,' the champ said. 'but I never thought anybody in the world could lick me. Once in a while, when I was training for a fight, the thought occurred to me, "What if this guy does beat me?" but that's as far as it went. It was a passing thought and passed quickly. Even during the progress of some of my toughest fights when I had to come from behind, I never did think I might lose. I never felt my strength was gone nor was I ever gasping for breath and I was never stunned enough that my brain wasn't clear.'[177]

Yet there were times when that undefeated record seemed like a terrible burden for the champ to bear, as he told the British sportswriter Peter Wilson in June 1954. Rocky was training for his first fight with Ezzard Charles at his camp in upstate New York. 'Marciano had some strange statements to make for a world champion,' wrote Wilson 'The Rock was sitting on the porch of the cabin at Grossinger's when, all at once, the man with the most famous fists in the world started to lather with his tongue. Among other things, he said, "I wish that I wasn't undefeated. Don't get me wrong. I don't mean I want to lose now. I don't intend to lose and I will fight harder than ever to keep the streak intact because as long as I'm unbeaten I'm still champion of the world. But I often wished to myself that somewhere along the line before I won the title, I would have lost a decision. I can't explain it but I would have liked to have been beaten only to know what the feeling is like. When it does happen, I don't want it to come as the shock that it will have to be for me because now the pressure is on. It's no longer just losing a fight. It's losing the title. Nobody knows the pressure a guy is under. Training for any fight is tough, although I like it. But when you've got something to protect, it's tougher. Nobody can know *how* tough and every year it gets a little tougher. Other guys can have faults or look bad one day, but with me they have begun to expect perfection. I'm not perfect and I'm not Superman."

'That doesn't sound much like a fighter who is boss man of the world,' observed Wilson, 'and another quote from Marciano is even more disillusioning.' "I thought there would be more glory and less work to being heavyweight champion of the world. I thought when

---

177 Reg Noble *Boxing Illustrated* Special 1979

I was champion people would stop me on the street and say, 'Hey, Rocky, you're some champ.' But people seldom stop me unless it is in my hometown of Brockton. In fact people generally don't even notice me at all unless I have been publicly introduced. But I still wish people would recognise me – it's a nice feeling to have them yell, 'Hey, champ, how're you feeling?"[178]

A week before the fight at Yankee Stadium in New York's Bronx, the champ was feeling great as he worked out with Willie Wilson, Toxie Hall and Keene Simmons. The boys were all wearing headguards like leather helmets, 16-ounce gloves, and were smeared with Vaseline and they all landed on Rocky enough times to earn their money, but the champion landed enough leather on them to make them think of changing their day job. Watching from outside the ring was the former champion Jersey Joe Walcott and he was not too impressed with Marciano, telling reporters, 'I think Charles has all the equipment and I believe he will beat Marciano on points.'

Yet, a few days before the fight, the challenger was looking somewhat less than impressive as he worked to be the first former champion to regain the heavyweight title, to go where men like James J. Corbett, Bob Fitzsimmons, James J. Jeffries, Jack Dempsey, Max Schmeling, Joe Louis, and Walcott himself had failed. Charles lost a rematch after Walcott knocked him out in a shock upset, now he was trying again to buck the odds. He was 33 going against 29 for the unbeaten champion and the smart money said he couldn't do it.

Charles had completed 128 rounds of sparring at Kutsher's Country Club, his camp in New York State, but a reporter watching the last four rounds a couple of days before the boys were due in the ring proper said he looked stale despite claims by his connections that Ezzard was in top shape. The former champion worked out with Gene Jones of Camden, New Jersey, and Al Smith of New York. Jones was allowed to push him around the training ring and score with heavy shots to the jaw. Charles kept backing to the ropes, where he looked like 'an old bluebottle trying to find a way out through a closed window'.

In that first week of June 1954, there was a strange face among the many sportswriters covering the training camps of Marciano and

178 Peter Wilson *Daily Mirror* London 11 June 1954

Charles. Edward R. Murrow temporarily left his observation post in the area of the world's larger struggles and made detours to the training camps where heavyweight world champion Rocky Marciano and contender Ezzard Charles were preparing for their 17 June title contest. Mr Murrow's purpose was to interview both boxers for a broadcast of his CBS Television programme *Person to Person* on Friday, 11 June. He reported his impressions of Marciano and Charles on CBS Radio's *Edward R. Murrow with the News*. The text of his radio broadcast was reported in newspapers across America, and the following extracts are from the *Rocky Mount Evening Telegram* of North Carolina, 17 June 1954.

'Being somewhat wearied of words and wrangling, of committee hearings and contention, this reporter betook himself to Grossinger's and Kutsher's in the Catskills. That's the rolling, lake-stuffed country of New York State. There, considerable conversation was had with two soft-spoken young men who are preparing to belabour each other about the head and body with six-ounce gloves come 17 June in Yankee Stadium. The two young men are Rocky Marciano, heavyweight champion of the world, and the challenger Ezzard Charles … Both men are given to understatement; they refrain from boasting, and they consider well before answering … Both men rose to fame and fortune from humble and obscure origins. As youngsters, they both day-dreamed about being the champ. Both have discovered that reality doesn't quite fit the dream.

'Rocky Marciano is proud of the fact that no one coddled him when he was in the army with the Combat Engineers; claims he dug more holes than any other GI in his outfit. Ezzard Charles served for 24 months in Italy, and learned to speak the language. He has the hands of a musician, plays the bass fiddle and the saxophone, and reads a lot, including poetry. But while he's in training he neither plays nor reads; says it takes his mind off his work, spoils his concentration. Marciano has been up there in the Catskills since January. He works and trains hard, except when a busload of kids turns up to visit his training camp; then he's more interested in fooling around with the kids than he is in doing road work or sparring.

'Both men agree that on fight night they are unconscious of the huge crowds surrounding them. Charles says, "I think only of the man in front of me; it's a poor time to be thinking of anything else …" Marciano thinks the best advice he ever received was from his mother, who told him simply that he ought to listen to people who knew what they were talking about. Charles remembers an army chaplain who told him when he was separated from the army that he should forget what he had been taught about war, and learn to live again as a citizen of the community. This reporter has seldom encountered less bombast, arrogance or personal pride. Perhaps it is because both men train by rules, and in the final test must rely only upon themselves. They cannot subpoena anyone to help them; cannot lie or equivocate their way to victory. If their preparation is inadequate, the result will be not merely embarrassment but defeat. They can seek refuge in no amendment. They cannot walk out of the ring if the tide of battle flows against them. They cannot violate the rules with impunity. There is a referee and not a chairman. And in the end, there is a decision that is clear cut and final.'

The esteemed Mr Murrow would not be drawn on a forecast, but the other gentlemen of the press were solidly behind the champion to remain so when the punches stopped flying. When 21 sportswriters in New York to cover the fight were asked their opinion, only two voted for Charles and most of the 19 who favoured Marciano picked him to win by a knockout inside of ten rounds. As usual, a number of former champions and contenders voiced their opinions. Even former heavyweight champion Tommy Burns, from his home in Coalinga, Fresno County in sunny California, took a few minutes out from celebrating his 73rd birthday to tell *United Press,* 'Rocky is young and hits hard. I think he has what it takes to be a champion for quite a while.' Tommy planned to listen to the fight on radio after a small birthday dinner with a few friends.

One guy who could speak with authority was Rocky's last victim, Roland LaStarza, who told reporters, 'Rocky looks easy to hit inside, but he has that left arm up and his chin down. He hits terrible punches to the body, and I don't think Charles can stand up under these. I know I couldn't.' Former light-heavyweight champion Bob Olin observed, 'The champ is in great shape.' Barney Ross, a triple champ at lightweight, junior welterweight and welterweight in the 1930s, was also impressed, saying, 'Look at the power that guy packs!' Alan Ward, sports editor of the *Oakland Tribune*, managed to get a few million words out of Max Baer, the former heavyweight champion, before going to press. 'Don't worry about Rocky,' said Max. 'He can protect himself. He's better than a green hand in the scientific department. Charles is the better boxer, but he isn't so good he can keep away from Rocky's punch and still be on his feet at the end of 15 rounds. Marciano is dangerous all the way. Ezzard will have two strikes on him realising that wallop is apt to land any time, and when it does – sweet dreams Ezzy!'[179]

Marciano was the puncher with 40 knockouts in 45 unbeaten fights, yet Charles had a more-than-respectable record in the power department with 48 knockouts in 85 winning fights. Harry Mendel, the IBC press agent for the fight, had drawn up a list of fighters Charles had knocked out with one punch, that is to say, one punch instead of a combination. Some impressive names were on the list – Anton Christoforidis, Archie Moore, Bernie Reynolds and Bob Satterfield succumbed to the left; Booker Beckwith, Jimmy Bivins, Fitzie Fitzpatrick, Oakland Billy Smith and Lloyd Marshall fell to the right hand. One month shy of 33, the man from Cincinnati had been fighting some 18 years, including a star-studded amateur career. Maybe this was a fight too far …

Ezzard had a strong ally in the British sportswriter Harold Mayes, who wrote, 'Marciano, the when-I-hit-them-they-drop fighter, gets his real chance to justify the legend of invincibility which has been built around him when he tackles Charles. Without any doubt, this can be his hardest contest. If there's one man in the world who is a good enough ring tradesman to tie up the Brockton battler and prevent him landing his H-bomb punch, it's Charles. Ezzard had one other great incentive for victory. He, a coloured man, would be the first in history to win back the title. And that, with his own people, would put him on a pedestal alongside the great Joe Louis.'[180]

Top New York columnist Jesse Abramson was also thinking Charles when he tapped out his preview for the 17 June 1954 issue of the *New York Herald Tribune*, writing, 'Skill has mastered brute strength in the ring before, and may do so again tonight … it is the conviction here that Charles has the skills, the flexibility, the reach, the speed, strength and

---

179 Alan Ward *Oakland Tribune* 17 June 1954
180 Harold Mayes *Rocky Marciano* 1956

cunning to beat the short-armed Marciano to a decision … The burden of proof is on Charles.'

On that cool June evening, a crowd of 47,585 paid $543,092 and they got value for every cent of every dollar watching one of the greatest world heavyweight championship fights in the history of the ring. At the noon weigh-in, Charles, an inch taller than the champion, scaled 185½ pounds to Marciano's 187½. As they waited in the ring, the officials appointed by the New York Commission, judges Artie Aidala and Harold Barnes, settled in their ringside seats as referee Ruby Goldstein climbed through the ropes. Johnny Addie made his announcements, the bell rang, and battle was joined.

The champion got off the mark first, short-jabbing Charles to the chest. Charles sent a light counter but Rocky came forward working both fists, though not very heavily. Ezzard scored two right hands to the ribs and avoided a swinging right from the champion. Charles was tying Rocky up as he tried to get an attack going, and near the end of the round sent a thudding left into Marciano's face. As the champion went to his corner at the bell his nose was bleeding. All three officials marked the round to Charles.

'At the start you would never have thought Marciano was the champion,' wrote Peter Wilson. 'In the first round his face was reddened and he kept licking his lips not tigerishly but like a schoolboy awaiting a flogging outside the headmaster's room.'[181]

Round two and Charles went straight on the attack with a right to the body. Rocky threw both hands to the body but the former champion smothered the blows. Now Ezzard jabbed twice to the mouth and followed with two quick lefts to the side of the head. Marciano fought back with left and right to the head but took four punches to the head and body as Charles again took the initiative. Rocky was wild with a big right and Charles smashed home a left and right before the bell. Referee Goldstein awarded the round to the champion but for the judges it was two rounds for the challenger. It was already that kind of fight.

'In the early rounds Charles hung grimly to the centre of the ring – he knew that to back up to the ropes against Marciano was as quick a way of committing suicide as jumping from the top of a skyscraper. He

---

181 Peter Wilson *Daily Mirror* London 19 June 1954

dug in crisp, deadly right hands to which Marciano appeared to have no answer. He was placing his punches just as he liked, and using his feet to keep out of the way of Rocky's bombs. Instead of running away when Marciano charged in, Charles went inside with him, holding him, digging him in the clinches, and at every opportunity putting punches into the champion's face.'[182]

In the third round, the crowd rose to their feet as both men traded lefts and rights to the head. A right hook to the head sent Charles's head back on his shoulders. They worked away at close quarters and Marciano kept wiping the blood from his nose. The champion increased the pace near the end of the round and a fast right to the head was partially blocked by Charles, who countered with a right to the head. An even round.

Into round four and Marciano thumped a right to the head. Charles countered smartly and a hard right to the face opened a cut on the side of Marciano's left eye. Another right from Charles caused the blood to flow from the eye injury and Marciano was forced to wipe the blood away. He appeared to have difficulty seeing from the damaged optic. On top and piling on the pressure, Charles whipped a right uppercut to the jaw then had the crowd roaring as he drove home four quick punches to the body. Marciano was at a loss to defend himself and, half blinded in the left eye, he was forced to take more lefts and rights to the head as Charles became confident.

The champion's corner were worried about the cut as Freddie Brown set to work. 'He used adrenalin to check the bleeding, a mineral jelly over the surface and a quick-hardening plastic shield over all, but he knew a good punch would wreck his repair job; the cut was two inches long and an inch deep. "With a cut like that, you got to be nervous," he said afterward. "A quarter of an inch further in and it would have run like a faucet."'[183]

'It was all Charles in the first four rounds,' reported Jack Hand, 'until Marciano began to come on in the fifth with a series of left hooks to the head. He finished the attack with a punch after the bell, drawing a shower of boos from the stands. Again in the sixth, Marciano poured it

---

182 Harold Mayes *Rocky Marciano* 1956
183 A. J. Liebling *The Sweet Science* 1987

on and the lumps began to appear on Charles' face. Charles was sliced around the right eye and an egg-sized bump began to emerge on the left side of his face. Although he tried to fire back resolutely and did score effectively when the Rock missed, he was unable to avoid the champ's heavy bombs the rest of the way.'[184]

'In the champion's corner between the fifth and sixth rounds, Charley Goldman urged his fighter to throw caution to the wind and revert to type. "He's blocking those left hooks … so forget about them from now on and start throwin' an overhand right," Goldman told Marciano. "You've got to punch your way out of this fight." Marciano started to do just that in the sixth round, which some ringside observers called one of the greatest in heavyweight history. About a minute into the round, Marciano connected with a short hook to the jaw that stopped Charles in his tracks and "made a sound like a steamroller passing over a soupbone". Now Marciano smelled blood – and not his own but that of Ezzard Charles. For the better part of the next minute he poured it on, chasing Charles from one end of the ring to the other while unleashing a steady, rapid-fire and furious stream of unanswered lefts and rights. The avalanche of punches wobbled Charles, but he managed to stay on his feet. After Marciano finally tired enough to halt his barrage, Charles even fought back at the end of the round, nailing Marciano with a left to the jaw.'[185]

Veteran scribe Oscar Fraley, at ringside for *United Press*, reported, 'From the sixth round on, Marciano took charge with a pounding, ripping attack which proved that while he might not have the punch of a Dempsey he has one of the most inexhaustible bodies in ring annals. He hit Charles with everything he had, powerful drives flush on the jaw and scorching shots to the body which smacked home with the sound of a mallet in an abbatoir. You winced in the safety of your seat as those relentless Marciano fists hammered time and again in a terrible tattoo against that battered face … No man, you felt, could stand such punishment from this muscular marvel rated as the greatest puncher since the immortal Dempsey. But Ezzard did. He took them, shook them off, and kept coming back with game little flurries of his own.

184 Jack Hand *Eau Clare Leader* Wisconsin 18 June 1954
185 Russell Sullivan *Rocky Marciano: The Rock of His Times* 2002

He couldn't win, but he didn't quit. He could have gone down and still been hailed as one of the gamest. But he stayed on his feet to prove it beyond doubt.'[186]

'They shook hands at the start of the 15th and although each must have hated the other for what each had suffered, there was respect in that leather handclasp,' wrote Peter Wilson. 'Then Marciano showed his brute strength. After being shaken by two left hooks, he bulldozed in and for the first time pinned Charles on the ropes and fairly clobbered him for the last half of the round until, neutral as a writer should be, I longed to ring the final bell and spare this courageous coloured guy any more punishment and the indignity of oblivion. Finally, like a rundown clock, it did sound, and they took Charles to the blessed relief of a locked dressing room and the healing hands of a doctor instead of the torturing fists of a Marciano.'[187] Rocky was the winner and still champion.

'In his Yankee Stadium dressing room, Rocky Marciano sat on a rubbing table, flanked by his father and his manager, Al Weill, and submitted to what has become a familiar ritual – a victory interview,' observed John Barrington. "Back up a little and give him a little room," Weill pleaded to the newsmen and photographers pushing close around Rocky. "What for?" quipped someone. "He's got more room now than Charles gave him all night." And it was the truth. Until Rocky's punches and his unbelievable strength and stamina wore Ez down, the ex-champion – who wanted so badly to win back the title – never gave Rocky an extra inch of fighting room. "He's the most courageous man I ever fought," said Rocky'. "I'd like to fight him again. He deserves it."'[188]

The gash over Rocky's left eye required ten stitches by Dr Vincent Nardiello. The physician cut away some old scar tissue in his post-fight operation at St Clare's Hospital. Charles's face was a mass of bruises and lumps and there was a nasty gash under his left eyebrow. He talked with difficulty, thanks to a Rocky uppercut that landed on his Adam's apple about the ninth round, but what he said was less than gracious to his conqueror. 'I want him again,' snarled the battered, unfazed Charles. 'I thought I won. I think I came closer to knocking him out than he did

---

186 Oscar Fraley *Long Beach Press-Telegram* California 18 June 1954

187 Peter Wilson *Daily Mirror* London 19 June 1954

188 John Barrington *Daily Review* Hayward, California 18 June 1954

me. The next time it will be different. He's strong and throws a lot of punches but he didn't give me as tough a fight as Walcott did. In fact, all four of my fights with Walcott were tougher. He didn't hurt me near as much as Walcott did.'[189]

To ease the pain he said he wasn't feeling, Ezzard took home a purse of $124,019 from the gate and an additional $23,726 from pay TV. To the victor the spoils – the champion had a nice piece of change in $200,586 from the gross gate plus $47,452 from pay TV. No wonder they both wanted to do it again, and the wheels were already turning along that road. 'Charles is entitled to the return,' said Al Weill, manager of the all-conquering Brockton bruiser. 'It was a great show and a great fight. If Rocky's cut comes out okay, I'd say a September fight with Charles in New York is a great possibility.'[190]

'If Rocky isn't great,' wrote Gayle Talbot from New York, 'he is a wonderful competitor. For the last 11 rounds, he fought under the handicap of a cut over his left eye that streamed blood off and on and soaked both fighters. There is no man in sight now to stand against him.'[191]

———
189 Murray Rose *Evening Independent* Massillon, Ohio 18 June 1954
190 *Lowell Sun* Mass. 18 June 1954
191 Gayle Talbot *Evening Independent* Massillon, Ohio 18 June 1954

17

WORDS, MORE THAN PUNCHES, HURT THE CHAMP

WHEN MARCIANO went into Grossinger's to train for the first fight with Charles, Barbara was pregnant again. 'As usual, Rocky seldom saw her during training. As he prepared to take on Charles, he arranged for Barbara to take a trip with friends. Rocky's brothers and some of his friends noticed a slight strain in the relationship between Marciano and his wife. Barbara had a glandular problem and had gained much weight. She had bleached her hair blonde, and friends recalled that she was almost a chain smoker and sometimes drank too much to relieve her loneliness. While Barbara was vacationing in Acapulco, she suffered a miscarriage. She never became pregnant again. High in the Catskills, Marciano was unaware of his wife's miscarriage. The training was going well ...[192]

It was about a year after the second Charles fight that Rocky took Barbara back to Acapulco. One night as they socialised with some people at the hotel, Barbara was talking about her last trip there without her husband. Rocky would recall later, 'I was ashamed and embarrassed. She was pregnant and she had a miscarriage down there, and I didn't even learn about it until after the fight. She had a real bad time, but she kept writing to me that she was having a fine time. It wasn't until later that I found out from the friends who had been with her ... In São Paulo I think it was, we met up with a lot of nice couples we got very friendly with.

192 Everett M. Skehan *Rocky Marciano: Biography of a First Son* 1977

165

Husbands and wives would tell about the places they'd been and the things they'd seen and done with each other. All of a sudden I realised I never really had any kind of family life. Everything I had done had to do with boxing. Everything Barbara had done she had to do herself, or with some of her girlfriends.

'Well, these people we met up with in Brazil couldn't understand the funny kind of life we led. Barbara tried to explain to them that it was necessary for a fellow who wanted to be a good fighter, but I could see she was embarrassed by it. She said that even after a fellow's a champion, he still owes a lot to the public and the fight fans, and one lady said, "Barbara, I wonder if you've ever considered that your husband also owes a lot to you and your daughter?" That hit me like a roundhouse right on the chin. Back at the hotel, I said to Barbara, "Honey, is it that bad?" And she said to me, "Really, it's no fun, you know, Rock. I get that from a lot of people."'

Rocky was starting to get it from his mother. 'One afternoon at Grossinger's in 1953, my mother said she'd like to have a little talk with me. "Sure, mom," I said, "I got ten minutes." "Ten minutes is no good," she said, but real annoyed. "Sometimes I think you not *figlio mio* no more. You not my son. You only the champ." "Mom," I said. "I got so many things on my mind." "Sure," she said. "What things? The last couple of years I know nothing about you. The family never see you. Your sister, Concetta, have a baby, you no see it 'til it's old, four months maybe. You don't see your sister Betty's baby for two months. Your old friend Snap get married, you don't come to the wedding. Your own baby is born, you not with your wife. Your own baby you don't see 'til she's old, seven days. Mary Anne growing up and you missing it. When there's going to be an end?"

'My god. I said to myself, I got to make up my mind. Even Mom's getting sore at me. Even Mary Anne doesn't know me. I thought of coming home after one of my fights. I tried to take the kid from Barbara's hands and Mary Anne started to cry and she wouldn't come to me … All of that stuff hit me all of a sudden. I never before tried to figure these things out.'[193]

---

193 *Saturday Evening Post* 20 October 1956

Rocky Marciano as a fighter? Champion, world champion … Rocco Francis Marchegiano as a husband, father, family man? Still a ten rounds pug.

Grossinger's, NY, 30 August 1954 – heavyweight champ Rocky Marciano was back at his workshop in the Catskills getting ready for his return bout with Ezzard Charles, scheduled for 16 September. Gnome-like trainer Charley Goldman abruptly interrupted the training session when he found Rocky to be one pound under his fighting weight. 'Get some rest and eat a big order of pasta fazoole,' he barked.

Meanwhile, from New York, Oscar Fraley was writing for *United Press*, 'I note in the latest bulletin of the New York State Athletic Commission that its doctors have indefinitely suspended a prizefighter from Brockton, Mass., named Rocco Marciano. This precautionary step was taken because of a laceration over the left eye. But there was no mention of any such action against a chap named Ezzard Charles. The puzzling part of all this is that Marciano is a gentleman known as Rocky who wears the heavyweight championship of the world. The unlisted Charles tried to take same from him one night recently and the collision was noteworthy.

'But as I remember the accident, officer, if Marciano is suspended indefinitely – Charles should be through for life. Because if you ever saw a thoroughly trampled, knocked down, worn-out, puffed-up, belaboured, swollen and thoroughly clobbered fellow in your life, it was Charles after his gallant stand against Marciano. If you saw the pictures after the fight, you'll recall vividly that Ezzard looked like a fellow who dropped a best-out-of-three falls decision to a steamroller. One eye was almost closed and the other was trying to catch up. There was a frightening lump on his left jaw and his lips were puffed grotesquely. For frills, he had minor scrapes and glove burns to set off a well-thumped nose. Certainly if Ezzard wasn't "ill", he'll never have to worry about a sick day in his life. And he can't be dead, which would be one logical way of accounting for his failure to make the list of "ill and unavailable".'[194]

A couple of weeks after the fight, Tom Tannas, co-manager of Charles, was telling reporters that Ezzard was in fine condition, he had no broken bones and the swelling on his face had disappeared. Tannas

---

194 Oscar Fraley *Ames Daily Tribune* 2 July 1954

was still of the opinion that if his boy hadn't been hit in the Adam's apple in the ninth round 'we would have moved right in and won the title again'. More fall-out from the fight – in Pittsburgh, the three theatres carrying the fight on the big screen were sold out long before the first bell rang. Detectives arrested four men trying to sell $3.50 tickets for $15. All four paid $50 fines and spent the night in jail. One guy complained bitterly because he was jailed before the fight started and they wouldn't let him go to the theatre to see it. At least Pittsburgh's Billy Conn got to see the fight. But he bet on Charles and blew $2,500, according to a Broadway columnist.

The winner of the Marciano-Charles rematch wouldn't have to look far for his next payday. In Madison Square Garden, Harry Grayson noted, 'Nino Valdes did boxing a tremendous favour with his two-round disposal of Hurricane Tommy Jackson. Had young Jackson outfumbled the big Cuban, The Beast would have been in position to challenge Rocky Marciano. That would have best illustrated to what extent the heavyweight division had fallen along with the rest of the beak-busting business.

'It is to be sincerely hoped that Valdes forever banished Jackson from the ranks of people we must put up with. Reduced to a small wind, the Hurricane won't be such a pounding headache with his totally unfunny antics. Valdes presents a fresh-faced challenger for Marciano, a huge man with a fine reach and a better right hand wallop than most suspect. He took a ten-rounds decision from Charles last year, looked excellent knocking out Heinz Neuhas in Germany. Nino Valdes now dresses like a fire engine and has a smile, which manager Bobby Gleason claims Liberace copied.'[195]

The big Cuban (6ft 4ins) was already on Al Weill's shortlist for Rocky's next job, as was the portly Englishman Don Cockell. With a 30-pound weight advantage over Harry 'Kid' Matthews, who never was a heavyweight, Cockell pounded out a one-sided third victory over the Kid in his Seattle hometown to claim a shot at the champ.

Cockell or Valdes. Leave those two on the backburner just now. Try Ezzard Charles. From New York, Jack Hand was writing, 'Ezzard Charles, the lithe Cincinatti negro, will be the first ex-champion ever to get three cracks at winning back his title. He lost the crown to Jersey

---

195 Harry Grayson *The News* Frederick, Maryland 20 July 1954

Joe Walcott, dropped a return decision to Jersey Joe, then lost another decision to Marciano six weeks ago. Now he's going to get a second crack at Marciano, here on either 15 or 21 September. And the Rock from Brockton, Mass., already is 1-3 favourite and is even money to stop the 33-year-old Charles. Marciano sat in Jim Norris' office at the IBC, where the doctors had just passed him as fit for action and pronounced his damaged eye completely healed.

"I think the guy's got guts," he said. "I kept pressing him all the time from the sixth round on. A lot of other guys fell apart. Some took 11 rounds, some 12 or 13 but most of them fell apart sooner or later. Only twice did I think I had him ready to go – the 10th round and the 15th." They tried to draw out Rocky on whether he thought he might have softened up Charles for a second fight. He wouldn't try to answer. "It was tough on both of us," he said. "He hurt me a few times and I hurt him. I wasn't exactly satisfied. This time I hope to do a little better. I was disappointed a little in not knocking him down."'[196]

There was a nice moment worth recording when the fighters arrived at the offices of the New York State Athletic Commission to sign for the fight. Whitney Martin, on hand for the *Associated Press*, wrote, 'The heavyweight champion got out of a car and greeted reporters cordially. A small boy held out his hand and Rocky Marciano took it in his massive fist, the boy withdrew it and gazed at it in unbelief. "Gee," he finally blurted. "Gee, I ain't gonna wash it."'[197]

Back in camp at Grossinger's, Tuesday 31 August, Rocky 'surprised onlookers when he loafed through four rounds of sparring. But trainer Charley Goldman said the champ was under wraps to prevent his catching cold in the drafty hangar he uses as a gymnasium.'[198]

Former heavyweight champion Jack Dempsey was present and agreed to don the gloves for the first time in years as he posed with Marciano for the photographers. But after Rocky shook hands with a youngster, he went on strike when he was asked to don greasepaint for the snappers. Next day, the heavyweight champion celebrated his 30th birthday with his wife Barbara and baby daughter.

———

196 Jack Hand *Billings Gazette* Montana 31 July 1954
197 Whitney Martin *Bluefield Daily Telegraph* West Virginia 5 August 1954
198 *Brownwood Bulletin* 1 September 1954

Sportswriter Scotty Stirling caught up with heavyweight Keene Simmons when he arrived in Oakland for a fight with Charley Powell at the Auditorium. Scotty was anxious to hear about Marciano, with whom Simmons had been sparring for the last three weeks. The Bayonne, New Jersey fighter had been an eighth-round victim of Rocky's back in 1951. 'It was a technical knockout,' he explained. 'I was never off my feet. They stopped the fight because my left eye was puffed and nearly closed. It wasn't a cut; in fact I had Marciano bleeding. I was winning the fight until the referee called a halt in the eighth round. He's a good puncher but he couldn't put me down … He's a much better fighter now than he was in 1951. Rocky punches shorter now. He throws them in combinations. When I fought him, he telegraphed almost all his punches. I'm in real good shape now,' said Simmons. 'Boxing with Rocky is almost as tough as a real fight. You have to be on your toes with him.'[199]

Well, he was still on his feet in round six of his fight with undefeated Powell but he was taking a pounding and the referee stopped the fight. So it was a TKO in *The Ring* magazine, but on the BoxRec website they have Powell winning on a sixth-round disqualification. Whatever, Keene was happy to be back heading east, back to the day job, swapping leather with the world heavyweight champion.

Marciano, as Simmons had mentioned, was punching shorter. 'Now and then he throws a looping right – his "Suzie Q", but most of his punches are delivered at short range when he is inside his sparmate's arms. The inside attack gives the advantage to a short-armed fighter, and Rocky has the shortest arms of any heavyweight champion. His reach is only 67 inches, from finger tip to finger tip. Charles' reach is 74 inches. Rocky discovered that Ezzard had a distinct advantage in long-range fighting in the early rounds of their June encounter because of his reach. After the fifth round, Marciano bulled forward constantly and tried to make a close-quarter fight of it. But he threw so many punches from the outside that he failed to stop Ezzard or even floor him.'[200]

Giving his impressions of the training camps of Charles and Marciano, Whitney Martin wrote for the *Associated Press*, 'The grim atmosphere surrounding the camp of the challenger just a dozen miles

<hr>

199 Scotty Stirling *Oakland Tribune* 30 August 1954
200 *Monessen Daily Independent* Pa. 9 September 1954

from Grossinger's, you sense it in the overly optimistic speech of Jake Mintz and the genial Tom Tannas, the co-managers, and in the quiet air of determination of Charles himself … In his small dressing room Charles, after posing patiently for a picture showing himself gazing into a glass bowl in which a photo of Marciano on the floor has been inserted, he talks with quiet conviction.

'Yes, he thought he could knock out the champion. No, he didn't have a cold, although he had had one when he first came to camp. He expected to weigh two or three more pounds for the fight at Yankee Stadium than he did for the June fight and he was close to the planned poundage. There was a sparse crowd to watch him work out and he went through his sparring chore with a methodical, almost bored air. He had explained that he did not try to punish his sparring partners, and watching him in his routine session with Coley Wallace you realise he must have been telling the truth. Nobody got hurt.

'The old galvanised airplane hangar high on a hilltop at Marciano's camp was jammed as the champion arrived for his daily sparring session. A singer was crooning, but loud, over a loud speaker, accompanied by the banging of a piano. The crowd was cheerful and noisy, and there was a carnival atmosphere about the place. Rocky went about his shadow boxing with a sureness and confidence which might be expected of an undefeated champion, and when he finally donned the big gloves, encased his head in a grotesque mask and went into action against his sparring partners, it *was* action. Gil Newkirk, a big, aggressive fellow, mixed with Marciano in what amounted to a small-scale war, several times connecting with Rocky's well-protected head and bouncing back with zest from the barrage of blows fired by the champion. The session was in marked contrast to the businesslike and coldly efficient workout at Charles' camp, and you saw in that contrast the *difference* in the two fighters. Charles is cool, calculating, thoughtful, with a purpose behind every move. Rocky is carefree and aggressive and impulsive … But you somehow got the idea that this fight might be a lot better fight than a lot of folks think it will be. There is something quite convincing in Charles' determination. Marciano? You never have to worry about him making a fight of it.'[201]

---

201 Whitney Martin *Uniontown Morning Herald* Pa. 11 September 1954

'There's a lot to Rocky Marciano as a fighter which not too many people know about,' Al Weill was telling NEA sportswriter Harry Grayson when he visited the camp a week before the fight. 'To begin with, my boy Rocky's got pride. The man who takes the championship away from Rocky will have to take a machine gun and empty it into him. Rocky knows what that title means. It took him from being a guy without any money in his Brockton neighbourhood right to the top. It means he can have dinner with the president and be somebody real big. It means his family ain't going to be broke at any time. Another thing that makes Rocky tough to beat is that he doesn't like to lose at anything. Something a lot of people don't notice is Rocky's ability to change his style, even in the middle of a fight. If the other guy begins to stop what Rocky's doing, my boy can do something else and bomb him out. Take this Charles fight coming up at Yankee Stadium. Ezzard knows he can't get himself ready for a certain type of fight that Rocky will make. Rocky can show him something new. In their last fight, I don't think Charles expected to see a left uppercut. But he got a whole series of them. All the things I just talked about all fit in with what most of you know about my boy Rocky's style. To begin with, he has that punch, of course. And what a punch! He has endurance like he was an automobile. He has a chin as tough as there ever was. He thinks pretty good in a ring. He knows where to throw them punches when he's not doing well and what to do about it. There's one other point in Rocky's favour. He don't ever lose a fight.'[202]

Hoping to change that situation and spoil Rocky's unbeaten record, Ezzard Charles was telling Ed Corrigan at his training camp at Kutcher's Country Club in Monticello, 'No sir, I'm not aiming to prove I can take a punch. In fact, I'm going to try not to get hit. Sure, he hurts, but he doesn't floor you with a single punch. I feel stronger this time. I've been punching the heavy bags more and I've added a mile or a mile and a half of roadwork to the three miles each morning I did in June. If Rocky couldn't punch, he'd be a bum in the ring.'[203]

As Mr Charles well knows, Mr Marciano can punch. He just had to look in the mirror after surviving 15 rounds with him in their last contest in June to realise that fact. And Rocky was no bum in the ring, he was the

______

202 Harry Grayson *Lowell Sun* 11 September 1954
203 Ed Corrigan *Lima News* Ohio 13 September 1954

champion of the world, undefeated in 46 fights with 40 knockouts. No bum comes into the ring with those figures on his dance card. No bum draws a crowd of 34,330 to the Yankee Stadium in New York City on a September evening in 1954. Considering the fight had been postponed two nights in a row because of rain, which resulted in a $60,000 refund by the promoters, that was a good crowd, with gate receipts of $352,654, not counting theatre and TV cash.

It was actually thought at one point that the fight would have to go on Saturday. 'Friday had been ignored in the original plans,' wrote Whitney Martin, 'because on that night a fight was to be televised from Washington, and neither rain, nor snow nor gloom of night shall stop a television show. That complication was straightened out as it was figured the Washington fight would be over when the championship fight started, but a new complication arose. The New York Giants had a game, originally scheduled for Friday afternoon, rescheduled for Friday night and there is an agreement that the Stadium and the Polo Grounds will not stage counter attractions. And baseball comes first. It was finally announced that an agreement had been reached. The fight would go on Friday night, weather permitting, at 11 o'clock, giving the baseball customers a chance to get from the Polo Grounds, over the Harlem River to the Stadium by bus, subway, taxi or kayak in time for the main event.'[204]

As one sportswriter said, they don't come to see the other guy. The guy they come to see was a 1-4 favourite, name of Rocky Marciano, so the customers who came over from the Polo Grounds having made a few bucks as the Giants beat the Phillies 9-1 could stick their winnings on a sure thing because Al Weill said his boy never loses a fight.

---

204 Whitney Martin *Titusville Herald* Pa. 18 September 1954

18

ROCKY WINS BY A NOSE

'IT IS champion Rocky Marciano and ex-champion and No.1 contender Ezzard Charles,' wrote Budd Schulberg for *Sports Illustrated*, 'in a rematch for the heavyweight supremacy of the civilised world, if you could call civilised what Marciano and Charles did to each other in their primitive, bloodied 15-round struggle three months ago. That night, Charles sleep-walked back to his dressing room resembling a man who had argued with and lost to the Super Chief and Marciano pushed his way back to his quarters with a close but justified decision and a torn left eye that had to be sewn back together like a sock with a three-inch rip.

'Studying the contestants at their training camps in the Catskills a few days ago, I saw them as the alpha and zeta of physical contrast ... Charles is drawn fine, as if by an artist with a sense of aesthetic proportion, with smooth-muscled shoulders and tapering legs. The skin on his body is as tight as that of a drum and he is so graceful that he seems ready to take his place with Sugar Ray Robinson and the Mambo Kid Gavilan as Fistiana's gift to terpsichore.

'No one will ever associate the rhythm of the dance with the heavy-footed, lumberingly powerful champion. He has weight-lifter's legs and thick, stubby arms. His moves are clumsy and awkward but purposeful. His flesh seems thick where Charles' is taut, and loose where the challenger's is tight. Looking at Rocky's back as he sat relaxed and freely sweating on a rubbing table after going five rounds with his sparring partners and twice that many with the newsreel cameras, you were reminded of the thick, hard fat covering a slab of country-smoked bacon.'[205]

Another visitor to the camps of Marciano and Charles was Dr J. L. Moreno, described by the *Associated Press* as a noted psychiatrist and author. Dr Moreno would write a series of three articles; one on Rocky; one on Charles and on the day of the fight give his prognosis.

'Marciano,' wrote the good doctor, 'has poise, charm, sensitivity, imagination, a remarkably retentive memory and a rugged handsomeness. He is friendly, warm, winning and appeals to women, especially when he smiles. Marciano has presence of mind. That is a most important thing – a most decisive factor in the ring. Absence of mind is most devastating to a pugilist. Marciano has the ability to concentrate immediately on the crisis. His concentration is intense … Unlike Ezzard Charles, Marciano has no inhibitions. Charles is the dreamer type. In his dreams, he is a mighty invincible fighter, who sweeps all before him in a reckless, savage, destructive fashion. In the ring, however, he loses the spontaneity he has in his dreams … If Charles can lose his inhibitions in a frenzy – for just 30 seconds – he might knock out Marciano. He would be like a tiger fighting for his mate. There are several mental blocks, however, that have held back the tiger. Because of this conflict, Charles is neither a primitive slugger nor is he a classic boxer.' In closing, Dr Moreno said, 'After weighing all the factors involved, I pick Marciano to knock out Charles tonight in one of the middle rounds, probably the seventh or eighth.'[206]

Dr Moreno was on safe ground with his prediction. Only one of the working press picked Charles to beat the champion. 'The others all picked Marciano,' Jake Mintz, Ezzard's co-manager, was telling anybody who would listen. 'There will be a lot of sour faces turn red when Charles wins.'

A week before the fight, the Charles camp had demanded that veteran Ruby Goldstein be banned as the referee for the Marciano fight because of 'past boners'. Jimmy Brown, Ezzard's trainer, told *United Press*, 'I think the New York State Boxing Commission should pick up the referee's card of Goldstein. He pulled a boner three times in title fights,

---

205 Budd Schulberg *Sports Illustrated* 13 September 1954
206 Dr. J.L. Moreno *Corpus Christi Times* 13,14,15 September 1954

each time not recognising the fact that the eight-count knockdown rule is waived in title fights. Just a year ago, he didn't adhere to the rules when Marciano knocked Roland LaStarza down, giving LaStarza an eight count. In the recent light-heavyweight championship fight between Archie Moore and Harold Johnson, he gave Moore an eight count on one occasion and Johnson the same thing on another knockdown. How can Goldstein expect the fighters to know and adhere to the rules when he doesn't know the rules himself?'[207]

Ruby Goldstein, one-time fighter and now one of America's most respected referees, had officiated in the first Marciano-Charles fight, so whether commissioner Robert Christenberry recognised the complaint from the challenger's camp is not known. On fight night, the judges announced were Frank Forbes and Artie Aidala, and referee Al Berl, in his first heavyweight championship contest. Weights were Marciano 187 pounds and Charles 192½, the heaviest of his career so far. As he took his place in Rocky's corner, manager Al Weill was feeling pretty good. Already that night, his middleweight Willie Troy had stopped Walter Cartier in the nationally televised fight from Washington and in a preliminary before Marciano's bout, heavyweight Joe Gannon had taken a six-round decision over Joe Rowan. Now for the big one and with the bell sounding at precisely 11.06pm, it was almost a midnight matinee.

'We gave Ezz the first round by a narrow margin,' reported Gayle Talbot, 'though realising that he was doing no part of what he had promised – meet Marciano in the middle and throw punches with him until something broke. He was using his long reach to wrap himself around Rock in the clinches, and was punching short instead of letting 'em go, as he had in the first battle. In other words, it looked as though here was the old, cute Charles.' [208]

Marciano came out quickly looking for an early knockout, but Ezz stopped him with a right to the head. Then there were two lefts by Charles, the second of which landed in Rocky's face. The champ seemed surprised and went into a clinch. Marciano threw a left to the jaw, but Charles got in several good punches and was able to

---

207 *Bridgeport Telegram* 8 September 1954
208 Gayle Talbot *Ogden Standard Examiner* 18 September 1954

dodge most coming his way. All three officials gave the round to the challenger.

'In the first round,' reported Dan Daniel in the November issue of *The Ring*, 'Marciano was the inquisitive one. He wanted to see what Charles had learned in the June brawl. Ezz hit him with a lead right to the jaw and a hard counter right to the same spot, and The Rock blinked. Charles manoeuvred well in the clinches, looked strong, and the press row wrote him down for the first round.'

'In the second round,' recalled essayist Joe Liebling, of the *New Yorker* magazine, 'to my amazement and, apparently, to Charles', the champion began to use a straight left, jabbing to the face with jolting force and then crossing a right, exactly as they teach in boxing school. For years, little Charley Goldman had refrained from trying to teach Rocky anything so fancy, on the ground that it might "spoil his natural leverage". Before Charles could react to this treacherous attack of orthodoxy, Rocky landed a right and he went sprawling down, forgetting to tread water, until he hit the bottom of the pool. The referee, Al Berl, counted to two and Charles got up … Marciano, moving in and swinging, the fancy stuff forgotten, appeared to have him headed for a quick knockout, but Ezzard rid himself of his emotional blocks for a fleeting second. He hit Marciano two dazzling left hooks, which, coming from a fighter apparently on his way out, gave the only intimation, however brief, that this could be a good fight.'[209]

'Charles was still boxing with some confidence in the second round,' reported Budd Schulberg, 'when Rocky hit him a terrible punch under the heart. The handsome, ebony-skinned, introverted challenger took an inadvertent half step backward. A different look came into his eyes. It wasn't fear that front-rowers read there so much as defeat … Charles, a sensitive man who talks to himself without moving his lips, felt more than a single punch as he shuddered under that blow to the heart … this Rocky has improved. He's hurting me early this time. Last time my ticket to Painville wasn't punched until the sixth round, when I was five big rounds in front. And this is only the second round.'[210]

---

209 A. J. Liebling *The Sweet Science* 1987
210 Budd Schulberg *Sports Illustrated* 27 September 1954

Into round three and Rocky out quick, only for Charles to box him off with a straight left. The champ landed a right to the head, but back came Ezz with two crisp punches to the body. Towards the end of the round, Marciano drove Charles to the ropes with a flurry of punches and Charles looked relieved to hear the bell. As the fourth round got under way, Marciano hammered a right to the body to put Charles on the defensive; his punches still landed and were scoring points but this fight wasn't going to be decided by arithmetic, not if Rocky had anything to do with it, and he did. Forcing the action, the champion sent thumping punches into the body and up to the head. Going to his corner at the bell, his nose was bleeding but he was happy at his work.

Into round five and he was in full flight, heavy punches from both hands hitting Charles in the body and to the head, and the former champion was forced to clinch and wrestle his way through the leather storm that threatened to engulf him. But Ezzard had no intention of succumbing easily, as he showed at the end of the round. Marciano struck his man after the bell and The Cincinnati Cobra, his features knotted in anger, hit back, hammering Rocky to the face. It was perhaps this punch that helped open up a gruesome gash on the end of Marciano's nose, which began to bleed heavily once the sixth got under way. Undaunted, the champion pressed on relentlessly, bulling the challenger around the ring as Ezzard tried in vain to cash in, hoping a stoppage would be called and he would be the first heavyweight champion to regain his title. But the referee allowed the fight to continue and at the bell there was work for Freddie Brown.

Joe Liebling recorded, 'The sixth round brought Freddie Brown his chance to operate. Marciano, for all his toughness, cuts easily, and in the first Charles fight got a long cut over the left eye. In this fight, Charles' right elbow collided with the champion's nose, inflicting a deep, wide cut. Marciano came back to his corner with an embarrassed grin, as if asking to be excused for putting his seconds to so much trouble. Brown, after stopping the chink with a quick-setting plastic called Thromboplastin, topped it off with a generous handful of Vaseline, which made the champion look as though he were wearing a Halloween false nose. I remember thinking, as I looked at Charles in his corner after the sixth round, that he was strong and unmarked, but I was perfectly sure he would be knocked out, and sure that he was sure of the same thing.'[211]

Coming out for the seventh round, Charles went straight for the champion and a right cross hit the spot, knocking the patch from Rocky's nose. As the blood poured down his face, Marciano ignored the pain and belted the ex-champ with lefts, right, swings, uppercuts. They didn't all land on target but the ones that did hurt like hell. Ezzard was forced to clinch, hang on, wrestle; his mantra now was staying alive, boxing through to the bell, making it through another round.

Describing Rocky's nose injury, Budd Schulberg wrote, 'It was just the sort of wound that a sharp-shooting, right-crossing Charles could have exploited, for if Rocky ever blows one it will be on cuts that are widened and deepened by a sharp-shooter. But Ezz was all out of ammunition.'[212]

'Marciano's manager Al Weill reportedly told Rocky before the bell for round eight, "This is it. You've got to stop him now or I'll have to stop the fight." The situation looked even bleaker for Marciano as the first exchange of round eight left him with a cut over the left eye. Charles scored with a right to Rocky's bleeding eye and caught a countering right from Marciano in return. A left hook turned Charles' legs rubbery and Marciano followed up with a three-punch flurry – left, right, left – to the jaw which sent Ezzard skidding sideways to the canvas. For reasons known only to himself, Charles elected to get up at four and it proved to be a mistake as Marciano unleashed a barrage of blows – right, left, right, left – sending Ezzard to the canvas in a kneeling position, and that's where he stayed as referee Berl tolled off the ten count with just 24 seconds remaining in the round.'[213]

Bob Considine, the *INS* columnist, wrote, 'The events of Friday night at the Yankee Stadium should convince Ezzard Charles that he ought always go to bed before 11 o'clock. He stayed up this night to be with the boys. By 11.30, he was strictly for the birds. The vultures.'[214]

211 A. J. Liebling *The Sweet Science* 1987
212 Budd Schulberg *Sports Illustrated* 27 September 1954
213 *Boxing Illustrated Tribute* 1979
214 Bob Considine *Charleston Gazette* 18 September 1954

'It wasn't until I dropped in at Stillman's the next day,' wrote Joe Liebling, 'that I got a reasonable non-Freudian explanation of Charles' conduct … I congratulated Mr Brown on his job on Marciano's nose, which had at least remained attached to the champion's face. When I propounded Dr Moreno's theory of the caged tiger within Charles' breast, it was met with polite scepticism from Mr Brown. "Why did he fight that way, then?" I asked. Mr Brown looked at me with placid, obliging condescension. "He fought the way he fought because Marciano fought the way *he* fought," he said. "Charles come in in a good mental condition, and he started right in to execute – biff! But Rocky is coming in. It is very hard to think when you are getting your brains knocked out. So Charles withdraws back to consider the situation. That puts him further from a position where he can execute. Meanwhile, Marciano is still coming in. He is cruel. Charles hits him a good right to the jaw, and Rocky hits him with a left hook and a right. First thing Charles knows, he is grabbing, and then he is just trying to hang on. Why? He don't know why. It is not like football. Rocky never gives you the ball."'[215]

'Heavyweight champion Rocky Marciano, his cut nose encased in a bandage that he said, "makes me look like Jimmy Durante," put his future plans in abeyance today pending the advice of medicos and movie producers,' wrote John Barrington for *INS*. 'Marciano's nose, cut along the top of the left nostril, may require plastic surgery, although manager Al Weill said "we don't think so." Dr Alexander Schiff of the New York State Athletic Commission staff took no stitches in the inch-long gash but pulled it together with tight bandages. Marciano, scheduled to arrive in Los Angeles by air tonight for a TV appearance on the Eddie Fisher show and discussion of a possible "life story" movie, probably will return to New York next Tuesday or Wednesday for further examination of his nose. Weill would like to have Dr Vincent Nardiello, who serves as Rocky's personal physician, participate in consultations with Schiff, but Nardiello currently is hospitalised with a virus attack and a heart condition. "Until then," said Weill, "we can't make any plans for another fight. If his nose is okay and we aren't tied up with a movie, we'd consider a winter fight. Like I said last night, Don Cockell and Nino Valdes are

---

215 A. J. Liebling *The Sweet Science* 1987

my two customers. But I don't want them sitting around waiting for Rocky. They should keep fighting in the meantime.'"[216]

'After the second Charles fight,' wrote Russell Sullivan in his Marciano biography, 'a Los Angeles doctor named Henry Ruben had performed plastic surgery on the badly split nose. Now, all that remained was a tiny scar and a minor national obsession. In March 1955, for example, *Life* ran a story entitled "Most Famous Nose in Sport," which featured large before-and-after photographs of Marciano's nose, as well as an image of Weill examining the nose with the aid of a magnifying glass. Despite all this attention, Marciano put on a brave public face. To another reporter, however, he confessed, "It's my big worry. I think about it a great deal. Every day after I get through boxing, I look into the mirror to see whether the slit is redder or wider."'[217]

The fight was the nearest the undefeated champion came to defeat. The left side of his nose was split like a walnut and pouring blood down his face on to his chest. Referee Al Berl would recall he was ready to stop the fight after giving Rocky his last chance. Al Weill would say he was ready to call it quits, although a lot of people doubted he would have done so.

Many of the sportswriters were calling it Rocky's greatest fight. This writer liked the way veteran scribe Oscar Fraley wrote it up for *United Press*. 'Rocky Marciano really can believe in himself as heavyweight champion of the world today. He proved it decisively under chill black skies at Yankee Stadium on Friday night when he knocked out Ezzard Charles at 2.36 of the eighth round. The Rock said later that it was "my best fight". For last night The Rock had to be good to win as impressively as he did … This was a tough fight. There was, actually, a great deal of the primeval in it. Up close, at the ringside, you could feel the almost venomous impact as their blows crunched home and the numerous times in which they kept swinging after the bell served only to emphasise their murderous attention to the job at hand.

'In the old days and in other fights, Marciano was a very inept champion. On his way to the title, only his iron constitution won against venerable Lee Savold. A lucky punch took out Walcott when he got his

<hr>

216 John Barrington *Charleston Gazette* 19 September 1954
217 Russell Sullivan *Rocky Marciano: The Rock of His Times* 2002

big chance. And since then there have been those, including me, who thought he was a poor picture of a heavyweight champion … But last night he came home as heavyweight champion of the world.'[218]

218 Oscar Fraley *Ogden Standard Examiner* 18 September 1954

19

THE NOSE WILL TAKE
THE BLOWS!

IT WAS late September 1954, some ten days after Rocky had knocked out Ezzard Charles, and Dave Lewis was writing in his column *Once Over Lightly,* 'The only reason Rocky Marciano will enjoy a long reign as heavyweight champion of the world is that there are no top-flight challengers on the scene. But even though there isn't a real valid contender around, many boxing observers believe Rocky is burning himself out. "He'll beat himself in the long run by the way he trains," Barney Ross was telling Lewis. "He's a doomed man. He'll reach his peak and rush downhill in a hurry before his time. No man can burn himself out the way Rocky does without paying a heavy price … A guy just can't keep up that pace, even when you're fighting bums."'[219]

Barney Ross had won the lightweight, junior welterweight and welterweight titles in the 1930s, losing only four of his 81 bouts on his way to the International Boxing Hall of Fame. He had spent a couple of days watching Marciano train for the last fight against Charles, telling columnist Lewis that Rocky was on the road at dawn, jogging and sprinting eight miles over 'hill and dale', not a flat road. 'I never did more than three miles when I was in hard training,' added Barney.

'As you know,' recorded Lewis, 'Marciano has never been beaten … and according to his handlers he's beginning to worry a little about the law of averages. "Rocky don't say nothing," says trainer Charley

219 Dave Lewis *Long Beach Independent* California 27 September 1954

Goldman, "but I know he's thinking how long can his streak last. Anybody that has won 47 straight fights and never been beaten has got to begin wondering about the odds. It's just like a crap game. After you make five or six passes, you start worrying. Rocky's like a man who has made 15 or 16 passes in a row. We keep trying to discount the odds, but he isn't any dumbbell. He knows he's going against the odds. There's been thousands of guys who boxed as pros, but there were only two of 'em who never got beat – Jack McAuliffe and Jimmy Barry – and both of 'em boxed in the last century.'"[220]

Rocky even boxed his way off the sports pages and into the Hollywood column of Louella Parsons, who wrote, 'The world champion Rocky Marciano, who came to Hollywood to appear on the *Colgate Comedy* hour with his friend Eddie Fisher, has gone to Lake Arrowhead for a rest. Then he returns here for plastic surgery on his nose, which was badly hurt in his fight with Ezzard Charles.'

Back on the sports pages was manager Al Weill, announcing from Los Angeles, 'The heavyweight champ will be returning, if not to fight, possibly to appear on television. The Rock may next defend his title in Los Angeles or in Las Vegas, San Francisco or Miami. He may also appear on a television show with Jimmy Durante or another with Phil Harris.'[221]

In the early days of 1955, the fans didn't want to see Rocky Marciano in there with Jimmy Durante or Phil Harris; they didn't really want to see him in there with Don Cockell either, but it was beginning to look as though the British heavyweight champion was being lined up as the next challenger for the world title, despite what Al Weill was saying. 'We ain't signed for nothing, I tell you, despite what you may read or hear about Rocky being signed for Cockell. How can we make any plans until we know how the nose is?'

The state of Marciano's nose was the subject of conflicting reports about this time. As related in Russell Sullivan's biography of the champion, a Los Angeles doctor named Henry Ruben had performed plastic surgery on Rocky's nose, leaving only a faint scar. According to British sportswriter Harold Mayes, in his biography of Marciano, a

---

220 Dave Lewis *Long Beach Independent* California 27 September 1954

221 *Idaho State Journal* 23 September 1954

former fighter from Boston named Johnny Indrisano, who had become a technical adviser on a number of Hollywood boxing films, made arrangements for Rocky to see Dr Ruben, a noted ear, nose and throat specialist.

Mayes had become quite friendly with the world champion and he recalled Rocky saying to him when he was training for the Cockell fight, 'Would you like to hear a secret?' Rocky went on, 'You've heard all about the plastic operations. Well, there weren't any plastic operations. There weren't any operations at all. I didn't even have a stitch in it. It just healed up by itself. And believe me when I tell you that even when I get hit by a good punch, all I know is that stinging feeling.'[222]

Rocky had already told his 'secret' to veteran sportswriter Dan Daniel in February 1955 during the course of a telephone call Daniel made to the champ at Grossinger's. 'As for my nose,' Marciano told the writer, 'I have had no plastic surgery on it as we had planned. I consulted a specialist in Los Angeles not so long ago and he advised against anything but sunshine. He kept me out in the sun as much as possible for ten days and now my nose looks OK. However, it has not been hit yet. Punching bags do not strike back.' 'Marciano is ready to resume boxing up at Grossinger's. If things go well with his "schnozz", he will box five rounds before assembled ring experts from New York next Tuesday.' [223]

So the big test was scheduled for 15 February. 'The Brockton Bomber said today he boxed four rounds over the weekend with Simmons, "but I didn't get hit square. The big show will be Tuesday," said Rocky. "I'm anxious to find out what's going to happen myself. I'm going four rounds with Simmons. We'll go all out. I've got to know." There's a red line on the left side of Marciano's nose where the cut has healed. "I massage it every day like the doc told me," said Rocky. "It feels all right when I do that. That's not much of a test."'[224]

The big day came and Jack Hand was writing for the *Associated Press*, 'Rocky Marciano is ready to defend his heavyweight boxing title against Britain's Don Cockell in May, probably in San Francisco's Kezar

---

222 Harold Mayes *Rocky Marciano* 1956
223 Dan Daniel *Newport Daily News* 9 February 1955
224 *Galveston Daily News* 15 February 1955

Stadium. The champ's celebrated nose passed a three-round test today without springing a leak, so manager Al Weill promptly pronounced him fit for duty. Actually it wasn't much of a test for the beak, sliced by Ezzard Charles last September before Marciano scored an eighth-round knockout in their title fight at Yankee Stadium. The champion wore a protective head guard as he has all along since his nose was injured at Holland, Michigan, when he was training for his rematch with Jersey Joe Walcott. The special mask has two protective prongs that fit over the cheeks and leave only a narrow gap at the nose. It would have been most difficult for sparmate Keene Simmons to get a clean crack at the schnozz today.

'After the workout, Marciano said he had been hit on the nose "a few punches, maybe five or six," but said it didn't worry him. He claimed he was convinced the nose wouldn't bother him in his next fight. There was no visible redness on the nose. Marciano had boxed privately three rounds on Saturday, three on Sunday and two on Monday so the outcome of the tests for the benefit of boxing writers wasn't much of a surprise.'[225]

'England's pudgy Don Cockell will get the first chance to put heavyweight champion Rocky Marciano's battered and valuable nose to the supreme test in a title fight in May. The site will probably be San Francisco's Kezar Stadium. After watching his heavily protected meal ticket box another three rounds with sparmate Keene Simmons yesterday, manager Al Weill said he was satisfied with the condition of the champ's "schnozzola". No blood was shed. Al surprised no one by announcing that Cockell, the 26-year-old British Empire king, would be the opponent. Although he mentioned London as a possibility for the site of Rocky's fifth title fight, the rotund manager quickly kissed off England by repeating his favourite gag at the moment. "Sure, we'll fight in England – New England." Asked about Nino Valdes and light-heavyweight champion Archie Moore, who have been clamouring for a crack at the title, Weill snapped, "They'll get their turn when we're ready. Rocky never ducked no one and he'll flatten them all in time."'[226]

It was announced that Cockell, manager John Simpson and London promoter Jack Solomons were due in New York on 24 February to meet

---

225 Jack Hand *Lubbock Morning Avalanche* Tx. 16 February 1955
226 Murray Rose *Biloxi Daily Herald* Mississippi 16 February 1955

with IBC promoter Jim Norris, Weill and Marciano to iron out the details. 'Then it will be up to Norris to decide what to do,' said Weill. 'After all, we have a contract with Norris.'

The news was not good for the giant Cuban Valdes, rated the number one contender for Rocky's title. 'What's the use of ratings in boxing if being the No.1 rival to the champion gets you nothing but an empty stomach and a dwindling bank account?' complained Bobby Gleason, the Cuban champion's manager. 'I am 63 years old. I have been in the boxing business for the past 43 years. How much longer can I hope to be around? I filed a challenge and a binder with the New York State Commission last October. It has done nothing to help us. Maybe the new chairman will run across the situation as he cleans up Bob Christenberry's desk. Imagine giving the next shot to a guy like Cockell and for what? Beating Harry Matthews three times. Marciano belted Harry out with one punch. Valdes beat Charles, he stopped Hurricane Jackson and he definitely is the best of the contenders.'[227]

Archie Moore, the veteran light-heavyweight champion, was already on Rocky's trail. A report by *United Press* from Cincinnati stated, 'The campaign by Archie Moore for a fight with Rocky Marciano gained some momentum here. Pat Harmon, sports editor of the *Cincinnati Post*, put the first signature to a petition which Moore plans to circulate among sports editors and writers who consider him the logical contender for Marciano's crown. The IBC favours either Don Cockell of England or Nino Valdes of Cuba as a summer opponent for Marciano. His supporters point out that Moore, 38, took a 10-round decision from Valdes in 1953. Moore carried the film of that fight with him on this first stop of his tour to gather signatures, but he has shown it to other supporters at Chicago, Boston, Providence and Lancaster, Pa.'[228]

'Now that the worst is known,' wrote Gayle Talbot from New York, 'and it practically is assured that Rocky Marciano will make the next defence of his heavyweight title against a pear-shaped Englishman named Don Cockell, it seems here that we should start slowly to accumulate a little information on the fellow who has proved himself a more worthy challenger than, say, Archie Moore ... What we want to

---

227 Dan Daniel *Newport Daily News* 9 February 1955
228 *Coshocton Tribune* 8 February 1955

know is, broadly, whether he can fight. Noting that Jim Braddock, the former champion, was the referee of Cockell's most recent victory over Matthews in Seattle last summer, we decided that was as good a place to start as any. "What do you think of him, Jim? Is it true he's built like Tony Galento?"

"Well, no, he's not like Tony. He carries a lot of weight for how short he is, but he's not fat the way Tony was. He's pretty solid. He gets around on his feet good for a big man. He throws a lot of punches, too. I wouldn't say he's a great puncher, what I saw of him. He's more the boxer type. He looks like he might take a good punch."

"Does he stand a chance against Rocky, or is that a silly question?" we asked Braddock.

"I'll say this much," said Jim, "he thinks he can beat Rocky. His manager told me he was sure of it. He's plenty cocky, and that never hurts a fighter if he's got anything to go with it."[229]

What Don Cockell had to go with his quiet confidence was a 78-fight record (66-11-1). At 26, he was the reigning British and Empire heavyweight champion and former British, Empire and European light-heavyweight titleholder. American fans knew of him through his three victories over Harry Matthews, two in his Seattle hometown, and his wins over Roland LaStarza, Nick Barone, Freddie Beshore and Lloyd Marshall. A good boxer, he had 38 knockouts on his win record.

With the champion already at his Calistoga training camp in California, challenger Cockell was being wined and dined by the IBC as he arrived in New York City. Whitney Martin was there for the *Associated Press*, writing, 'It was dim and shadowy in Leone's wine cellar, and if one of the neat racks of dust-covered bottles had swung open silently to disclose a mysterious passageway, you had the idea Don Cockell would have been very happy about it. It would have given him an escape hatch, for here he was trapped in a situation beyond his comprehension, hemmed in by sportswriters with questioning tongues and facing the cyclopic eyes of cameras and the blinding glare of flash bulbs at every turn.

'Cockell conducted himself admirably through the ordeal, even coming up with a whimsical little smile as he was posed eyeing a

---

229 Gayle Talbot *Indiana Evening Gazette* 17 February 1955

tremendous platter of spaghetti, a tempting dish but not exactly ideal for anyone expecting to fade from a robust 217 pounds to an anaemic 210 in the next few weeks … The idea of the party was to give the New York writers a chance to see him in the flesh and perhaps see something in him which would change their minds about his futility as an opponent for the heavyweight champion. What they saw was a round-faced, stubby sort of fellow who might double as a guard on a pro football team, but whose general construction didn't seem to be that of a man making his living in a sport requiring the agility of boxing. That is, he seemed downright plump … It is doubtful that his hello and goodbye here during his brief stop-over on his way to the west coast changed anyone's opinion of his chances in Kezar Stadium on 16 May. But he got through the reception without losing his poise. Anyone who can do that should be able to face nearly anything without wavering.'[230]

Before he left for California, the champion was impressing the newspapermen who showed up at Grossinger's for his final workouts. Al Cartwright recorded, 'The champion looks good, if there are any around who might be concerned with this Cockell thing. He seemed a little droopy while Goldman was taping his hands before the workout, but this was attributed to the daily nap he had just finished. There was nothing droopy about the stuff he threw at Keene Simmons and Felix Antonio later that afternoon nor when he belted the Spalding out of four specialised punching bags. Marciano is heavy at 195 but carries it well, even on that sawed-off frame. He will be in the [1]80s for Cockell, and will be there fast at his present gait. The Marciano of Grossinger's appears no different than the Marciano of Yankee Stadium – murderous, looping puncher, improving as a defensive fighter, still inclined to lunge at times. Trainer Goldman was asked if Rocky had any flaws that might need special attention. "No," grunted the little old pug. "He don't do nothin' wrong – because he never loses."'[231]

'He's now only a trainer, but some 35 years ago Charley Goldman used to be a partner of Al Weill, who runs the show. "In more than 50 years in sports," says Charley, "I've never seen an athlete who can deny himself like Rocky. It's the reason he's great." Says Cus D'Amato, the

___

230 Whitney Martin *Titusville Herald* Pa. 15 April 1955

231 Al Cartwright *Kingsport Times* Tennessee 10 March 1955

prominent fight manager (Floyd Patterson), "You had to see Marciano when he started, the crudeness of him, to appreciate the job Charley Goldman has done in making him a champion." Cus thinks Rocky would have licked Jack Dempsey. They don't advertise it, but Grossinger's, where Marciano is training until he goes to the coast at the end of March, contributes its half of the take at the sparring sessions to charity.'[232]

Ed Rosenthal, a former reporter with the *San Francisco Call-Bulletin* and now with *Reuters* in London, sent a letter to his old sports editor, Jack McDonald. It was about Donald John Cockell, the British and Empire heavyweight champion, who was to challenge Rocky Marciano in San Francisco on 16 May. 'Cockell is a bumpkin, yes,' wrote Ed, 'but not a bum. He'd rather have hayseed than resin in his hair. He's crazy about farming, bought a 40-acre farm at Horam in 1953 and spent a small fortune modernising it … already has an option on more farmland.

'He's smart, knows where he is going, when to fight, when to quit and how not to get punished. Fleet Street is in an uproar over the New York view that the Cockell-Marciano go is no match. London boxing writers admit Don is too fat (present weight 210), too devoted to his tractors to train on traditional lines and is too short in arm, leg and torso to counter punch much. But the very best ring experts in England tell me Cockell is one of the most underrated boys in the business, probably because of his record as a light-heavy. Seems he was fighting the weight problem as well as his opponents throughout his light-heavy career. But he has not been licked by a heavy since he let his metabolism take its natural course and balloon his weight to over 200.

'He feels better as a heavy, actually is faster of eye and foot, and owns a dangerous left. He's a converted southpaw, knows how to box and he won't climb on a bicycle and try to stay away from a Marciano slaughter. The info, straight from Cockell's camp, is that he'll try to go forward and get inside Rocky's punches. This could make for a real good brawl. A thing to remember, Jack, is that Cockell has surprising speed in spite of his stature. And Don has a pair of blacksmith's shoulders to power his punches … Only yesterday, at his Sussex farm, Cockell told me, "The Americans hate the idea of losing the world title. Why worry over what they say? Maybe Marciano has more than I've got as a fighter. Anyway,

---

232 Murray Olderman *Fitchburg Sentinel* Mass. 7 March 1955

I'm going out there to show him what I can do." The consensus here, Jack, is that Donald John Cockell will put up at least as good a showing as Tommy Farr did when he rode out 15 rounds with Joe Louis in 1937, to the amazement of the boxing world.'[233]

From San Francisco, 5 April, 'Jimmy Murray, co-promoter with Jim Norris of the Rocky Marciano-Don Cockell title fight at Kezar Stadium on 16 May, gives some solid reasons for selecting the Englishman as Rocky's opponent. Norris, president of the IBC, has first call on Rocky's services. He offered Murray his choice of the number one and two contenders, Nino Valdes of Cuba or Don Cockell of England. Without hesitation, Murray tabbed Cockell.

"We'll draw more money with Cockell," he stated. "Valdes is a question mark as a box office attraction. Look what Cockell did in three fights with Harry 'Kid' Matthews: in two Seattle fights over $200,000. In London $150,000 – a total of more than $350,000. On the other hand, the most Valdes ever drew to the best of my knowledge was that $14,286 gate in the Garden last year, when he fought Hurricane Jackson.

"As for their ratings: well, Cockell has not been defeated since 1952. In that same period, Valdes suffered four defeats. Moreover, Cockell is idolised in England, has never been defeated as a heavyweight. Important to the promoter, who's risking his dough, is the international angle. Why, the first two million-gates in boxing were internationals, Dempsey-Carpentier and Dempsey-Firpo … These guys shedding tears because Valdes was bypassed, would they cry for me if I took it on the chin financially? Tex Rickard was a wonder when he made money on his first five million-dollar shows. But did anyone weep when he dropped over $200,000 with the Tunney-Heeney show? The public will support a fight it wants to see. That's the kind I want to promote. The figures prove Cockell's value to the box office, and well all know Marciano's terrific drawing power."'[234]

For all Jimmy Murray's optimism, the British champion was still going to be a hard sell to the American fans. Which is why Jim Norris called Harry Mendel, told him to pack his beachwear and head for California. Harry Mendel was 61, a portly little Jewish guy who had been

233 *Humboldt Standard* Eureka, California 13 April 1955

234 *Nevada State Journal* 5 April 1955

around sports forever. A newspaperman, sports editor and promoter of six-day bicycle races before getting into the public relations field, Harry knew everybody in the fight business and they all knew him. When he drew the Cockell job, he was still dining out on the great job he did for Joe Louis, promoting the champ's exhibition tour.

'I knew the tour couldn't miss when I put Louis in with Bob Foxworth in Chicago after his first bad fight with Walcott and drew $35,000. One week we drew $48,000 with Jimmy Bivins in Cleveland, and just three nights later came into Detroit and drew $38,000 with Verne Mitchell. Joe got more dough for himself out of what was taken in from my tour than he ever got for any fight or anything else he was ever mixed up in. For his own end, he got $220,000.'[235]

For Harry Mendel, selling Joe Louis was one thing, selling Don Cockell was something else. 'The fact that he was chosen to handle the publicity at the British fighter's camp is a tribute to his ability. That's always the toughest job and in the current situation he sees a challenge, as Cockell generally is conceded no chance against the champion … Just before Mendel took his Davey Crockett role, guiding Don Cockell through the wild west to the haven of a training camp at San Rafael, California, he rifled through a huge stack of pictures at International Boxing Club headquarters. 'Ammunition,' he grinned slyly. The pictures all were alike. They were copies of a photograph of Rocky Marciano's towel-swathed head taken immediately after the champion's last fight with Ezzard Charles, and the long, gaping slit in his nose stood out, well, like a sore nose … The pictures Harry was toting west in his knapsack were part of his campaign to play up the possibility of the re-opening of the cut on Rocky's nose.

'In due course we received one of the pictures by mail from San Rafael, sharing such a reception with 249 other sportswriters on Mendel's mailing list. It came in the form of a huge postcard. There was a scrawled note of greeting, but no mention of the picture. A man familiar with the part the injured beak might play in the fight would have to be quite dense not to get the inference that Cockell would be using that nose for target practice come 16 May.'[236]

---

235 Ted Carroll *The Ring* October 1950
236 Whitney Martin *Anderson Herald Bulletin* Indiana 1 May 1955

CHAPTER 20

UNCLE SAM vs JOHN BULL

CALISTOGA IS a city in Napa County, California, with a population of just over 5,000, its economy based on silver and mercury mining, agriculture, growing grapes, prunes and walnuts, and tourism, with the natural hot springs a big attraction. In 1955 it was a town boasting a population of 1,418, but in April that year there was a population explosion that peaked at 2,300, with visitors thronging Lincoln Avenue, where the hotels, restaurants and saloons were doing record business. All because of one man: Rocky Marciano, heavyweight champion of the world, who was putting Calistoga on the map as his training camp for his title defence against British champion Don Cockell at San Francisco on 16 May.

When news of the fight broke, Calistoga's chamber of commerce raised $4,500 to outbid neighbouring towns and host Rocky's training camp. The champion left Grossinger's on 26 March, stopped off in Scranton and Carbondale in Pennsylvania, then to Chicago, arriving in San Francisco five days later.

'Marciano and his entourage set off for Calistoga at noon on 2 April, and the reception was presidential. Napa County Sheriff's Department cruisers met him at the county line and escorted him into the town of Napa. He sat in the rear of a long, wax-shined convertible, followed by more than a dozen cars, their horns honking, and preceded by police cars and fire trucks with sirens blaring. He smiled and waved as champions do. A grammar-school band serenaded the famous man as he turned on

193

to the main drag. People ascended to rooftops and clung to poles to see him. It was only a slight exaggeration to say the whole town was there. "I was running the gas station on the corner," said Jack Smith, a lad of 15 at the time. "I shut it down to go watch, and everybody else did too. Everything was shut down." It was Calistoga, it was April of 1955, and Rocky Marciano had arrived.'[237]

'I think the biggest thing of my whole career for Pop came when I trained last year for the Don Cockell fight in Calistoga, California. That's out in the Napa Valley country, which is just like Italy. They got vineyards out there all grown by Italian people, and Pop really was in his glory. Every winery kept supplying him with cases, and the wine kept piling up in one of the rooms. This wasn't like Grossinger's, where Pop still was a little uncomfortable. Here, there were Italians with long moustaches, like my grandfather used to wear. A four-piece orchestra with accordions and a violin serenaded us with old-time songs. They played when I made my entrance to the gym and they played when I left after a workout, and Pop was like the boss of the whole shebang.'[238]

'Well, if old Pete Marchegiano was happy out there in sunny California, his first son was far from happy. "I just can't get excited about this fight, Allie," Rocky told Colombo, "Everybody says the guy's nothing. If he's nothing, what am I fighting him for?" "How could he be nothing?" Colombo said. "A guy who's been British and European champ can't be just nothing." "That doesn't mean anything," Rocky said. "I don't know. I just can't get up for this fight." "But the guy's a good fighter, Rock," Colombo said. "You've got to get that out of your mind. This is for the title."'[239]

'The English are supposed to be models of restraint, as their American cousins are wielders of hyperbole,' wrote Budd Schulberg in his preview for *Sports Illustrated* magazine, 'but happening to glance at a British sporting journal the other day I saw that the impending Marciano-Cockell match for the championship of the world is being heralded over there as the battle of the century. Not even the loyal percussion section who beat the drums and clash the cymbals for the

---

237 Phil Barber *Press Democrat* Santa Rosa, California 2 May 2015

238 *Saturday Evening Post* 20 October 1956

239 Everett M. Skehan *Rocky Marciano: Biography of a First Son* 1977

IBC have gone that far … The truth is Don Cockell, for all his Empire laurels, is a manufactured opponent, hand-picked by Al Weill as the least menacing of the heavyweight contenders … In a way you can't blame the manager. He's protecting his merchandise. But you can't blame the fans for squalling either. They come to see a fight. Maybe they'll see one in San Francisco next Monday night. Maybe the soft-spoken fat boy from Battersea will stand up to the appealing, gutsy Italian shoemaker's son from Brockton, Mass. Maybe Cockell will cross up us wisenheimers and go all the way like his hardy predecessor Tommy Farr … But I don't think so. Rocky is easy to hit and he's a bleeder and he still has moments when he looks like a six-round preliminary fighter. But he's got the dedication, he's got the confidence, he's got the pride. I'm ready to risk a bob or two he'll mess around with the English importation for three or four rounds, and then give him a leveller, as they used to say, in the fifth or sixth. And so another hand-picked opponent bites the dust.' [240]

At Don Cockell's training camp at San Rafael, the hand of Harry Mendel was all over the place. The walls were festooned with blown-up photos of Marciano's nose and the gory cut opened by Ezzard Charles in Rocky's last fight. New York columnist Red Smith was on hand to see Harry at work when Cockell was sparring Grant Butcher, a former heavyweight champion of California. 'Once Butcher took what looked like a counter-feint into the ropes,' wrote Smith, 'but a little later the big sparmate was dropped legitimately on to the blouse of his long woollen drawers. A fine one-two combination put him down … As Butcher struck the floor, Harry Mendel, the camp publicist, leaped as though hit by a battery. He was at his typewriter in one bound, composing a prose poem in praise of Cockell's punch … Wilfred Smith of the *Chicago Tribune* told Cockell, "You know, Marciano isn't in the class of Dempsey, Louis or Tunney in their prime." "Neither am I," Don said.'[241]

Harry Mendel's job was not helped by Los Angeles heavyweight Bob Albright, who knocked Cockell to the canvas in a sparring bout. The news 'struck the champion's camp here like the bubonic plague,' reported *United Press*. 'Maybe I'll have Rocky knocked down this week,' groaned manager Al Weill, as visions of a sellout in San Francisco's Kezar

240 Budd Schulberg *Sports Illustrated* 16 May 1955
241 Red Smith *Oakland Tribune* 14 May 1955

Stadium faded a little faster. Cockell's camp later denied that Albright had been fired for upsetting the boss. Cockell's manager John Simpson said, Allbright left for home in Los Angeles on Thursday when he received word of his wife's illness. Bob left his gear here; in fact Cockell is using his headguard.'

That item of news would have heartened promoter Jimmy Murray, who had been chewing over the fact that the Englishman had arrived in camp without a headguard or mouthpiece. Don caused further anguish to Murray when he went into town to obtain a driver's licence, and immediately after receiving the permit got behind the wheel and drove back to camp. 'First he trained without a headguard, then he passed up a mouthpiece and now he's driving a motor car,' moaned Jimmy. 'I got few hairs left on my head now, and I'll lose them before this fight comes off.'[242]

Ten days before the fight, the British sportswriters covering the camps had some good news for their readers back home. 'Heavyweight champion Rocky Marciano was "properly nailed" and floored by a sparring mate's left hook to the jaw. "It was a knockdown, no question about it," said Peter Wilson of the London *Daily Mirror*. Wilson was one of five British boxing writers watching Rocky work out with Toxie Hall of Chicago, a 200-pounder. There was no question, either, that the second knockdown in Rocky's career couldn't have come at a better time in the build-up for Marciano's 16 May title defence against Don Cockell … In London, the knockdown of Marciano was given front-page headlines. In their stories from California, British sportswriters were quick to seize on the incident as a good omen for Cockell when he faces Marciano.'[243]

The knockdown of Rocky was widely reported as the second of his career, the other being the first-round knockdown by Jersey Joe Walcott in their championship fight in September 1952.

Second knockdown, or third? The writer is looking at a press cutting from the 10 July 1952 issue of the *Long Beach Independent*, California, headed 'Rocky Floored by Sparring Mate – Marciano Suffers 1st Knockdown – Rocky Marciano was floored for the first time in his

242 *Oakland Tribune* 4 May 1955

243 *Evening Independent* Massillon, Ohio 5 May 1955

career yesterday … Marciano was hit on the chin by an overhand right thrown by sparmate Jimmy Cerello … Marciano was driven to one knee for what would have been a count of three had there been an official in the ring … Rocky insisted he had not been knocked down, that he had merely slipped. But trainer Charley Goldman said, "Quit kiddin', Rocky – it was a definite knockdown."'

Jimmy Cerello; Jersey Joe Walcott; Toxie Hall – three knockdowns and Charley Goldman saw all three. That's good enough for this writer.

United Press reported from Calistoga on 6 May, 'Rocky Marciano worked over sparmate Toxie Hall in a vicious two-round boxing session on Thursday as he almost evened the score for Wednesday's surprising knockdown by Hall. After one round with Keene Simmons, manager Al Weill ordered Hall into the ring with the champion. Marciano tore after Hall from the opening bell, hitting the Chicagoan with vicious right-hand smashes to the head and body. At one point, Rocky threw a right at Hall's head that almost tore Toxie's headgear off.'[244]

While the fighters were doing what they do, the managers were going head to head with the California commission. Cockell's manager, John Simpson, was complaining about a small ring that would favour Marciano and Al Weill was crying about big gloves. 'They wanna put eight-ounce gloves on us,' he said. 'We fight always with six-ounce gloves. I'm gonna demand the California commission that they change the law. A heavyweight championship fight this is. They wanna roon [ruin] it?'[245]

John Simpson wired the California commission claiming that the 16½ft ring would be 'a tremendous handicap' to his boxer. 'We were promised a 20ft ring and we get a 16-footer,' Simpson said. At least both managers agreed on the size of the gloves. Both wanted six-ounce gloves but in California, eight-ounce gloves were mandatory for all championship fights.

British sportswriter Harold Mayes, reporting the fight for *Kemsley newspapers*, wrote, 'When Simpson was told that the ring would be 16½ft inside the ropes, he threatened to protest to President Eisenhower downwards. Harry Mendel, Cockell's camp publicist, said, "What the

---

244 *Independent* Long Beach California 6 May 1955

245 Bob Myers *Abilene Reporter News* Texas 12 May 1955

hell do they want the guy to do – fight in a phone booth?" By the time the war broke out on this subject, considered so vital to Cockell, who was regarded as being likely to need all the floor space available to keep Marciano at bay, the ring platform had already been erected. I took a rough check with a groundsman's tape measure, and decided that the size of the ring inside the ropes would be around 17ft 6in.'[246]

Sports cartoonist/columnist Arthur 'Bugs' Baer chipped in his two-cents worth, writing, 'Cockell's manager is complaining about the size of the ring and demanding one that measures 20ft. What difference does it make? His man isn't that tall.'[247]

Whatever the size of the battle pit, the crowd that gathered around it that night in May 1955 was somewhat disappointing for a heavyweight championship fight. Fleischer's *Ring Record Book* listed a gate of $196,720 paid by 15,235 hardy fans, who braved the seagulls and a chilly night to sit in Kezar Stadium. Closed-circuit TV boosted the revenue when shown in 83 theatres in 59 cities. They saw a good fight.

The champion scaled the heaviest of his career at 189 pounds against 205 for Cockell. Referee Frankie Brown soon got them on their way in what was termed an even round. The fighters rushed to close quarters at the opening bell into two clinches. Marciano flicked light rights to the body, then Cockell shot over a hard left jab as Rocky missed an overhand right. Rocky let loose a one-two combination that Cockell took on his gloves. Cockell had the best of the trading at close quarters. Cockell socked home two good left hooks. Marciano opened up with both hands and had the better of the infighting. Cockell grazed Rocky's head with a vicious left as the champion ducked. Cockell scored a good one-two to the top of the head and Rocky retaliated with a stiff right uppercut.[248]

'In Rocky Marciano's corner,' wrote Red Smith, 'they were screaming, "Come on, come on. Dig in. Double up, Rock. Keep punching. Two hooks – let him hold ya." The heavyweight champion of the world was moving in on Don Cockell, swatting him soundly one blow at a time, but his handlers weren't satisfied. The challenger from England was boxing

---

246 Harold Mayes *Rocky Marciano* 1956
247 *The Book of Boxing* edited Heinz/Ward 1999
248 *Nevada State Journal* 17 May 1955

better than you'd think a fat man could, and countering well enough to hold the boss even.'[249]

Round two and Cockell showed a livid bruise on his left cheekbone. Rocky missed a hard volley of blows at long range. Cockell made Rocky blink with a jarring jab. Rocky came back with his own straight jabs to the face. Rocky rushed in and was jarred by Cockell's chopping rights to the jaw. Cockell seemed strong at close quarters and was blocking Rocky's body blows. Referee Brown and judge Jack Downey gave Cockell the round, with judge Johnny Bassenelli scoring it even.

'Cockell opened round three with hard lefts to the body. Marciano blocked most of them with his gloves and countered with a left hook. Rocky's straight right to the jaw jarred the challenger. Cockell flared back with a one-two to the head and sank a hard right to the forehead. Marciano had a trickle of blood from the nose from a left hook thrown by Cockell. Rocky landed a terrific right to the jaw, hammering Cockell into the ropes. Cockell weaved out of trouble as Rocky let go with both hands. Marciano's round.'[250]

'In the third round,' wrote Smith, 'Cockell was backing away into a neutral corner. The champion stepped in with a left hook that caught him full in the features. For just an instant, the Briton's expression seemed to come all apart. He rocked back against the ropes, his face a moon of startled blankness. He seemed shocked rather than stunned, as though he had realised something for the first time. He might have been saying , "Blimey, I didn't know a man could hit like that". Rocky was on him swiftly, swinging wildly for an early knockout, but Cockell was by no means ready for that. Recovering his wits he was fighting back at the bell, and after it. This was going to be a long, arduous job, not altogether unlike chipping Gibraltar away with a nail file, and witnesses in Kezar Stadium were going to see a bloody definition of British pluck.'[251]

'Round four and the pace was quickening,' wrote Keith Howard for the London *Boxing News,* 'Both scored with rights to the head, then came a collision of heads. Don emerged with a cut forehead and his nose was bleeding. Marciano was now punching viciously. A left hook, two

---

249 Red Smith *Oakland Tribune* 17 May 1955
250 *Nevada State Journal* 17 May 1955
251 Red Smith *Oakland Tribune* 17 May 1955

rights to the body and two more lefts to the chin. But Cockell, although hurt, fought back giving blow for blow. The blood from his forehead was getting in his eyes. Marciano's round. Round five and Marciano came in as if he could see victory in sight. Moving forward the whole time, he used every blow in the book and even more that wouldn't get in any book. Cockell left-jabbed to good effect, but not for nothing did they call his opponent "The Rock". Marciano slung right after right, some wild but some accurate. Still Don was fighting back with good lefts and a right uppercut, but he might have been using a powder puff for all the effect his blows had. Marciano's round.

'The sixth round saw the mixture as before, Marciano attacking relentlessly to the body and then switching over-arm blows to the head. Then came an amazing comeback by the British champion. Two right uppercuts slowed up Rocky and Don followed up with two left hooks and a vicious right cross, one of the best punches of the fight so far. Momentarily, Don was the guv'nor, but Rocky soon came back again, driving his opponent to the ropes. Cockell's round'[252]

'Just before the bell ending the sixth, a right to the jaw sent Cockell walking unsteadily to his handlers. Don's manager, John Simpson, admitted later that the referee came over and asked if the fight should go on, and he himself suggested to Don that he give up. Cockell refused and made it plain he did not want his manager to stop the fight under any circumstances.'[253]

'Seventh round and Rocky rushed in like a wild bull, pounding to the body. Cockell side-stepped and landed a one, two, three combination to the face, although blood was streaming into his eyes from his cut forehead. Rocky butted his opponent in the face again then scored a wide right to the side. Cockell dropped his hands to his waist in a corner as Rocky unleashed a wicked barrage to the midsection. Rocky shook Cockell with an overhand right to the head, threw a low left hook and then sent Cockell reeling back with a right to the face just at the gong. Marciano's round.'[254]

---

252 Keith Howard *Boxing News* London 20 May 1955
253 Bob Myers *Rocky Mount Evening Telegram* North Carolina 17 May 1955
254 *Nevada State Journal* 17 May 1955

'After taking that right hand in the sixth, Marciano threw some whistling right hands at Cockell's ample stomach – a large target. It sounded as if [Gene] Krupa was beating it out eight to the bar on a tight bass drum. When Cockell returned to his corner he was seasick – and no Dramimine in sight.'[255]

Peter Wilson, ringside for the London *Daily Mirror,* dipped into his vocabulary and came up with this … 'The movie stars and politicians and the big business tycoons and the maidens in mink – white *café au lait* and lemon-coloured ones from San Francisco's Chinatown – are surging and bubbling and effervescing out of their seats. For this is the eighth round of the world heavyweight championship battle. Not what the bullfighters call the moment of truth, but three minutes of dissection and amputation and the use of the leather truncheons which The Rock calls gloves – without benefit of anaesthetic. And that is why the high and the mighty, the men with riches and the men with power, the women with beauty and vast possessions, are rising in a kind of primeval mass – sympathy and acclamation for a man from thousands of miles away, whose tongue they can hardly understand.

'They rise to him because they know he is exhibiting something which power cannot command, beauty cannot achieve nor money buy. The kind of courage which refuses to bandage in front of the firing squad … Now we knew he couldn't win. Marciano caught him with a hard right and then two more. A left to the jaw made a corkscrew of his neck. Still he tried to box back. He produced and delivered punches, correct punches, punches out of the text book. But in the ring, Marciano can't read … Killer Marciano was crowding in now, head down like a gorilla, except that a gorilla does not eat meat, and Marciano is the most carnivorous fighter I have ever seen.'[256]

'Marciano must have clobbered him 50 times in the eighth,' observed Red Smith, 'with full shots to head and body. The body blows made him stoop like a fat woman over a washtub. The head shots had him weaving like a cobra. Yet he was on his feet until, just at the bell, a right hung him over the middle rope near his own corner. Seconds after the ninth began, he was sitting under the ropes. Up again, he tottered in upon his

---

255 Ray Haywood *Oakland Tribune* 17 May 1955
256 Peter Wilson *Daily Mirror* London 20 May 1955

punching opponent, clawing at Rocky's body for support, sliding slowly to hands and knees. Still he got up, still he got slugged, until Frankie Brown got a conscience.'[257]

Brown stopped the fight at 54 seconds of round nine and Rocky Marciano was still heavyweight champion of the world, still undefeated after 48 bouts, 42 by knockout.

Marciano won the fight but Cockell won the hearts of the spectators.

Rocky may not have liked the press he received, not only by the British reporters but by the leading American sportswriters. The champion's *modus operandi* leaves a lot to be desired. A boxer he will never be. He is a fighter, a rough fighter, but not deliberately a foul fighter. The London *Boxing News*, in its coverage of the fight listed what the world champion was allowed to get away with under the California State rules – kidney punch, punches after the bell, (third and sixth rounds), butt that gashed Don's forehead, low blows (fifth, sixth and seventh), Cockell hit while down in the ninth – commenting, 'Marciano was never once reprimanded by Referee Frankie Brown.'

The American *Newsweek* magazine stated, 'Rocky Marciano's world heavyweight boxing title needed less defending than his fair name … Among most of the 15,235 customers at the scene, the impression was that Marciano was guilty of a scalp-opening butt, some low blows, and rude elbows and shoulders, in addition to striking the challenger while he was down or on the way down. But dirty? "On my wife and baby," Marciano solemnly swore, "I don't do one of those things knowing I do it."'[258]

The day after the fight, even America's leading sportswriters criticised the champ. Joe Williams of the *New York World Telegram & Sun* wrote, 'Marciano violated practically every rule in the book. He hit after the bell, used his elbows and head in close quarters, several times punched below the belt, and once hit Cockell when he was down. If Cockell should get the idea that anything goes in the American ring, short of wielding a knife or pulling a gun, you couldn't blame him.'

Jesse Abramson of the *New York Herald Tribune* reported, 'Cockell had courage far beyond the call of ring duty. How he stood up so long under that stunning, shattering bombardment was a mystery.'

---

257 Red Smith *Oakland Tribune* 17 May 1955
258 *Newsweek* 23 May 1955

Joseph Nichols of the *New York Times* wrote, 'Those present witnessed one of the most inspiring exhibitions of gameness in the history of the heavyweight championship.'

Perhaps the most damning comment came from columnist Jack Slattery in the *Syracuse Herald Journal*. 'In World War II, I saw a lot of men die. But I never saw a murder. Last night for three dollars I came so close to seeing a man murdered as I ever hope to. To allow Rocky Marciano to batter a helpless, offensively and defensively, Don Cockell as he was permitted to last night in San Francisco borders on the criminal.

'There weren't more than a half dozen people in the world who thought Cockell had a chance to defeat Marciano. But few of that great number in Marciano's corner knew what a horrible mismatch it really was ... There are a lot of men in jail for less cause than Cockell's handlers showed last night.

'I have sat at ringside and watched Marciano batter Roland LaStarza, Joe Louis and Ezzard Charles into pulp. I have been close enough and seen enough of his punches to appreciate the tremendous power the man has. And to sit in a theatre 3,000 miles removed from the scene of the action and still be nauseated by the beating Cockell took is a new emotion in my book.'[259]

In his Marciano biography, Harold Mayes wrote, 'We pride ourselves on English justice. But I think that some of the statements levelled at Rocky were less than justice to him and, in the circumstances, were much less than justice to Cockell himself, in the light of his gallant stand ... Rocky's style of fighting is such that he is a problem-and-a-half for any opponent, whatever methods are taken to combat it. He's rough. He's tough. He's a power hitter. He doesn't mind what he takes as long as he can give. Is that wrong for a man who is heavyweight champion of the world, the king of them all? Because no one really expects the man at the top of the heap to be other than a ruthless individual, surely.

'Ruthless, even callous cruelty, in a boxing ring is not a crime. However brutal his efforts may have appeared, I do not believe that the charge of dirty fighting against Marciano is one which can be sustained. For, knowing this mildest of men, outside the ring, as I do, I find it

---

259 Jack Slattery *Syracuse Herald Journal* 17 May 1955

incomprehensible that at any time when he is fighting he kicks over the traces deliberately.'[260]

Don Cockell, who earned a total purse of $65,062, said cheerily, 'I'd like to fight him again. But I must say that Rocky is the most persistent fellow I ever fought.' Don never did fight Marciano again. Like several of Rocky's victims, he was never the same again and stoppage defeats by Nino Valdes and Kitione Lave saw him hang up his gloves in July 1956. He retired to Diamond Farm, a 45-acre tract in Sussex near the sea, where he built his own pigpens and tended his 400 hens and 12 cows with his wife Irene and their boys, Pat and Peter. He liked what champ Marciano told the press. 'England should be proud. He's a great boy and very much under-rated. I hit him something awful.'

That you did, Rocky, that you did.

---

260 Harold Mayes *Rocky Marciano* 1956

ARCHIE'S SHIP COMES IN – AT LAST!

ROCKY COULD now boast an unbeaten ring record of 48 fights with 42 knockouts after his fifth title defence against British champion Don Cockell. But he wasn't really happy, as Daniel M. Daniel recorded in *The Ring* magazine. 'No matter what Rocky accomplishes, it isn't enough for those who write for the sports pages. Their stories are not about Rocky's knockout victory, but about the amazing gameness of the vanquished. He has been left in the background of every one of his major bouts. That has irked him. When Marciano stopped Don Cockell of England in nine rounds, it wasn't his success that the experts wrote about. They sang the praises of the Briton for a game and dramatic stand and panned The Rock for alleged rough work and fouling. The game Briton was thrashed as he never feared he would be by any man. His quick demise in the fight with Nino Valdes proved how badly beaten he had been by Marciano.

'A man wants some appreciation of his worth. But this is not being given to Marciano, and if he weren't chagrined and miffed, he would not be human. This tendency to play down the winning, knockout-producing champion in waves of gush over the losers is without precedent. It is very odd, too, and for thousands of ring followers is distasteful and unjust. It is odd because Marciano's public relations are so ideal. His relationship with the press is reminiscent of that which made Jack Dempsey so popular. The fans like Rocky, he conducts himself like a gentleman, he hasn't gone Park Avenue. In fact, out of the ring, everything considered, he is just about the all-round No. 1 champion of all time. But the writers go right on bubbling over about the gameness of the guy who finished up on the canvas.'[261]

Just before the Cockell fight, writer W. C. Heinz interviewed Rocky for an article on 'How It Feels to be Champion,' which ran in *Colliers* magazine. 'Rocky finds after three years as heavyweight king, that, "in some ways it's everything you think it's going to be, and in other ways it's different". One thing he has discovered, says Rocky, is that "you end up a lonesome guy in a crowd, because people, even your family, are overawed by the title". He finds that the "influence you have, goes so far beyond what you think sometimes it frightens you".'[262]

As early as July 1954, Walter Winchell had an item in his Broadway gossip column; 'Rocky Marciano is telling pals he will quit after two more fights.'

Before he knocked out Don Cockell in San Francisco, Rocky told a newspaper friend, Mike Thomas of the *Providence Bulletin*, 'Mike, I'm getting fed up with this.' Nicky Sylvester, one of Marciano's closest pals from Brockton, would recall, 'I was driving along and I run into Rocky. "Hey, Nick," he says, "give me a ride home, will ya?" We were about two miles from his house. Always before, wherever he went in Brockton, he walked. It was part of his training. Now, he was asking for rides. Then and there, I says to myself: "Rocky's never going to fight again."'

Rocky did fight again, but the doubts were creeping in. 'After I had the title for three years, I got a chance to look around, and I began to appreciate that keeping the championship wasn't everything. It helped all of us, but it hurt us too. When I was away I had no privacy, and when I was home I didn't have it either. I could feel the unrest growing in me – and it was a funny thing. I remember at Grossinger's when they built a wire fence around the cottage I lived in. I looked out the window and I saw that fence, and I wondered, "Is that to keep the people out or is it to keep me in?" The few times I got home and visited Mom, I'd always have a gang with me. One day she said, "Rocky, you're never alone no more. When you going to come home by yourself and sit down?"

'Another time, at my own home in Brockton, the bell rang at 7.30 in

---

261 Daniel M. Daniel *The Ring* December 1955
262 W. C. Heinz *Colliers* magazine April 1955

the morning. It woke up all of us – the baby, Barbara and me. It was two kids wanting my autograph. I signed it and went back to bed. I never refused an autograph in my life. But the baby couldn't go back to sleep, and my wife couldn't either. I got used to that sort of thing, but it was tough on Barbara. Until the time in South America when she got sick. Barbara never said a word to me about it, but I'd already begun to see that our life was unnatural. I couldn't quit, though, until I'd cleaned up all the fighters around who had a right to be in there with me.'[263]

In the issue of *The Ring* magazine reporting the Marciano-Cockell fight, editor Nat Fleischer rated the top five heavyweights as 1) Archie Moore 2) Bob Baker 3) Don Cockell 4) Nino Valdes and 5) Tommy Jackson. Though knocked out by Rocky in their title fight, Cockell had gone home to Battersea to a civic reception he protested he just didn't deserve. 'I would have if I had won,' he said.

The erratic Hurricane Jackson, so-called because he blew hot and cold, had some good names on his dance card, stopping Rex Layne and Dan Bucceroni and beating Clarence Henry, the guy Joe Louis thought a lot of, but Nino Valdes had crushed him inside two rounds. Jackson had spent a week in Marciano's training camp before the second Walcott fight. A week was too long for Rocky and they parted after agreeing to disagree.

Pittsburgh puncher Bob Baker appeared to be flavour of the month with Al Weill, the champ's manager, and IBC promoter Jim Norris, but he didn't figure better than a 6 to 1 shot against the champion. Yet matchmaker Billy Brown, who succeeded Al Weill in the Garden, said, 'Baker is a real good fighter. He can box, punch and now seems to be taking training seriously. I wouldn't be surprised if he gets a crack at Marciano in September.'

Cuban giant Nino Valdes had fought himself into the number one spot to Rocky's throne but risked his rating when taking on Archie Moore in Las Vegas. They fought 15 rounds under a hot sun that the canny Moore kept in Nino's eyes for half of the fight. At the final bell, referee Jimmy Braddock, the former heavyweight champion, gave it to Archie 8-5-2. Moore told reporters, 'This was a big strong boy, but he died in the last three rounds.' Archie, the 38-year-old veteran light-

———
263 *Saturday Evening Post* 26 October 1956

heavyweight champion, had been clamouring for a crack at Rocky and now, in a rather bizarre scenario, was one fight away. It would be against middleweight champion Carl Bobo Olson, who was moving up a division to go for Moore's title at the Polo Grounds in New York City on 22 June.

From ringside, Nat Fleischer wrote, 'Knocking out Carl Bobo Olson in one minute 19 seconds of the third round … the light-heavyweight king gained the right to challenge Rocky Marciano for the heavyweight title. That Moore, at long last, will get his delayed shot at Marciano either in New York or Chicago on 22 September appears quite certain. Plans for a fight between The Rock and Bob Baker definitely were cast into the trash basket by Moore's summary disposal of the middleweight leader with a terrific left hook to the jaw. It was the only knockdown of the fight. It was Moore's 120th victory in a career that has carried him around the world and his 21st straight conquest. It also marked the 82nd knockout on the way to his biggest payday.'[264]

It had been a strange few months for the Old Mongoose. In March, the California Commission issued a statement from San Diego saying, 'Archie Moore, world's light-heavyweight champion, is under observation for a possible heart condition. Moore said from his hospital bed, "All I got is a broken heart because I can't get a fight with Rocky Marciano." Clayton Frye, state athletic commissioner, confirmed in Sacramento that Moore was held unfit to fight after an examination Tuesday night by Dr James Ryan, commission doctor, disclosed a heart murmur.'[265]

Less than three weeks later, the *Provo Daily Herald* reported, 'Examining physicians for the California Athletic Commission said today that world light-heavyweight champion Archie Moore was a "perfect physical specimen" despite the fact he had been banned from fighting last month because of a bad heart. Athletic commissioner Dr Robert Laddon said that he would "recommend that Moore be issued a licence to box in this state on the basis of this examination". Dr Laddon called into consultation here Dr Meyer Friedman, well-known local heart specialist. Dr Friedman said a cardiograph showed no heart deficiency and that Moore's chest and lungs were in fine shape.'[266]

---

264 Nat Fleischer *The Ring* August 1955

265 *Hutchinson News Herald* Kansas 19 March 1955

266 *Provo Daily Herald* Utah 5 April 1955

The veteran proved that in whipping Valdes over 15 rounds in May and chastising Olson inside three rounds in June. Archie was ready for the fight of his dreams. From New York on the first day of July, *United Press* reported, 'Moore and Marciano were matched today for a world heavyweight championship fight at Yankee Stadium on 20 September.' Marciano would receive 40 per cent of the total net receipts and Moore 20 per cent.

There would be no home television but the fight would be made available on theatre-television throughout the country. In addition, Norris would be negotiating for radio to the homes. Tickets would range from $10 to $40. However, on the night of the fight, a limited number of $5 tickets would go on sale.

'Marciano was present at today's signing of the contracts by the managers of the two fighters and by Norris. However, Moore was either in Toledo or en route to San Diego, California. Manager Charley Johnston wasn't certain which. Rocky said he may go to his usual training quarters at the Grossinger resort early next week for preliminary conditioning. He said, however, he would not start actual training until the last week in July. Bookmakers quoted Marciano the favourite at 13 to 5.'[267]

Moore arrived in New York a few days later to scout for a training camp. 'I've got my agents looking over the mountains,' he said. 'I should know by Saturday where I'm going to go.' He guessed he weighed under 200 pounds and said he would probably come in between 181 and 187. He had arranged for one sparring partner, Clint Bacon of Denver, but planned to hire three.

'It'll be some fight,' he said. 'Sure, I'm going to win. I believe I can knock Rocky out.'

Pat Robinson reported from New York, 'Although he is built like a Falstaff, Al Weill had the lean and hungry look of a Cassius as he entered the sanctum of fight promoter Jim Norris. An hour later, Al left grinning like an oil man who has just got word that six new gushers have come in on his property. Norris gave Al a look at the cheques and money orders that have come in for the $40 ringside pews and the total was an astonishing $50,000. This led Norris to raise his sights to $1.5m for the fight, but when asked if thought the gate would hit that mark,

---

267 *Syracuse Herald Journal* 1 July 1955

he said, "No, but I think the gate, plus the take from radio and TV, will surely do that much."'[268]

Norris made no mention of Chicago, Los Angeles, Houston or New Orleans, which had been mentioned as possible sites for the big fight. He settled for New York, where the last million dollar fight was held on 19 June 1946, when the Joe Louis-Billy Conn rematch drew $1,925,564 at a $100 top. New York suited Al Weill because he could draw heavily on Rocky's New England supporters. 'This is a hot fight and I gotta get what we can,' said Weill. 'Rocky's the champ, ain't he?'

'Al Weill takes the Moore match reluctantly,' wrote NEA sports editor Harry Grayson. 'After taking Charles to the pork barrel twice, Marciano's manager was asked about Moore. "He won't draw a quarter," he replied. "We'll go with Don Cockell. The international angle will bring money." Weill had an out and would prefer big and slow Bob Baker with the sign of welcome on his chin this trip, but now there is a public demand for the Moore fight.'[269] Rocky's manager never had shown a fondness for putting his tiger in with Old Man Moore.

Archie's backers had tape recorder evidence that Weill, in the most vehement language possible, said he would never let Marciano fight Moore. Now, in July 1955, Al was singing a different song. 'With these two punchers in there, it'll be murder,' he said. Then he quickly asked, 'Think it'll draw a million?' It was starting to look that way, Al, as veteran sportswriter Bill Corum noted in his column.

'In spite of the dog days, vacation time and the virtually nationwide and prolonged heatwave, the demand for tickets for the Marciano-Moore fight on 22 September continues to be astonishing. True or false, the public seems to believe that ancient Archie is going to give Rocky the fight of the latter's charmed boxing life, and it intends to be there to see it.

'Why everybody wants to see Moore now, when for years they couldn't see him with the Lick Observatory telescope, is hard to explain. But that's the way it appears to be and it isn't likely that promoter Jim Norris is lying awake nights trying to figure it out. James D will just take the money, mail out the tickets, and thank his stars that he finally has come up with a heavyweight championship match for which fans

---

268 Pat Robinson *Greensburg Daily News* Indiana 20 July 1955
269 Harry Grayson *Centralia Daily Chronicle* Washington 18 July 1955

from all parts of the country were writing for tickets even before the contracts were signed.'[270]

Marciano was at Grossinger's by the end of July, where he was cornered by columnist-cartoonist Murray Olderman, who wanted to talk about the allegations of dirty fighting and rough stuff when the champ swings into action. 'Once that bell rings, I'm a different man,' he said. 'Of course I'm not so far gone I don't know what's going on, but I've never been conscious of using any dirty stuff on another guy, even unintentionally. It's too late in the game for me to change my style. I've got short arms, and when I throw a punch all the leverage comes from my shoulders. That's how I get power.

'If I miss, my elbows got to come around. The way I'm built it's out ahead of my fist. But, brother, I'd sooner hit him with my fist first. They talk about butting. I'm a small guy. The only chance I have is to get in close. I have to use a crouch. With that style, you can't help but bump heads sometimes. That was no glove that opened the cut on top of my head in the first Walcott fight … You know, in my three years as champion, no referee has even warned me. They took only one round away from me ever since I been a fighter – in that first LaStarza fight, and that had to be the round I knocked him down, too.

'Many times on the day of a fight, I gotta lot of personal things on my mind. Right away, Al Weill and Charley Goldman start worrying. "You shouldn't concern yourself with that. You should be thinking of the fight." I say to them, "Don't worry, once the fight starts I haven't got room for anything else on my mind." The results bear him out.'[271]

From Pittsburgh, the *Associated Press* reported that Archie's mother wanted him to quit boxing whether he won the world heavyweight championship or not. Mrs Lorena Reynolds said, 'I hope Archie quits. He's getting too old. If he wins this one, I'd be for a return bout – then quit.' She said she's not counting on it, but she thinks Archie can beat Rocky 'with proper training and rest. I don't get my hopes up. I just pray for him.'[272]

---

270 Bill Corum *Ogden Standard Examiner* 6 August 1955

271 Murray Olderman *Mount Vernon Register-News* Illinois 26 July 1955

272 *Logansport Press* Indiana 20 July 1955

Meanwhile, her 38-year-old son had just picked his new training camp at North Adams, Massachusetts, much to the satisfaction of the sporting press. 'Now that Moore has established training headquarters,' wrote Harry Grayson, 'we'll be able to give you a more detailed line on the venerable challenger. "Where's Archie?" we asked Walter Smallshaw, who minds Charley Johnston's Broadway office while the manager of record is away.

"I don't know, nobody ever knows," replied Smallshaw. "but I just read about him in the paper. He could be in Toledo running a sports centre, whatever that is, or St Louis, or San Diego, where he had a chicken shack, or Miami, or leading an orchestra somewhere. I don't know. But he sure gets in them papers and sells this fight." Manager Charley Johnston wanted Archie the Ancient to go to Atlantic City or a resort near Grossinger, New York, where Al Weill keeps Marciano in hiding. "It's easier for the newspaper guys to come around," the old geezer was told. So, of course, Moore picked North Adams, a beautiful ski centre and summer resort in the Berkshire Hills.

"I don't want to train near Marciano," he explained. "My camp would be second fiddle, and at this stage of the game Old Archie doesn't play second fiddle to anybody. The newspaper boys would drop by my place on the way to or from Marciano's camp. I wouldn't get a fair shake. I'd be secondary and I'm running first as usual."[273]

On Saturday, 30 July, Rocky Marciano put on boxing gloves for the first time in more than two months and started training for his title defence against Archie Moore at Yankee Stadium on 20 September. Rocky sparred two rounds with Felix Antonio of Dayton, Ohio, a 180-pound heavyweight. The champ appeared sharp in his timing for a boxer who had been idle for so long. Marciano weighed 194 pounds, five pounds more than his fighting weight for Cockell. 'I know I'm in for one of the toughest fights of my career,' said Marciano, referring to the Moore match. 'I've been resting for several weeks, but from now on, it's all grind.'

Later that week, Rocky stopped grinding and made his mother a very happy woman. He left Grossinger's and headed home for Brockton. Lena had often berated her champion son. 'When you going to come home

---

273 Harry Grayson *Long Beach Independent* California 3 August 1955

by yourself and sit down?' she would say. Rocky was going home to be an usher at the wedding of his sister Betty. Elizabeth Ann Marchegiano was married in St Patrick's Church to Armando C. Colombo, a coach at Archbishop Williams high school in Braintree. It was hard to see who was the happiest woman in Brockton that day, bride Betty or Mama Marchegiano.

Rocky's car was knocked out that week, as the *Associated Press* reported. 'The champ's car with the registration plate "KO" was knocked for a loop Tuesday night but Mrs Barbara Marciano and a friend escaped with minor injuries. Police said Mrs Marciano, wife of the world heavyweight champion, reported she was teaching Miss Margaret Fay to drive when the latter became confused by the lights of an oncoming car, lost control and crashed into a tree.'[274]

A week later, *United Press* reported from Grossinger's, 'Heavyweight champion Rocky Marciano shaved off two pounds and reduced his weight to 195 today by boxing three rounds with two sparring partners. Marciano, speeding up preparation for his title bout with Archie Moore, stalked Felix Antonio of Dayton, Ohio, for two rounds. Then he went one with Keene Simmons, a Providence, Rhode Island heavyweight who arrived in camp today. Simmons imitated Moore's style of shielding his head behind his arms. Marciano stood flat footed and concentrated on punching his way through the defence.'[275]

At his North Adams camp, Moore went through three fast rounds of sparring. 'Archie seemed to concentrate on the faces of his partners, indicating that he might be thinking of trying to centre his attack in this direction when he faces Rocky Marciano, mindful of the fact that Marciano's nose is regarded as vulnerable.' One of those faces feeling the weight of Archie's gloves was familiar to fans of a decade earlier, heavyweight Joe Baksi, who had fought such topliners as Ezzard Charles, Tami Mauriello, Lee Oma, Lee Savold, Lou Nova and Jersey Joe Walcott. Baksi was cuffed about the face and his cheekbones were reddened and slightly puffed when he left the ring. Working as a bouncer in a small, noisy side street barroom in Albany, New York, times had been rough of late and trying to pick up a few extra bucks, Joe asked Archie Moore

---

274 *Benton Harbour News Palladium* 3 August 1955

275 *Nevada State Journal* 11 August 1955

to use him as a sparring partner. He did. But after a couple of days with noticeable bruises showing above both eyes, Joe decided to call it a day, this time for good. 'Besides,' he said, 'it wasn't good for my prestige.'

'Moore said he will start working on his "come on" punch, the one that KO'd Bobo Olson. The "come on" punch, he explained, is a right hand lead much on the style of an amateur and in the trade is known as the "sucker punch". "Olson fell for it," Moore went on, "and I think Marciano will do the same. When Olson came in after me, after throwing the right, I countered with a left hook and that was the punch that did the damage. In spite of the fact that I am giving one of my secrets away, I am sure that Rocky will rush in after me when I lead with my right."[276]

Heavyweight champion Rocky Marciano said after reading the sports pages, 'Archie Moore talks too much,' prompting trainer Charley Goldman to cool things down as he warned that loss of his temper in his title defence against Moore might be followed by loss of the title. 'All Moore wants is for you to lose your temper, Rocky,' said Goldman. 'Look what he did to Bobo Olson when he got him to fall for a sucker punch. It would happen to you, too.'

Manager Al Weill was singing from the same hymn book when he said he 'was afraid Rocky may lose his temper and start swinging wildly. That could be very dangerous against a sharpshooter like Moore. That's why I want the sparring partners to shake Rocky up and see if he can control himself.'

'Today is the champ's 31st birthday, but there'll be little celebrating. Archie Moore, as quick with a quip as he is with his hands when boxing, said today he has a birthday present for Rocky but he'll deliver it on the night of their title bout – 20 September. "I'm going to give him a punch right on the button for a birthday present," Moore promised.'[277]

---

276 *North Adams Transcript* Mass. 11 August 1955
277 *Dunkirk Evening Observer* New York 1 September 1955

22

IONE WAS A LADY!

'AFTER I got the title,' Rocky recalled, 'I was so proud of it. It was like Jerry Lewis, the comedian, told me one night when we went for a walk. "Do you realise what you are, Rock?" he said. "You are the boss of the world – the whole world."

'What a feeling that gives you! You lay there in bed at night sometimes, and you think of what a wonderful thing it is. You think of what you had to go through to get there, and you say to yourself, "It *was* worth it. It was worth everything."'[278]

Now it was September 1955 and a dark cloud had appeared in Rocky's blue sky in the shape of Archie Moore. The 38-year-old veteran of 140 professional fights had battled prejudice and illness to eventually be given his chance at a world title, taking a 15-round decision over light-heavyweight champion Joey Maxim in December 1952. Now he wanted Marciano's title. Now *he* wanted to be the boss of the whole world. The odds were against him. Previous holders of the light-heavy laurels had failed to move up and win the big one, from Jack Root in 1905 to Philadelphia Jack O'Brien, Georges Carpentier, Tommy Loughran, John Henry Lewis, Billy Conn, Gus Lesnevich and Joey Maxim. Also, no heavyweight champ had ever lost his title in Yankee Stadium.

Could Archie succeed where they had failed? The old guy had no doubts as to that one as he regaled the press boys with his theoretical analysis of the situation. 'I have watched Marciano fight and have taken him apart like a watchmaker takes a watch apart. Marciano won't be

---

278 *Saturday Evening Post* 20 October 1956

able to solve my defensive style, he can't and won't hit me. Marciano will miss more punches against me than he ever has before because I have the right style to beat him. Marciano lacks defence and I will pour it on when he misses.' The usually unflappable Marciano countered, 'It was silly of Moore to say I'd never hit him. He may be the best boxer in the world, but the ring is only so big and he can't hide for 15 rounds.'[279] The bookies and the ring experts were almost unanimous in thinking that Rocky would hit Archie often enough and hard enough to make him a believer.

'If Archie Moore does what he keeps saying he'll do,' wrote Budd Schulberg – 'relieve Rocky Marciano of his heavyweight title – he'll be the first man to write as well as fight his way to the championship. When he climbs into the ring, sporting his resplendent robe and Mephistophelian moustache on the night of the 20th, it will not only climax a notable 20-year career but a personal publicity campaign that has poured across the desk of American sportswriters, literally bushels of telegrams, letters, posters, circulars – some $50,000 of words calling all sports editors to come to the aid of Archie Moore in his quest to tangle with Rocky for the championship of the world.[280]

'Rocky Marciano planned this fight with Archie Moore very carefully,' wrote Murray Rose in his preview for *The Ring*. 'Conceivably more carefully than he had plotted the five previous defences of his heavyweight title. Marciano sat on the rubbing table at his training camp. "I learned a lot in my two fights with Ezzard Charles and Roland LaStarza," he said. "I'm not underrating Moore by any means but he's human and he's going to be 39 years old in December. Experience is a great thing to have but experience alone doesn't win fights. You've got to fight and I don't think he hits that hard that he can knock me out early enough to get away from me."

'Rocky seemed happier and more content than he has been for a good many of his fights. Was there any special reason for that? "It isn't that I'm happier," he added. "It's just that I haven't slopped up the way I did when I had a lot of time between fights. I have weighed around 194 pounds constantly and haven't got too much weight to

---

279 *Boxing Illustrated Special* 1979
280 Budd Schulberg *Sports Illustrated* 5 September 1955

take off. I wasn't happy with my performance against Don Cockell and attribute that to the long lay-off between September and May. Now that I've got the Cockell fight under my belt, I'm about rounding into the form I should be for Moore. I should weigh around 185 to 187 for Moore, which is my best fighting weight. I feel a lot sharper even in my early training than I did for the Cockell fight. This is the way it should be. When you work up to a thing properly, there is a peace between mind and body. I'll be ready for Mr Moore, more ready than I've been for anybody.'"[281]

Veteran fight handler Dan Florio had been in the opposite corner to Rocky six times and recalled for Whitney Martin, 'Only once did my guy return under his own power. The first man I had to face Rocky was Joe Dominic, up in Providence. That ended in the second round and I never saw a harder punch than the one which put him out. Then I had Roland LaStarza in his first fight with Rocky. That one went the limit and really was pretty close, although Rocky won a split decision. Then came Louis, and you remember how Joe went out in the eighth round when Rocky finally got to him. Jersey Joe Walcott was next, in two fights. That first was a thriller, and Walcott was full of confidence until Marciano connected with that tremendous right in the 13th round. The next fight was different. Walcott got old on me overnight. Maybe it was the memory of how he had landed his best punches in the first fight, and Rocky just keep coming and finally knocked him out. I had LaStarza in his second fight with Rocky too, and he really thought he would win. He went out in the 11th round.

'Anyone going into the ring with Rocky is in for a real Pier Sixer. I don't see anyone around right now who can beat him, although there always is the chance Rocky might get cut and lose that way. Rocky hits so hard that wherever he hits it hurts, and an opponent is liable to have lumps on his head for two or three weeks afterward. Moore is a good fighter, and for five or six rounds it should be a heck of a fight. After that, Archie is liable to get run over, as Marciano just keeps coming at you.'[282]

Red Smith was at Moore's camp at North Adams to see the challenger work three rounds with a stocky California heavyweight named Gorilla

---

281 Murray Rose *The Ring* October 1955
282 Whitney Martin *Oneonta Star* New York 8 September 1955

Brown. 'Brown is a snorter who came weaving in fairly low, giving off sounds like the mating call of a bull hippo. He threw roundhouse punches, mostly towards the ribs, which Moore blocked, slipped and rolled under. Backing away most of the time, rocking back to ride with occasional shots at his head, Archie threw relatively few right hands. His left hand was busy, jabbing and hooking. As Marciano has said, "Moore is all elbows and hands."

'Presumably the Gorilla's job was to impersonate Marciano. Squatty and thickset, he kept moving forward as the champion does, swinging whenever he was within reach. Playing Marciano's role, he looked less like Rocky than like the late Mayor Fiorello LaGuardia. "The longer the fight goes," Charley Johnston was saying, "the better it is for this guy, you know. He finishes strong." Charley manages Moore when the fighter is otherwise occupied. "He is the best fighter Marciano has met," said Bertie Briscoe, who would be the head trainer if Moore weren't. "This fellow does things you don't see a fighter do in the last 25 years."'[283]

Little Charley Goldman was equally confident that he had the better man, saying he wasn't worried one bit over what style Archie Moore used against the heavyweight champion. 'It all adds up to the same thing,' said Charley. 'Rocky will beat him. You know, almost every guy who has fought Rocky has said before how he was going to whip him. But you notice Rocky has won all of his 48 pro fights and he's fought guys with all kinds of styles. I don't think Moore can surprise him with anything. I've seen every heavyweight champion from Jim Jeffries [1899-1905] down and Rocky could have taken any of them.'[284]

* * * *

For many years, hurricanes and other tropical storms bore only girls' names. In an era when political correctness had never been heard of, the exclusively male meteorological community in the USA considered female names appropriate for such unpredictable and dangerous phenomena. In 1953, the National Weather Service began using female names for storms. In September 1955, Hurricane Ione was raging up

---

283 Red Smith *Oakland Tribune* 11 September 1955
284 *Bridgeport Telegram* Conn. 15 September 1955

the eastern seaboard of the United States, heading northtowards New York City.

From New York, columnist Jack Slattery wrote, 'With the possible exception of a recent visit by Marilyn Monroe, no entrance on the part of a gal has created so much fuss in New York as has the lady known as Ione. And no single group or organisation is as concerned about her appearance as is the International Boxing Club. Ione's flirtation, and at this writing there isn't the slightest indication that she's even in the area, has put a furrow of concern on the figurative face of the IBC.'[285]

It was the face of promoter James D. Norris and at 10am on fight day he announced that the Rocky Marciano-Archie Moore heavyweight championship fight, scheduled for Yankee Stadium, would be postponed 24 hours. Norris was uncertain how much a one-day washout would hurt the gate. He had expected at least $750,000 from 50,000 fans. The advance sale approximated $600,000 and he figured additionally that at least $50,000 worth of tickets already had been sold in outside consignments.

'Usually a postponement hurts a gate,' wrote Murray Rose on Wednesday 21 September, the new fight date, 'but this fight seems almost certain to benefit. "We refunded about $5,900 by late evening," said Harry Markson, a Norris aide. "We had close to $700,000 in before the postponement and I'm confident we'll do at least $750,000 and maybe $800,000." The odds favouring the all-conquering 31-year-old Brockton Bomber lengthened to 19-5 after the one-day setback caused by Hurricane Ione's threat. "No Moore money has showed," said one bookmaker in explaining the rise. "As a betting fight, this one has fizzled out like Ione."

'Weight is another factor. The 38-year-old challenger scaled 188, about three pounds more than he had been expected to carry. Rocky tipped the beam at 188¼, about a pound more than he had aimed at. There will be no further weigh-in unless the weather kicks up again and forces another postponement until tomorrow.'[286]

Ed Corrigan had been putting a few items together for the *Associated Press.* 'In the opinion of Ezzard Charles, an expert if ever there was one,

---

285 Jack Slattery *Syracuse Herald Journal* 20 September 1955
286 Murray Rose *Sheboygan Press,* Wisconsin 21 September 1955

the one-day postponement will hurt the challenger more. "I think Moore will be the worried one," said Charles. "He has more imagination than Rocky." That's a new way of putting it.'

'Hotel men and restaurateurs were the happiest men in town over the postponement. You couldn't get a closet in the metropolitan area and the eateries were jammed into the early hours this morning … International Boxing Club President Jim Norris has his problems too, consider: "Four different guys called me insisting they got good seats because they were bringing the governor of New Jersey. If all of them are right, the governor must want to lie down."

"Rocky's not going to get cut up like in the Charles fight," proclaimed manager Al Weill. "That was a lucky one. I even asked Charles if he butted Rocky and he said no. It was just one of these freak things. When did you ever see a fighter get a cut alongside the nose like that one? Moore may puzzle us for three or four rounds, but we'll catch up with him."

'Moore had his usual gem when asked how the postponement would affect him. "One day is a little piece of 20 years," he commented, apparently referring to the length of time he has spent in the ring."'

As fight day loomed, there was talk around town that this would be Rocky's last fight, that he had spent enough time in the ring and the training camps. Caswell Adams had the story in his column in the *New York Journal American*. Adams said he was told this by Rocky's life-long friend and assistant trainer, Allie Colombo. 'Rocky wants to quit. He's dead tired of all this training stuff. If he wins, he will have approximately half a million dollars in the bank, which, with conservative investments, will net him $15,000 a year for life. What more can a man want? He has been living the life of a hermit for the last four years and, although outwardly satisfied with this way of living, has inwardly rebelled. He will quit for sure if he beats Moore.'[287]

'The fighters arrived in New York yesterday,' reported Bob Considine – Rocky from Grossinger's, a Catskill resort, and Archie from North Adams, Massachusetts. 'Some attempt was made at seclusion. The champion was stashed away in the Concourse Plaza Hotel, within jabbing distance of the Stadium, and Moore was put away – yachting cap and all – in the Warwick Hotel. He didn't expect to leave his room until

---

287 Caswell Adams *New York Journal American* 20 September 1955

he weighs in. Rocky was torn between taking in a movie or buying a new comic book. Their work is behind them. Rival camps issued statements today.

'Al Weill, speaking for the champion, said, "Rocky's going out there to take charge of the fight from the opening bell and when he gets the range he'll knock him out."

'Jack Kearns, who has a piece of Moore, said, "Archie's going out there and take charge of the fight from the first bell and when he gets the range he'll knock him out."

'Moore's reach of 75½ inches is seven inches longer than Rocky's, allowing him to jab away at will. The pick here is the 31-year-old Marciano by a knockout inside ten rounds.'[288]

Speaking for themselves, Rocky and Archie each issued a pre-battle statement in which he predicted victory. Moore declared, 'I've said a lot of things about Rocky and this fight, and I meant every word of them.' He apparently referred to his charge that Rocky was not merely a rough fighter but a foul fighter. Rocky, denying, said, 'I've never been a dirty fighter. Nothing, not even the heavyweight title, would make me stray from the way my parents trained me.'[289]

Jack Cuddy, for *United Press,* reported, 'Many boxing men figured promoter Jim Norris had "pulled a boner" on Tuesday when he deferred the fight 24 hours because of a bad weather threat that never materialised. He announced the washout at 10am but less than an hour later the skies were clearing and Hurricane Ione veered out to sea. It was the first time an important title bout had been postponed before the weigh-in. Norris denied any boner. He explained, "I would do it again. We had no choice. Forecasts from all weather bureaus – government, navy and flying fields – were hopelessly gloomy. And we were being bombarded by railroad and air companies for instructions whether to start their special fight trains and planes for New York."'[290]

Wednesday dawned with clear skies and the trains and planes started their journeys into the city. By fight time, a buzzing crowd of 61,574 fans were settling into Yankee Stadium, having paid a gross gate of

---

288 Bob Considine *Arizona Republic* 20 September 1955

289 *Syracuse Herald Journal* 20 September 1955

290 Jack Cuddy *Idaho State Journal* 21 September 1955

$948,117.95. The frown had disappeared from the face of Jim Norris, to be replaced by a beaming smile. With thousands watching the fight on the big screen in 133 theatres in 92 cities, and untold millions tuning into the radio broadcast, Mr Norris knew this was going to be a million-dollar fight, a knockout before the first bell had even sounded.

23

A ROCK SINKS ARCHIE'S SHIP

JOE LIEBLING, the writer for the *New Yorker* magazine, was jammed into his press seat at Yankee Stadium that Wednesday night in September 1955 for the battle of the champions, heavyweight Rocky Marciano versus light-heavyweight Archie Moore. 'At about 10.30pm,' Liebling wrote, 'the champion and his faction entered the ring. It is not customary for the champion to come in first, but Marciano has never been a stickler for protocol. He does not mind waiting five or ten minutes to give anybody a punch in the nose. In any case, once launched from his dressing room under the grandstand, he could not have arrested his progress to the ring, because he had about 40 policemen pushing behind him, and three more clearing a path in front of him. Marciano, tucked in behind the third cop like a football ball-carrier behind his interference, had to run or be trampled to death.

'Wrapped in a heavy blue bathrobe and with a blue monk's cowl pulled over his head, he climbed the steps to the ring with the cumbrous agility of a medieval executioner ascending the scaffold ... His attendants – quick, battered little Goldman; Al Weill, the stout, excitable manager, always stricken just before the bell with the suspicion that he may have made a bad match; Al Colombo, the boyhood friend from Brockton – are all as familiar to the crowd as he is.'[291]

Rocky's blue bathrobe looked more like a remnant from a charity shop compared to that of his challenger. Archie entered the ring in a

---

291 A. J. Liebliing *New Yorker* 8 October 1955

beautiful black silk robe with a gold lamé collar and belt. One writer commented the splendid outfit would have made Liberace envious while Budd Schulberg declared, 'No Othello was ever more lavishly costumed.'

Well, this wasn't a fashion show, it was a fight, although they started quietly in the opening round. The man from the *Associated Press* reported, 'Rocky missed a light jab and they clinched quickly. They each missed with lefts. Rocky landed a left high on Moore's temple as Moore moved away. They exchanged light jabs. Moore jabbed a left to the jaw and Rocky sent over a right to Moore's left shoulder. Moore got in two jabs and a right to the body. Moore scored with two light left jabs to the head. Rocky sent a left to Moore's left arm. Rocky got in a short right as they worked at each other inside. [292] The *AP* man gave the round to Moore.

'In the second round,' reported Joseph C. Nichols for the *New York Times,* '"Old Archie" worked the magic. He tricked Rocky into a lead and cracked him on the jaw with a solid right. He feinted. Rocky moved in, and Moore sneaked over a pinpoint sneak right to the jaw and down went the champion. When Rocky resumed fighting, he was not groggy, but he was puzzled. Moore moved in and out on him and punished him with both hands, but could not get on the target again.'[293]

Nat Fleischer, *The Ring* magazine editor, wrote, 'For a few moments in the second round, after Marciano had gained a clean margin in the opening session, it seemed that the vast crowd would be treated to the biggest heavyweight championship upset since Jimmy Braddock dethroned Max Baer. Fighting cleverly, Moore, stepping back as Rocky tried to nail him with a left hook, caught the champion with a short right to the jaw and dropped him amidst a howl from the thousands who packed the stadium. Though The Rock got up at the count of two, he was dazed and that's where Archie, with his knowledge of boxing gained through almost two decades against the world's best, made his mistake.

'Instead of stepping out of range and depending on his long reach to take full advantage of the situation he had created, Moore went in for the kill. He went after Rocky and brought claret from The Rock's nose ... But the champion, in close, was able to check the attack that might

---

292 *Daily Capital News* Jefferson City, Miss. 22 September 1955
293 Joseph C. Nichols *New York Times* 22 September 1955

have proved fatal to him. Then, suddenly coming to life, he bounced a powerful right off Archie's chin and followed with an attack that ended only when the bell sounded.'[294]

'He had hit him right if ever I saw a boxer hit right, with a classic brevity and conciseness,' recorded Liebling. 'Marciano stayed down for two seconds. I do not know what took place in Mr Moore's breast when he saw him get up. Anyway, he hesitated a couple of seconds, and that was reasonable. A man who took nine to come up after a punch like that would be doing well, and the correct tactic would be to go straight in and finish him. But a fellow who came up on two was so strong he would bear investigation.'[295]

'The challenger showed boxing skill in the highest degree in the third round. Depending on Marciano to force the fighting, the challenger moved competently and with virtuosity as he capitalised on Rocky's crude lunges by scoring with repeated counters. It was evident in that session that Marciano was far from being a polished boxer. Moore just about made him do anything he wanted to.'[296]

Round four and the *AP* man reported, 'Archie came after Rocky and they clinched. Rocky bulled in and scored with a short right to the head, a right to the ribs and a left to the body. Rocky smashed a right to the jaw as Moore backed away. Another Marciano right buckled Moore's knees. Rocky drove Moore to the ropes and whaled away with a barrage of short left and right punches. Rocky smashed another terrific right to the jaw. Rocky manoeuvred Moore to the ropes and Archie lashed back with a short left and right to the jaw. Rocky drove Archie back to the ropes again and let loose with over 15 punches but some of them were blocked. Rocky hit Archie with a right to the head after the bell and Archie replied with a right of his own. Marciano's round.'[297]

'Fifth round up,' wrote Peter Wilson of the London *Daily Mirror*. 'Marciano is working, but I do not think I have ever seen him miss so much or – at this stage having lost the rhythm again – punch with such little effect. But now, with the fight one-third of its scheduled distance

294 Nat Fleischer *The Ring* November 1955
295 A. J. Liebling *New Yorker* 8 October 1955
296 Joseph C. Nichols *New York Times* 22 September 1955
297 *Jefferson Capital News* Jefferson City Miss. 22 September 1955

completed, you realise just how exceptional Marciano is. Those punches keep winging in. Crude, slow and lumbering – why, you could avoid them yourself! Sure you could, if you weren't being crowded the whole time, pushed, butted, shoved so that no square foot of the ring is yours, so that you are never out of sweaty physical contact with this runaway truck.'[298]

'Abounding in highlights as the fight was, it contained one that will probably be referred to by this generation as comparable to any single round in heavyweight title history,' wrote Nichols of the *New York Times*. 'That was the sixth round when Archie was floored twice. It started as a reasonably easy round for Rocky as his powerful punches pounded Archie about the head. A right to the jaw floored the challenger, who arose at four. A combination of rights and lefts sent Archie down again, this time for eight. Sensing that this was his time, Rocky sprang at Archie, prepared to blast him into the ranks of the also-rans.

'Moore was neither of a mood nor of a consistency to be blasted out, at least not then. He met the savage onslaughts of the champion bravely, and in kind. For every punch Rocky threw, Archie threw one back. All semblance of boxing was forgotten as the tremendously strong athletes flailed away at each other with a fury that bordered on the heroic. Most of the fans expected Archie to go down with every exchange, and some of them hoped that one of Archie's blows would find the mysterious "button" and put the champion out. When the bell rang the combatants stopped, automatically, and started for their corners. They could not walk steadily, out of sheer exhaustion, and it was almost ludicrous to see them wobble to their respective corners, Archie across the ring and Rocky along the side, helping himself by grabbing the top rope with his left hand.'[299]

'In the seventh,' recorded Liebling, 'after that near approach to obliteration, the embattled intellect put up its finest stand. Marciano piled out of his corner to finish Moore, and the stylist made him miss so often that it looked, for a fleeting moment, as if the champion were indeed punching himself arm-weary. In fact, Moore began to beat him to the punch. It was Moore's round, certainly, but an old-timer I talked to

---

298 Peter Wilson *Daily Mirror* London 23 September 1955
299 Joseph C. Nichols *New York Times* 22 September 1955

later averred that one of the body blows Marciano landed in that round was the hardest of the fight.'[300]

'Marciano had Moore on the verge of a KO in the eighth,' wrote Fleischer, 'when a looping right that landed somewhat as did the punches of Luis Firpo – sort of a chop – spilled Archie to the canvas in a squatting position. It didn't seem possible he could get up on time. He was still down when the bell came to his rescue at the count of six. Had it not, he would undoubtedly have been counted out. Dr Nardiello raced into the ring for a quick examination of Archie and after advising Referee Kessler, let Moore come out for a worse fate in the ninth. The end came as Marciano, bleeding from the nose and a cut over the left eye sustained in the second round, rushed out for the kill.

'Moore, weary but refusing to yield, stood his ground for a few seconds then was pounded into his own corner and there, with a hellish cross-fire of lefts and rights that came so rapidly one couldn't keep up with the count, [Marciano] felled him again. Two pulverising left hooks, one following quickly on the heels of the other, turned the trick. Moore sank to the canvas. He sat with legs crossed, listening to the count of the referee through glazed eyes, his right half-closed and claret coming from his nose. When the count reached eight, he made an attempt to rise, but sank back exhausted. He couldn't make it.'[301]

Referee Harry Kessler, the millionaire metallurgist, called the knockout at one minute, 19 seconds of the ninth round. He had marked the contest two rounds, the second and seventh, for Moore, one even and five to Marciano; judge Harold Barnes scored five rounds to Rocky, giving Moore rounds two, three and five; judge Artie Aidala made it almost a whitewash for Rocky, giving Moore only the second round.

In his crowded dressing room after the fight, Archie told the press, 'If you fellows think I put up a good fight, then I'm extremely happy. I think Rocky fought a great fight. I'm not making any excuses … When the doctor asked me if I wanted to quit, I said, "No champion should lose except in the centre of the ring. I wouldn't want to lose sitting in my corner."' Unfortunately, that is where the Old Mongoose was sitting, but he was sitting on the floor, not on his stool.

---

300 A. J. Liebling *New Yorker* 8 October 1955

301 Nat Fleischer *The Ring* November 1955

Joe Louis, the old Brown Bomber, never had much schooling as a kid growing up in Alabama, but he had a knack for saying the right thing at the right time. Before the fight, he told veteran sportswriter Bill Corum, 'I pick Marciano by a knockout, because he can take more from Archie than Archie can take from him. He hits harder and takes better and that's his edge.' As usual, Joe was right on the money.

'Marciano's dressing room was a bedlam of flashing lights and question-shooting newsmen, who had been pushed and shoved by billy-threatening cops a full 40 minutes before they were admitted to the champion's quarters. It was Marciano's toughest fight and the Brockton brawler indicated tonight it might have been his last.

"My mother wants me to retire, my wife wants me to retire – my whole family wants me to quit. It's been a tough life for them all. I don't know what I will do. I want time to think it over." At Rocky's elbow, Al Weill, his little snow-haired manager, tugged at a towel and yelled, "No, no, Rocky will fight again."

"How about that knockdown in the second round," somebody asked. "Did it daze you, champ?"

"Sure, it was a hard right hand to the head. I blacked out just a second, but I snapped out of it. I got up at the count of four, you know. Then I knew I could take him."

'The swarthy son of an immigrant Italian bootmaker had an ugly gash, by now half-covered, over his left eye and there were noticeable bruises about his nose, which bled freely in the early rounds. "Was he the toughest man you ever fought?" somebody asked.

"One of the toughest. I'd have to include Jersey Joe Walcott and Ezzard Charles," Marciano replied. "But I'll say this, he was certainly the cleverest."[302]

'After he knocked out Moore, Rocky squatted down beside him and said, "Archie, you put up a great fight. The crowd loved it." Newspapers carried a picture of that scene. One fellow in Brockton, who saw it, said to Rocky, "I know what you were saying to Archie." "What?" asked the Rock. "Why," the fellow said, "you were saying, 'Have you had enough or do you want some more?' "Can you imagine him thinking I'd say something like that?" says The Rock. "I told him nothing was farther

---

302 *Daily Capital News* Jefferson City, Miss. 22 September 1955

from my mind. Some people don't seem to understand about professional boxers. They have a job to do. They try to take each other out of there. But once the fight is over, they seldom have any feeling of dislike toward each other. It's usually the other way around.'"[303]

Archie Moore thought the same way about his conqueror. In his 1960 autobiography, he wrote, 'When two fighters who respect each other have fought a hard, tough go, they usually develop a camaraderie that lasts forever. It is the feeling that they have shared something no other people have, and it is a binding tie.' However, the Old Mongoose did not have the same feelings about the other guy in the ring with Rocky and himself, the referee appointed by the New York Commission, Harry Kessler. 'In the second round I spotted an opening. Rocky lunged in with a wide right hand, and I pivoted away, then came back with a half right uppercut. Though I was too far out to get the best leverage, he dropped like a pound of mashed potatoes on a tile floor. I went to the farthest neutral corner. Kessler began counting. One, two, Rocky was up but Kessler went on, three, four. The mandatory count does not apply in championship bouts, but Kessler must have been excited, too. My seconds were shouting for me to finish him and I moved to do so, but Kessler got there ahead of me.

'He carefully wiped off Rocky's gloves, giving him another few seconds, and then when he released him he gave him a sort of stiff jerk, which may have helped Rocky clear his head. When Rocky first got back on his feet, he had an elbow on the ropes and was staring out at the crowd. I know. I was there. I was so furious at Kessler I thought I better hit him first and get that obstacle out of the way. But as it was, I turned to fight Rocky and I was blind and stupid with rage. And my rage wasn't directed at Marciano, because so far he was the only one cooperating with me.'[304]

In his biography of Marciano, Russell Sullivan wrote, 'Nothing happened in the first round. Then, in the second, Archie Moore nearly won the fight. A wild Marciano miss left him wide open, and Moore seized the moment, delivering a short, well-timed and powerful right to Marciano's jaw. Before anyone realised what had happened, the

---

303 Tim Cohane *Look* magazine October 1956
304 Archie Moore *The Archie Moore Story* 1960

champion was down on the canvas on all fours … Fans in Yankee Stadium and around the country were stunned. So was Marciano. Some ringside observers thought he was in real trouble and had never been closer to defeat. Marciano later admitted that he "blacked out just a second." He also said, however, "I was dazed but my head cleared quickly." Indeed he was quickly up at the count of two. He wore a look of confusion and puzzlement and was halfway turned to the ropes, but he was on his feet.

'The knockdown also took referee Harry Kessler by surprise, so much so that he made a significant blunder. At the time, the mandatory eight-count was not in effect for championship bouts in New York. Kessler forgot. After Marciano had gotten up at the count of two, Kessler remained in front of him, continuing the count for two or three more seconds as he wiped the dazed Marciano's gloves and blocked Moore's entry. Then Kessler realised his error, stepped aside, and finally let Moore move in for the kill. Moore, however, had lost a few precious seconds. Some felt that Kessler's mental lapse may have disconcerted Moore and cost him a shot at finishing the dazed Marciano. In later years Moore himself advanced that claim, and with much bitterness. In 1985 he recalled "standing there looking Kessler right in the eyes and he's looking in my eyes. And he see the hate in my eyes, he sees it all right. And he knows I hate him. I hate him to this day."'[305]

Author Sullivan, in common with this writer, did not see the fight from a seat in the stadium. Harry Kessler saw the fight, he had the best view of all of us, being in the ring with Rocky and Archie. In his 1982 autobiography, *Million Dollar Referee,* Mr Kessler wrote, 'I have shown a film of the fight hundreds of times when lecturing to foundry organisations, service clubs or charitable groups. After Moore had gone home to San Diego and had nothing better to do one day, Archie came up with the idea that I had protected Rocky Marciano after Archie had knocked him down in the second round. According to the ancient one, I gave Rocky an extra two seconds after he had resurrected himself from the canvas. The film disproves Moore's charges. It shows that Moore went to the far corner. I gave Marciano a normal count and when he got up, I gave the two of them the signal to begin mixing it up again. Archie

---

305 Russell Sullivan *Rocky Marciano The Rock of His Times* 2002

Moore moved in – but with a slight hesitation. Remember, he had taken a strong shot to the stomach before he decked Marciano.'

Viewing the film of round two, Moore fires a right to Rocky's jaw and he drops on to his right knee, gloves in front of him on the canvas. Marciano gets up almost in the same movement at the count of two, takes a couple of steps to the nearest ropes, touches them with his right glove and turns to face Kessler as the count of four is heard, either from the referee or the knockdown timekeeper, Al Berl. Kessler does *not* wipe Rocky's gloves (he later said they weren't dirty), steps away and the fight goes on.

Reporting for the London *Daily Mail,* Harry Carpenter wrote, 'It was as hard a punch as I've ever seen one man inflict on another. Years of pent-up frustration were behind that mighty single blow, a perfect counterpunch which took Marciano full on the jaw and dropped him in an untidy heap on the canvas. Moore must have believed then he was only a ten-second count away from being champion of the world. And then what were his feelings when the human lump of rock came up off the floor, not at nine, eight, seven, six, five or even four, but at three? At three – after perhaps the hardest punch Moore had delivered in 19 crowded years. Moore could not possibly win after this. He had smashed Marciano with all his might, the man had shrugged it off and was actually fighting back.'[306]

Boxing writer-historian Lee Groves recorded, 'From the time Marciano's knee hit the floor to when Kessler resumed the fight, less than five seconds had elapsed.' This writer found no controversial reports of the knockdown in the next day's newspapers and Moore did not remark upon it when the reporters crowded his dressing room after the fight. Next morning at the Warwick Hotel, Tom McShane reported, 'Bitter words were exchanged between Archie Moore and his manager Charley Johnston, when the beaten challenger accused Johnston of having been lax in not protesting earlier against the Vaseline smeared over Rocky Marciano before last night's fight. This unexpected outburst came in the midst of a press conference where Marciano's 49th victim sought to explain his defeat. Moore charged that Johnston offered no protest until after his trainer, "Cheerful" Norman, had been ordered from the ring

---

306 Harry Carpenter *Daily Mail* London 23 September 1955

under the threat of losing his licence when he complained vigorously about the Vaseline application.'

Moore was also angry that Johnston hadn't protested the appointment of Harry Kessler to referee the fight. Kessler was the third man in the ring on that December night in 1952, when Archie finally landed his shot at a world title, challenging Joey Maxim for the light-heavyweight crown. 'I won 13 of the 15 rounds,' recalled Archie, 'and it was a clean decision. My "old friend" from the St Louis days, Harry Kessler, was the referee. He gave me the decision by only two points, while the other judges were unanimously in my favour. And even after this, Johnston didn't protest when Kessler was announced as referee in my fight with Marciano.'[307]

Harry Kessler made the right decision when he stopped Rocky Marciano hitting Archie in the ninth round of their heroic battle at Yankee Stadium and allowed Moore's handlers to haul him back to his corner.

Little Charley Goldman had the last word when he told his champion protégé, 'Rocky, that was your peak fight.' Charley didn't know it that night, but it would also be Rocky's last fight.

---

307 Archie Moore *The Archie Moore Story* 1960

ROCKY SAYS 'NO MORE!'

'IN MY dressing room that night after I beat Archie,' Rocky would recall, 'the reporters started throwing questions at me about retirement. "Yeah," I started to say, "my mother, father and wife would like to see me stop fighting." But then Weill hustled me right into the shower room. "What's this about retirement?" he asked. I says, "Al, I've been thinking about it."

"I can't make you fight if you don't want to," he says, "but don't tell these guys. Let them think you're going to fight some more. There's plenty of dough can be made while you're still the champ. You can retire if you want to but don't say it. You don't have to say it for a year. Once you retire, there's no money for you."

"Yeah, Al," I said, "I'll tell them it's just talk."[308] But it wasn't just talk. Rocky was thinking seriously about hanging up his gloves in the weeks after his greatest fight, the knockout of Archie Moore in September 1955. There were several reasons moving him towards retirement. Rocky had just passed his 32nd birthday; that wasn't old for a heavyweight, but his eight years as a professional fighter had been hard years, hard years of monastic living in training camps around the country, hard years of sweat and toil as he worked his body to peak physical condition.

'He was eager to get away from boxing,' wrote Tim Cohane. 'He was weary of the sacrifices it demanded of him. No man in the history of athletics could have subjected himself to more sustained Spartanism than

---

308 *Saturday Evening Post* 15 September 1956

The Rock did. He had to, because his physical make-up, relatively short and blocky for a heavyweight, with the shortest reach in championship history, 68 inches, demanded a pattern of all-out attack and a concurrent hardihood to absorb punishment and keep coming on. This, in turn, demanded invincible condition. The Rock was gifted with extraordinary natural strength and stamina. He built on to it by ceaseless training for eight years until his physical resources seemed almost unnatural. But the bill he paid was steep.'[309]

He had a recurring back problem, as Ernie Clivio, a boyhood pal of the champ, recalled. 'Rocky and I discussed it. Several times his back had gone out on him, and he was really crippled up when that happened. He knew the back could go any time in the ring, and Rock was too proud to use that as an excuse. The Rock was no dummy. I believe you'd have had to kill him to stop him, but he knew he wasn't getting any younger and that a fight can end with one punch.'[310]

He hated the time it took him away from his family in Brockton. His wife Barbara was having health problems, which she had kept from him, and his baby daughter Mary Anne saw him as a stranger. He remembered one time coming home from a fight and trying to take her from Barbara. The child cried and wouldn't go to him.

The night he knocked out Moore, Rocky was in his suite at the Concourse Plaza Hotel, near Yankee Stadium. 'I was sitting in the kitchen of the suite, resting my head in my hand, when Pop walked in. My father was always a great one for making me proud of my wins. He was a sickly man who never made better than 75 dollars a week in his best days. But when I started fighting, it was like a whole new world opened up for him. He became a big man in Brockton. In the training camps he did a lot of little jobs for me, and he felt important. After every fight he was usually the happiest man at the celebration, but this time Pop looked terrible. His face was pale. He looked terrible tired.

"Pop," I said, "what's the matter with you? You look worried."

"I'm all right," he said. "I'm all right now." I pulled out a kitchen chair for him. Pop couldn't sit down. He walked out into the living room and I watched how nervous he was. He kept walking back and forth. One

---

309 Tim Cohane *Look* magazine October 1956
310 Everett M. Skehan *Rocky Marciano, Biography of a First Son* 1977

of the fellows in there told him to rest, and I heard Pop say, "This is my son. He fight a toughest man. Toughest like Walcott. This is not an easy life my boy has." I'd never realised how tough it was on him, seeing me in the ring,'[311]

Rocky Marciano started to retire that night in New York after seeing how distressed his father was. A couple of days after the fight, he was in Weill's office and Al, never breaking stride, started talking about an exhibition tour he had planned for Italy without Barbara going along. The champion thought about that one for a few days before telling his manager he didn't want go to Italy, to call the whole thing off as he was going home to spend some time with his wife and family. He and Barbara had their own idea of a tour, but in South America, without Weill going along. Even then, Al started figuring the angles … he had connections down there. 'We'll pick up your expenses and maybe make a few dollars out of it too,' Al said. But Rocky was adamant, telling Al, 'I'm going on this trip. I'll see you when we get back.'

All went well as Rocky and Barbara hit the high spots, but one night in Rio Barbara woke Rocky and told him she didn't feel well. She had a glandular condition and it worried her; she thought she might have cancer. There was a lump on her neck and Rocky knew what he had to do. He booked flights back to the States as soon as possible and sent his wife off to the doctors. When he met Al, the manager wanted to talk about their trip, but Rocky told him Barbara was sick and how he had found out how this thing was bothering her.

'Al,' he said, 'I think I've had my last fight.'

Rocky would recall later, 'I thought I might get a big argument from my manager, Al Weill. He'd been practically running my life for me ever since I turned pro in 1948. When I told him I was going to retire, though, he actually didn't make too much of a fuss. He seemed to accept that my mind was made up. He said he wouldn't stand in my way, but that we could still make money on exhibitions if I'd hold off on announcing the retirement. I refused, because I'd promised my wife to make a clean break. "Al," I said. "I want to get it over with. You set up any kind of arrangement you want for me to announce it."'[312]

311 *Saturday Evening Post* 15 September 1956
312 *Saturday Evening Post* 22 September 1956

Early on the morning of 27 April 1956, world heavyweight champion Rocky Marciano called his wife Barbara from somewhere in Michigan and told her something that brought tears to her eyes. Her husband was retiring from boxing, hanging up his gloves and putting his championship on the market. He was coming home to her and three-year-old daughter Mary Anne.

Several hours later, at what was widely reported as a 'hastily arranged press conference' at the Hotel Shelton in Manhattan, Rocky sat between Al Weill and Charley Goldman on one side and International Boxing Club promoter Jim Norris on the other, and formally announced his retirement from boxing as undefeated heavyweight champion of the world.

'In typical fashion,' wrote *Lowell Sun* columnist Vic Wood, 'Marciano's thoughts yesterday were of Brockton and those who had done much for him when he was a nobody in the ring. We feel certain that he himself set up the timing of his retirement press conference for 12.30 yesterday noon. In the meantime, he had phoned his wife in Brockton confirming his decision to retire and, most likely, instructing her to relay the information to Vic Dubois, sports editor of the *Brockton Enterprise* right away. This she did, because the first flash shortly before noon came over the *United Press* wire out of Brockton. In this way, Rocky gave his hometown paper the "scoop" by a couple of hours. Then, later on, the New York writers were given the formal announcement by Rocky himself. It was neatly handled and typically Rocky. Others in a similar situation would have catered for the big city press.'[313]

Red Smith was one of the 'big city press guys' and a couple of days later he wrote in his column, 'After Rocky Marciano racked up his cue, Bill Heinz had Allie Colombo on the telephone up in Brockton, Mass. Allie is Rocky's pal … "I can't feel bad about it, Bill," Allie said. "I can't feel bad because the fella did what he wanted. He wanted to win the championship and retire undefeated. So he did that and I'm glad. Now the job will be to keep him out. The only thing, though, I don't know where he is. I've been looking out the window all morning and I haven't seen him. I don't know where he is."

---

313 Gil Wood *Lowell Sun* Mass. 28 April 1956

'This made a picture, too. For years, wherever Rocky was, so was Allie. This morning Rocky was news in ever newspaper in the United States. Since early Friday afternoon, his name had been coming across the radio no matter where you set the dial. All evening his face has kept coming up on television screens. And there was Allie up in Brockton looking out the window.'[314]

'It really wasn't the family that was pushing Rocky into retirement. "There were many reasons why Rocky retired," the champ's brother, Louis (Sonny) Marciano, said. "But the absolute main one was Al Weill. He just hated the guy and didn't trust him." That spring, the investigation of boxing in California confirmed Rocky's suspicions that Weill had cheated him on the Cockell fight.'[315]

'During the investigation by the Governor's Committee, James E. Cox, principal investigator for the committee, charged in a report to the governor that Weill had received $10,000 from Jim Murray [who co-promoted the fight with the International Boxing Club] in an "under the table" deal. Cox further charged that the money was taken from the top of the profits. He had unearthed documents with the interesting expense item: "Exp. A. W. 10,000." Cox apparently did not believe the "A. W." stood for "All's Well." Murray tried to explain he had an agreement with the IBC to take the first $10,000. He denied he gave the money to Weill.

'Asked what he did with it, he said he lost it betting at the Golden Fields race track. A check revealed the track was closed at the time. After this was pointed out to him, he still denied that he had given the money to Weill and claimed he had forgotten what he did with it. Whatever happened to it, Marciano didn't get his share of it: $2,000. The Governor's Committee report also stated that both boxers were shorted in computation of the percentage of the gate, Marciano to the extent of $4,170.56.'[316]

'Weill got that dough, the son of a bitch,' Rocky said. 'I don't care what it costs me, I'm not fighting for that guy again.' Sam Silverman recalled that Rocky showed up at a boxing show he was promoting in

---

314 Red Smith *Mansfield News Journal* Ohio 1 May 1956

315 Everett M. Skehan *Rocky Marciano: Biography of a First Son* 1977

316 Tim Cohane *Look* magazine October 1956

Holyoke a short while later. 'I'm gonna quit fighting,' Rocky said. 'But I'll take one more fight for you if you can handle it with Weill.'

'Weill and I are bad friends,' Silverman said. 'He'll never go for it.'"

Silverman said later, 'Rocky wanted me to give him 25,000 dollars under the table that Weill wouldn't get a cut on, because he figured Weill screwed him on the promotion money for the Cockell fight.' [317]

Weill denied the allegations and Rocky publicly accepted his manager's explanation. 'I believe Al is an honest guy,' he said. 'We've been together for nine years, and Al wouldn't do that to me.' But Rocky was determined to take control of his own affairs. Although his contract with Weill was still in force until July 1957, the ex-champ told Al that, 'I don't intend to sit up here in Brockton and have you keep cutting me up the middle on everything. You can take 20 per cent or nothing.'

Magazines were bidding for Rocky's story, which the *Saturday Evening Post* would eventually secure for $75,000. Milton Gross, sports columnist for the *New York Post*, had priority on the Marciano story. When he asked writer Al Hirshberg to assist him, Al said, 'It was like handing me a diamond on a silver platter.' When Weill accepted the 20 per cent deal, Rocky had scored another knockout. Al wasn't so happy when the magazine's six-part series hit the newsstands. Rocky had told the writers how the manager had ruled his life from the day he signed a contract to become a professional fighter.

'Weill was a manager from the old school,' wrote Russell Sullivan in his 2002 biography. 'He believed that he – and not the fighter – was the main attraction. Concerning an upcoming fight, for instance, Marciano once mentioned to Weill in passing, "I'm glad I got this match." "You're glad *who* got this match?" Weill retorted angrily. "You think *you* got it. *I* got it. I made this match for you. You ought to pay me for making this match. What are you? You're just the fighter. Without me, you're nothing."[318]

'That's the way Al Weill was,' recalled Rocky in his memoirs. 'When we travelled, he had the suite and I had the single room. He controlled everything I did. He told me when to go to bed, when to get up, what to eat, what to drink, what to read, who to talk to, where to go, who

317 Everett M. Skehan *Rocky Marciano: Biography of a First Son* 1977
318 Russell Sullivan *Rocky Marciano: The Rock of His Times* 2002

to do favours for. My family was nothing. He decided when I could get married to Barbara, when I could see her, when we could talk to each other on the phone, when we could write [to] each other, when we could raise a family. The only decision I ever made for myself was when I decided to retire.'[319]

Oscar Fraley, *United Press* sports columnist, visited the veteran fight manager a few weeks later to get his reaction. 'Those who were there the night Rocky Marciano knocked out Jersey Joe Walcott to win boxing's greatest prize remember the grateful appreciation with which Rocky draped an arm around Al Weill and praised him profusely. I was one of those who heard him say: "I can't give too much credit to my manager. Without him, maybe I never get a chance to be champion."

'Those words echoed in my ears once again as I walked into Weill's tiny office in a mid-Manhattan hotel to see his reaction to "The Rock's" biographical baiting. The rotund figure rocked angrily back and forth in a creaking swivel chair. Swinging halfway around, Weill raised one stubby arm and stabbed an accusing finger at the life-sized colour photo on the wall over his head. In vivid, dramatic colours, the picture showed Rocky Marciano sledging home the right hand which twisted old Jersey Joe Walcott's face into a grotesque mask and tore the heavyweight crown from his battered head on a September night in 1952.

'Al Weill, the man who guided "The Rock" to that historic moment and through an undefeated career, was plainly irate as he stormed, *"Rocky Marciano is an ingrate!"* Weill slumped in his chair and the fire left his eyes, to be replaced by a hurt, almost disbelieving look. "Sure I'm hurt," admitted the man who, at 62, can look back on 40 years of managing fighters, including four world champions. "Who wouldn't be? I'm very hurt – down deep. I brought him all the way from nowhere. I like to think that the man who wrote this put the squeeze on Rocky and made him say these things, stories being stories. But I don't know. All I do know is that I always did the best I knew how for him, and while I've taken a lot of raps before, this time it's different."'[320]

'Sometimes people ask me if I had a son, would I want him to be a fighter?' Rocky told his biographers near the end of the *Post* series.

---

319 *Saturday Evening Post* 13 October 1956

320 Oscar Fraley *Man's Magazine* March 1957

'For a trainer I'd want him to have someone like Allie Colombo … for a teacher I'd want him to have someone like Charley Goldman … and for a manager I'd want him to have someone like Al Weill. I wouldn't have been champ without him.'[321]

I wonder if Al read those last few words.

---

321 *Saturday Evening Post* 13 October 1956

25

ONE MORE FIGHT

ONE DAY in May 1956, ex-champ Rocky Marciano was working on his golf game at the Blue Hill Country Club in Canton, Massachusetts, taking lessons from pro Ed 'Porky' Oliver as his friend, singer Frankie Laine, looked on. At the grubby St Nicholas Arena at 66th Street and Columbus Avenue, a few steps east of Broadway, Charley Goldman was back working at the day job. It was a far cry from Yankee Stadium but it was a living. The little trainer had his new kid, middleweight Rory Calhoun, in the ring with Randy Sandy, and Charley allowed himself a smile as Calhoun stopped his man inside three rounds. In her 'Voice of Broadway' column, Dorothy Kilgallen noted, 'A garment centre manufacturer has bet $10,000 at 3 to 1 odds that Rocky Marciano will make a comeback within a year.'

It looked a good bet. Rocky's Uncle Mike thought so. 'Do me a favour, Rocky,' he said. 'Stay in shape. Maybe you don't want it now, but someday they're going to offer you a lot of money to fight again. And you're going to want to make a comeback. Remember I told you so. Because all fighters want to make a comeback.'[322]

Uncle Mike had called it right. Jim Norris, missing his number one attraction, offered Rocky a million dollars to fight again. But Rocky proved Mike wrong when he turned Norris down flat. He had made his decision and he was sticking with it.

---

322 Everett M. Skehan *Rocky Marciano: Biography of a First Son* 1977

'The best I could get out of fighting again is more money,' Rocky told his biographers in 1956. 'What good is money when I'm worried about whether my little girl's eyes can be straightened and she won't be cross-eyed? What good's another bankbook or another stock when my wife has a glandular condition which almost choked her to death last year? What good are all the headlines in the papers – and I admit I got a bang out of reading them – when I'm scared that my own back is so bad I may be kind of a cripple for the rest of my life?

'I received a letter from Buff Donelli, the football coach at Boston University. He wrote, "Retirement is not a normal thing. Don't think in terms of retirement. Think in terms of a new vocation." That's what I'm doing. In the meantime, I've still got income coming in from the Moore fight, which was spread over several years. That fight earned better than $1m at the gate and from theatre TV and the movies. Our end was 40 per cent. Of course expenses and the manager's cut take a big bite out of this, and income taxes take still more. Even so, with the Moore payoff added to what I've already made, you can see I'm pretty well off. If I never got anything more than the income from my capital, which is invested real good, I'd still have enough to live conservatively for the rest of my life.'[323]

Manager Al Weill had booked Rocky Marciano through 49 professional fights in a nine-year career and his slugger came out the other end undefeated. He was heavyweight champion for three years with seven championship purses going into retirement. Their gross take from those was almost $1.5m with Rocky's share, including radio, TV and movies, approximating $750,000. When he got through paying taxes, he ended up with about $300,000.

'In the old days,' Rocky told Tim Cohane, sports editor of *Look* magazine, 'any fighter who had as many tough fights as I've had – fights that brought in so much money – would have had three times what I have to show for it.'

'Marciano was eminently correct. To begin with, of course, the Government was taking tax bites unknown in the days of such regal predecessors as Jack Dempsey and Gene Tunney. Then there is the fact that Marciano was "cut down the middle" by Weill. That is, Weill got

---

323 *Saturday Evening Post* 15 September 1956

50 per cent of what Rocky earned. Weill, however, did pay all expenses from his share. Aside from the 50 per cent for Weill and the take by the government, Marciano definitely came out on the short end of several important fights, not only before he was champion but afterward.'[324]

When Marciano fought Joe Louis, the veteran Brown Bomber insisted on 45 per cent of the 60 per cent purse the Garden was putting up. Promoter Jim Norris made Rocky an offer he couldn't refuse – take it or leave it. Marciano took the 15 per cent and he took Louis in eight rounds. Even after Rocky knocked Walcott out to win the title, he was tied into a rematch deal that saw the former champ walk away with a $250,000 guarantee, after being flattened in the first round. Rocky's purse for that one came to $83,962 *less* than Jersey Joe took home for his first round flop. Rocky certainly did have a legitimate beef.

It was a bad time for James Dougan Norris. The federal government had filed an antitrust suit against the International Boxing Club for conspiring to monopolise championship boxing in the United States, and in June 1957 the court finally ordered the IBC be dissolved.

Rocky never did fight again. 'In 1959, though, Marciano did briefly contemplate a return to the ring,' as related by Russell Sullivan in his biography of The Rock. 'Lou Duva reveals that Marciano came close to signing a deal to fight Ingemar Johansson, the big Swede who had knocked out Patterson to become the new champion. Negotiations took place at the Victoria Hotel in New York, with Marciano slated to receive $1.4 million ("a tremendous figure at that time," says Duva) and Duva set to work Marciano's corner. In preparation, Marciano underwent secret training sessions in Ocala, Florida. For a while he was serious, cutting down on meals and doing roadwork with his old zeal. Eventually, though, his various business interests interfered. Besides, Cus D'Amato, Patterson's manager, successfully managed to block the Marciano-Johansson deal from being consummated. After a month, Marciano called off the comeback.'[325]

Besides, Rocky was having too good a time to go back to the training grind. There were cracks starting to show in the Marciano marriage. In the lonely hours, days, weeks, months that Barbara spent at home while

324 Tom Cohane *Look* magazine October 1956

325 Russell Sullivan *Rocky Marciano: The Rock of His Times* 2002

Rocky was in camp driving his body to fighting perfection, she began drinking, smoking and putting on weight. When he retired, Rocky wanted to do things, go places. Barbara didn't. Rocky went anyhow. He began building a network that would eventually stretch across the continent, a network of businessmen, showbusiness people and mob guys, all more than willing to bask in the reflected glory of the retired former heavyweight champion of the world. Rocky was on a roller-coaster ride that would end in a cornfield in Iowa. It was a free ride but it would cost him dearly in the long run.

Dale Miltimore was along for the ride. A former cab driver and short order cook he became Rocky's valet, chauffeur, secretary, cook, butler and bodyguard. 'You name it, whatever the situation called for, I was it,' he recalled. 'Rocky was the world's greatest schemer. He could leave town with 30 cents in his pocket and tour the country and he'd come back with the same 30 cents. He never had transportation, money or a system, just the connections to get all of those things. The plane tickets, the hotel rooms, the meals were always on somebody, but never Rocky. He considered the rich guys strictly from the standpoint of survival. You lived each day on zero expenses, and everything you took in was profit. In order to do this you had to have connections with hotel owners, restaurateurs, lawyers, legitimate businessmen, syndicate people, celebrities and so on. Rocky had all of these.'[326]

'It was a strange, fantastic world he had built for himself,' wrote William Nack in his 2003 book *My Turf*, 'one shaped in considerable part by the obsessive, relentless quest for $100 bills for cash to feed his lending business, for cash to buy his way into multitudes of deals, for cash to toss on to Pasqualena Marchegiano's dining room table. "He'd come home sometimes with two large bags of money, and he'd give his mother one." Marciano's longtime accountant and travelling companion, Frank Saccone, recalls. "Five or six thousand dollars in each bag. His mother would count it all over the table." She would then stack it neatly in piles. "What do you want me to do with it, Rocky?"

"Keep it, Ma, for spending money."

---

326 Everett M. Skekan *Rocky Marciano: Biography of a First Son* 1977

"He had this crazy, crazy need for cash," Saccone said. "He loved the sight of cash. A cheque was just a little piece of paper."[327]

Saccone would recall being in Montreal with Rocky, who had made a speech at a large function. Afterwards, one of the organisers handed Rocky an envelope containing a cheque for $5,000. Rocky insisted on getting cash, even telling the man that he would take $2,500 in exchange for the cheque. The poor guy went away and returned with the cash, handing it to Rocky. Marciano happily handed over the cheque, pocketed the cash and was on his way. And he wasn't on his way to the nearest bank. The cash he made was stored in the most unlikely places; old-fashioned toilets, inside curtain rods, light fixtures, anywhere. Rocky didn't trust banks; he never had contracts for the deals he made with this guy or that guy. No paper trails. The head office for Marciano Loans Inc. was in Rocky's head. He didn't forget many of the deals he made, be it for a few dollars, a few hundred or a few thousand.

Rocky was a great friend and admirer of former featherweight champion Willie Pep and he got Willie a public relations job with the Soundex Company in Brockton. He called in one day to see Willie.

'I just made a big score, Willie,' Rocky said, taking a fat roll of hundred-dollar bills from his pocket. 'You need some cash?' 'I'll tell you what, Rock,' Pep said, 'Loan me a hundred and I'll pay it back when I get paid on Friday.' But on Friday Willie was out of town. The following Monday, he went to the office to pick up his pay. He was handed an envelope that contained just $100 instead of the usual $200. "Where's the other hundred?" Willie asked. "Rocky took it," the company paymaster said.

'Rocky?' questioned Willie. 'Rocky came in and said you owed it to him,' the paymaster said. 'Then he took it out of the envelope.' 'Yeah, that's right,' Willie said. 'Rocky would always loan me anything I wanted,' Pep said. 'He'd hold out the cash and tell me to take as much as I wanted. If you were a man of your word, The Rock was always right there any time you needed him.'[328]

Of course there were guys who forgot where they got the cash and they tried to stay out of Rocky's way. But he would get in *their* way and

---

327 William Nack *My Turf: Horses, Boxes, Blood Money, and the Sporting Life* 2003
328 Everett M. Skehan *Rocky Marciano: Biography of a First Son* 1977

it was paytime. Eddie Massod ran the Liberty Club in Brockton with a bookies business on the side. Rocky loaned Eddie $5,000 and he had a lot of trouble getting Eddie to pay the money back. He cornered Eddie at the club one day and when the guy said he didn't have the money 'right now', Marciano hit him with a left and down he dropped. Rocky went through his pockets taking every cent. A few weeks later, Eddie met Peter Marciano on Main Street in Brockton. His jaw had been cracked and he could barely speak, but he was still grinning. 'I'm lucky he used the left,' he told Peter, 'With the right he might have killed me.'

Along with his addiction for dollar bills, Rocky had developed the same passion for dolly birds. Maybe it was all those months of spartan living in a training camp, being without what he now wanted more than ever: sex.

'Richie Paterniti, one of Rocky's best friends in those retirement days, would recall, 'Rocky liked girls, know what I mean. Forget about the fights. He was crazy about the girls, that's all he wanted to do. A friend of mine in New York got me and Rocky thousands of girls. We had girls every single day and night.' There were women for Marciano everywhere he went in those days after his retirement. That a woman be waiting for him was as requisite for his appearance as the folded $100 bills. 'He never had an affair,' says Santarelli, his Chicago underworld pal, who booked him to make appearances and advertisements all over. 'If he ever went to some place and there was not a girl waiting for him, he'd never come back.'[329]

'Mob guys tended to have a high degree of respect for The Rock,' recorded Sullivan in his book. 'To a large extent the respect was mutual … Marciano became friendly with underworld figures throughout the country. He became a business associate of Cleveland racketeer Pete DeGravio and was on his way to visit him when DeGravio was shot to death on a golf course in 1968. He became close friends with Chicago mobster Frankie Fratto, who possessed a long and inglorious criminal record. He even visited the notorious Mafia don Vito Genovese in prison shortly before the latter's death in early 1969.

'And he became friends with Frankie Carbo. After meeting Carbo through Weill, Marciano developed a fairly close relationship with the

---

329 William Nack *My Turf: Horses, Boxes, Blood Money, and the Sporting Life* 2003

"underworld commissioner of boxing." He saw Carbo as having class, someone who knew how to dress, how to live, how to move, how to command respect and how to treat other Italians. Moreover, Marciano liked the aura of danger and excitement that surrounded Carbo, although he hated Carbo's control, and often abuse, of fighters.'[330]

In 1969, Murry Woroner managed to do what Al Weill and Jim Norris couldn't do with all of their power and money – get Rocky Marciano back into a boxing ring. Woroner was not a boxing promoter but a radio producer and in 1967 he had the idea of determining the all-time greatest heavyweight champion of the world by matching boxing champions of different eras in a series of fantasy fights. Woroner sent out a survey to 250 boxing experts and writers to determine which boxers would be used. Punch-by-punch details of the boxers' records during their prime were entered into an NCR 315 computer. Their strengths, weaknesses, fighting styles and patterns and other factors and scenarios were converted into formulas.

A year and a half later, the All-Time Heavyweight Computer Tournament was broadcast nationwide, producing Rocky Marciano as the champion after he defeated Jack Dempsey in the final. Woroner awarded Rocky a gold and diamond championship belt worth $10,000. A year later, the All-Time Middleweight Computer Championship was put on air, with Sugar Ray Robinson emerging as champion.

'Perhaps the most pertinent arguments resulted from the fact that the two undefeated heavyweight champions – Marciano and Clay [Ali] – did not meet each other in the tournament,' wrote Woroner for *The Ring* magazine. 'Clay took violent reaction to Marciano's winning the tournament and filed a one million dollar damage suit against Woroner Productions. The suit was settled in Chicago Superior Court for one dollar, but it was the out-of-court manoeuvring that really tells the story. Clay wanted a computer shot at all-time champ Marciano, and, the price being right, Marciano was willing to give him the opportunity.'[331]

Marciano went into intensive training, along with a rigid diet, and got himself into comparatively good condition. Both fighters were

330 Russell Sullivan *Rocky Marciano: The Rock of His Times* 2002
331 Murry Woroner *The Ring* February 1970

serious. Clay said, 'I'll drop him in five.' Marciano replied, 'I think if I can get him into a corner I can KO him.'

In December 1968, with only the necessary film crew in attendance at a sealed Miami motion picture studio, they climbed into the ring for the 'Super Fight', as it was named. Rocky had shed 50 pounds and sported a new toupee that Angelo Dundee said 'looked like a dead cat'. Dundee, as usual, worked Clay's corner, while Mel Ziegler seconded Rocky in place of the late Charley Goldman. Referee was Chris Dundee.

Woroner stated that more than 70 three-minute rounds were filmed during a five-day shooting schedule. The last filming took place just three weeks prior to Marciano's tragic death. As the filming progressed, it became apparent that neither fighter was following the script, while according to the computer readouts they were, nonetheless, landing good punches. Clay complained of the deadening effects of Marciano's shots to his arms and body, and Rocky was incredulous over Clay's speed.

On a visit to Miami Beach in November 1969, I called at Woroner's studio in Miami and was given a short viewing of some of the film. Marciano and Clay weren't murdering each other but they weren't playing pat-a-cake either. Rocky's toupee looked, well, like a toupee. During filming, a looping left from Clay apparently sent the hairpiece flying, with Rocky yelling to the cameramen to switch off. They did.

The result of three years of planning and effort was given a one-day screening on 20 January 1970 and it was a smash hit at the box offices of 1,500 theatres over closed-circuit television in the United States and Canada and throughout Europe, grossing around $2.5m. American and Canadian audiences saw Rocky a knockout winner in 13 rounds, while European audiences were shown another ending with Clay the winner, also by KO in 13 rounds. Interviewed in 1976, Cassius Clay, who would became Muhammad Ali, said, 'I truly think on my best day and his best day I would have beaten him, probably not knocked him out. I think he was better than Joe Frazier, put it that way. And you know what Joe Frazier did to me.'

'The filmed version of a meeting between Marciano and Clay,' wrote Nat Loubert in *The Ring* 'was as exciting as any Hollywood script of a boxing match. It had its flaws but to the man in the theatre it was believable. Rocky took an early beating and was dropped in the eighth round. The Rock was unable to catch his foe in those early rounds as a fast-stepping and quick-handed Clay stabbed Rocky's face into a red mask. Rocky's right eye was "cut" in the third round, his left eye and nose were "sliced" in the fifth session and ketchup poured from these wounds from then on.

'Marciano started back towards the winner's circle when he belted Clay to the canvas in the tenth and 12th rounds. When the bell rang for the 13th, both men were even on points 114-114 each. The round was only 57 seconds old when Rocky culminated a swarming rush with two rights and a left to Clay's head and Cassius went to one knee. He attempted to rise and then collapsed to be counted out. The KO was believable, with Clay giving the impression of being on rubbery legs before being knocked out. The charge to witness the show was $5 per head and the theatres were packed, contrary to many boxing people who scoffed that the venture would not be a success. Clay, Marciano's family and Woroner all made a parcel of green stuff out of the "Super Fight". You never can tell, can you?'[332]

So Rocky Marciano beat the man they call The Greatest, Muhammad Ali, but that was a fantasy fight and yet many still call Rocky the greatest. Veteran promoter-manager Lou Duva, who died in 2017, said, 'In raw terms of fighting, you had to go with Marciano. Louis was a stylist, Ali was the guy for Fancy Dan and promotion.' Nat Fleischer, editor of *The Ring* for 50 years, rated Rocky number ten in his all-time listing of heavyweight champions, behind Jack Johnson, Jim Jeffries, Bob Fitzsimmons, Jack Dempsey, James J. Corbett, Joe Louis, Sam Langford, Gene Tunney and Max Schmeling.

Abe Attell, in boxing's Hall of Fame as featherweight champion, saw them all from the start of his career in 1900 until his death in 1970, and had this to say about Marciano when he retired in 1956. 'It's laughable what the so-called experts are saying about him. According to them, Rocky did everything wrong in the ring. Well, he may have done everything wrong, but he also did something no other heavyweight champion has done – win all his fights. I happened to be around in the

---

332 Nat Loubert *The Ring* April 1970

halcyon days of Corbett, Fitzsimmons, Jeffries and Johnson, and I've been familiar with all the rest of the champions up to now.

'Of all the heavyweights who preceded Marciano under the Marquis of Queensberry rules, what fighter do you think could battle successfully with Rocky for 20 or 25 rounds, assuming all of them were at their peak? Not one in my opinion. Marciano's greatness lay in the fact that he was the greatest conditioned heavyweight ever to hold the title. His power in setting and carrying the pace was such that none of the modern heavyweights since John L. Sullivan's time could endure his offence for the distance I have mentioned.'[333]

Although it's impossible to give an absolute answer to the age-old question, 'Who was the greatest heavyweight champion of all time?' Marciano's supporters can always ask, 'Who ever beat him?'

Look at the guy's record, 49-0. That'll do for this writer.

333 *Boxing Illustrated* 1979

EPILOGUE

THEY FOUND Charley Goldman dead in his one-room apartment on the Upper West Side of Manhattan, wearing an old robe of Rocky's. He'd been taken by a heart attack, aged 79. The date was 11 November 1968.

Allie Columbo, aged 49, died after an accident at work. He was crushed by a trailer-truck as it was reversed up to the loading dock of a supermarket in the Readville section of Boston. Allie was dead on arrival at City Hospital. The date was 6 January 1969.

Rocky Marciano was killed in a light aircraft crash in Iowa. It was the eve of Rocky's 46th birthday. The date was 31 August 1969.

His manager Al Weill, aged 75, died in Miami Beach Nursing Home. The date was 20 October 1969.

The world title-winning team of 1952 were all dead within 11 months in 1968/1969.

Rocky's wife, Barbara M. Cousins Marchegiano, aged 46, died of cancer in Florida. The date was 15 September 1974. She was interred at the Forest Lawn Memorial Gardens, in Fort Lauderdale, Florida, five years to the day after Rocky was laid to rest.